Higher Education at Oldham College

EXPLORING EXISTENTIAL MEANING

OPTIMIZING HUMAN DEVELOPMENT ACROSS THE LIFE SPAN

GARY T. REKER / KERRY CHAMBERLAIN

EDITORS

Sage Publications, Inc.
International Educational and Professional Publisher
Thousand Oaks ▪ London ▪ New Delhi

For information:

Sage Publications, Inc.
2455 Teller Road
Thousand Oaks, California 91320
E-mail: order@sagepub.com

Sage Publications Ltd.
6 Bonhill Street
London EC2A 4PU
United Kingdom

Sage Publications India Pvt. Ltd.
M-32 Market
Greater Kailash I
New Delhi 110 048 India

Printed in the United States of America

Library of Congress Cataloging-in-Publication Data

Reker, Gary T.
  Exploring Existential Meaning: Optimizing human development across the life span / by Gary T. Reker and Kerry Chamberlain.
    p. cm.
  Includes bibliographical references and index.
  ISBN 0-7619-0993-1 (cloth; alk. paper)
  ISBN 0-7619-0994-X (pbk.; alk. paper)
  1. Life. 2. Meaning (Philosophy) 3. Meaning (Psychology) 4. Existentialism. 5. Life change events. I. Chamberlain, Kerry. II. Title.
  BD431 .R38 1999
  128—dc21

                                        99-6281

This book is printed on acid-free paper.

00 01 02 03 04 05 06 7 6 5 4 3 2 1

Production Editor: Wendy Westgate
Cover Designer: Candice Harman

Contents

Acknowledgments

The production of an edited book requires the cooperation and collaboration of many people if the Editors are to achieve their objectives successfully. We express our deepest appreciation to our contributors. Their work and commitment were crucial to the success of this endeavor. They met our demands for clarifications and revisions of their contributions promptly, with good humor and scholarship. Their cooperation made our task as editors much easier than it would otherwise have been.

We are indebted to Dr. James E. Birren for graciously consenting to write the Foreword. He has captured the true spirit of the content of this book.

We are also indebted to Jim Nageotte of Sage Publications for making *Exploring Existential Meaning: Optimizing Human Development Across the Life Span* a reality. His original interest and ongoing assistance for our project is very much appreciated. Our thanks must go also to our Production Editor at Sage, Wendy Westgate, who handled the myriad of production issues with efficiency and ineffable good humor.

The success of any worthwhile endeavor rests, in part, on the working relationship established between the principal editors. We are both thankful for a meaningful experience that was realized in a climate of mutual trust, support, and encouragement throughout the entire term of this project.

About the Contributors

Liora Bar-Tur, PhD, is a clinical psychologist and affiliated with both the Department of Psychology and the Bob Shapell School of Social Work at Tel Aviv University in Israel. Her research and teaching interests include the psychology of adulthood and aging as well as clinical issues in working with post midlife adults. Recent publications include: Sources of personal meaning in a sample of old-old Israelis (*Activities, Adaptation and Aging*) and mental engagements as a moderator of losses of elderly men (*Journal of Aging Studies*, in press).

Kerry Chamberlain is a Senior Lecturer in the School of Psychology at Massey University in New Zealand. His current research interests are centered in health psychology, including research on meaning in life in chronic illness and death and dying. He is also interested in general issues of existential meaning and the involvement of personal meaning in psychological well-being. He also has interests in research methodology, and specifically in varieties of qualitative research. He is coeditor (with Michael Murray) of *Qualitative Health Psychology: Theories and Methods* and author of several articles on meaning in life.

Doris D. Coward, RN, PhD, is an Associate Professor at The University of Texas at Austin School of Nursing in the USA. She teaches nursing research and health promotion to advanced practice nurse graduate students. Her research interests focus on how persons find meaning and healing within the context of life-threatening illnesses. She is a member of the Medical Advisory Board of the Breast Cancer Resource Center of Austin, a breast cancer survivor established facility that provides educational and emotional support to women with newly diagnosed breast cancer and their families.

Dominique L. Debats, PhD, is a clinical psychologist and psychotherapist. He is a senior staff member of the Department of Clinical Psychology at the University of

Groningen, The Netherlands, and is a supervisor therapist at the regional institution for mental health. Dr. Debats has been active in the practice and teaching of the experiential and cognitive/behavioral psychotherapies for over 20 years. His research and publications have addressed the role of personal values in psychotherapy and the psychometric, clinical, and phenomenological aspects of meaning in life.

Freya Dittmann-Kohli, born 1942 in Berlin, is full-time professor and head of the Department of Psychogerontology at the University of Nijmegen in The Netherlands. She is also director of a research program on personal meaning systems in the second half of life. This program comprises research on life-span development, cross-cultural comparisons between European and non-Western countries, and interdisciplinary large-scale survey research with open and closed methods. In her former position as a staff member of the Max-Planck-Institute for Human Development and Education in Berlin, she conducted theoretical and empirical research on late life intelligence training, wisdom, and personal meaning systems. In prior phases of her career she headed a large-scale project on development-in-context of apprentices. Another field of present interest and former research is cross-cultural psychology in African countries. Educational and curriculum research was the topic of her work in France, Canada, and the United States. She has published books, articles, and reports on all of these and other topics, such as the older worker.

Carol J. Farran, DNSc, RN, FAAN, is Professor in the College of Nursing and Rush Alzheimer's Disease Center, at Rush-Presbyterian-St. Lukes' Medical Center, Chicago, USA. Her earlier research focused on hope in healthy community-based older adults and in geropsychiatric inpatients. Her more recent research has focused on caregivers of persons with Alzheimer's disease, including intervention studies, studies on caregivers' ability to find meaning through difficult life circumstances, and a comparison of caregiver differences by race and gender. She has published in *The Gerontologist, American Journal of Alzheimer's Care and Research, Western Journal of Nursing Research, Archives of Psychiatric Nursing, Journal of Psychosocial Nursing, Issues in Mental Health Nursing,* and *Clinical Nursing Research.*

Karen Lowe Graham, MA, is Outreach Coordinator at Rush Alzheimer's Disease Center, Rush-Presbyterian-St.Lukes' Medical Center, Chicago, USA. Her current position focuses on work with diverse populations, in which she regularly participates in the training of health and social service providers and family caregivers about various aspects of Alzheimer's disease. Most recently, she was selected as a 1997-1998 New Ventures in Leadership Partner for the American Society on Aging.

David Guttmann, Associate Professor at the University of Haifa, Faculty of Health and Welfare Studies, School of Social Work in Israel, was born in Hungary in 1932. He received his doctorate from the National Catholic School of Social Service, the Catholic University of America in 1974, and since then has been engaged in research, teaching, training, and consultation in social work, gerontology, and logotherapy. Dr. Guttmann is the former Dean of the School of Social Work at the University of Haifa. In 1981 he was the organizer of mini-conferences for the White House Conference on Aging. In his 24 years of academic career he has authored, co-authored, co-edited, and translated altogether 10 books, 3 among them in logotherapy. His books, *Logotherapy for the Helping Professional: Meaningful Social Work* and *Homecoming* have been translated into other languages. He is also the author of over 40 articles, 12 book chapters, and many other publications in social work, gerontology, and logotherapy, which constitute his main academic interests.

Hubert J. M. Hermans is Professor of Personality Psychology at the University of Nijmegen in The Netherlands. His early work was on achievement motivation and fear of failure. Partly as a reaction, he later developed a valuation theory, together with a self-confrontation method. He is the chairman of a Foundation that has developed national and international training programs for this theory and method. Recently, he published, together with Harry Kempen, *The Dialogical Self: Meaning as Movement* (1993), and together with Els Hermans-Jansen, *Self-Narratives: The Construction of Meaning in Psychotherapy* (1995). He is the first International Associate of the Society for Personology.

Gary M. Kenyon, PhD, was born in Montreal and received his education at Concordia University. He did his doctoral work at the University of British Columbia in Vancouver. He is married and has two children. Dr. Kenyon is founder and Director of Gerontology at St. Thomas University, Fredericton, N.B., Canada, where he is responsible for a certificate and a degree program. He is also Adjunct Professor, Centre on Aging, Faculty of Medicine at McGill University, Montreal, and Honorary Research Associate at the University of New Brunswick. Dr. Kenyon is listed in *Who's Who* in Canada and America. He is a Fellow of the Andrew Norman Institute for Advanced Studies in Gerontology and Geriatrics, University of Southern California, has been a Postdoctoral Scholar at the University of Linköping, Sweden, and is a frequent visiting scholar in Sweden and Finland. His recent publications include: *Metaphors of Aging* (1991, coedited with J. Birren & H. Schroots), a special issue of the *Canadian Journal on Aging* (1993, Guest Editor), *Aging and Biography: Explorations in Adult Development* (1996, coedited with J. Birren, J. E. Ruth, H. Schroots & T. Svensson), and a special issue of *Ageing and Society* (1996, co-edited with J. E. Ruth). Most recently, Dr. Kenyon completed a volume with Bill Randall entitled *Restoring our Lives: Personal Growth Through Autobiographical Reflection* (1997). He is currently working on a second volume with Randall, entitled *Ordinary Wisdom: Biographical Aging and the Journey of Life.*

Dimitra Loukissa, PhD, is a Postdoctoral Fellow in the College of Nursing, Rush-Presbyterian-St.Lukes' Medical Center, Chicago, USA. Her research has focused on caregivers of persons with chronic mental illness and immunological health of family caregivers of persons with dementia. She has published in the *Journal of Advanced Nursing, Journal of Clinical Nursing, Journal of Psychiatric and Mental Health Nursing,* and *Nursing Science Quarterly.*

Alfons Marcoen is a Professor of Developmental Psychology at the Catholic University of Leuven (K. U. Leuven), Belgium. He obtained his PhD in psychology from the same university. His research interest is in life-span developmental research. He has published on loneliness and solitude in adolescence, personal meaning, and well-being and spirituality in the elderly. His recent research focuses on filial maturity in adult children, parental maturity in aging parents, and attachment representations in children and adults.

Susan H. McFadden, PhD, is Professor of Psychology at the University of Wisconsin, Oshkosh, in the USA. Her research and scholarship focuses on the psychology of religion and aging, particularly in terms of developmental trends in later life. She coedited *Aging, Spirituality, and Religion: A Handbook* and is the author of many papers on religion, spirituality, and aging. She is actively involved in the American Society on Aging, the Gerontological Society of America, and the American Psychological Association, where she seeks to bring researchers together with practitioners to examine the opportunities and challenges older adults encounter in securing and maintaining meaning in life.

Kay O'Connor is a lecturer in Counselling in the School of Community Studies at Unitec Institute of Technology, Auckland, New Zealand. Her interests are in counseling psychology, especially narrative therapy, and critical psychology. Specific research interests include meaning in life and the social constitution of emotion.

Edward Prager, PhD, is a Senior Lecturer and Chairman of social work programs in gerontology at the Bob Shapell School of Social Work, Tel Aviv University in Israel. Among his research and teaching interests are cultural and environmental issues in social gerontology and phenomenological and existentialist social work orientations with aging populations. Recent publications include: The Sources of Meaning Profile (SOMP) with Aged Subjects Exhibiting Depressive Symptomatology (*Clinical Gerontologist*); Exploring Personal Meaning in an Age-Differentiated Australian Sample: Another Look at the Sources of Meaning Profile-SOMP *(Journal of Aging Studies)*; and Correlates of War-Induced Stress Responses Among Late Middle-Aged and Elderly Israelis (*International Journal of Aging and Human Development*).

Gary T. Reker, PhD, is a Professor in the Department of Psychology, Trent University, Peterborough, Ontario, Canada. As a life-span developmental psychologist, his research interests have focused on the aging process, particularly on the role of personal meaning, optimism, subjective well-being, death attitudes, and creative coping in the promotion of successful aging. His recent research focuses on the conceptualization and measurement of existential guilt and humanistic spirituality. He has published in the *Canadian Journal of Behavioural Science, Canadian Journal on Aging, Journal of Clinical Psychology, The Gerontologist, Journal of Gerontology, Journal of the Gerontological Nursing Association, International Forum for Logotherapy, Omega,* and *Revue Québécoise de Psychologie.*

Rivka Savaya, PhD, is a lecturer at the Bob Shapell School of Social Work at Tel Aviv University in Israel. Her two main professional interests are help-seeking among Israeli Arabs, including the development of culturally sensitive interventions for this minority group, and the evaluation of clinical and social intervention. Among her recent publications are: Attitudes Towards Family and Marital Counselling among Israeli Arab Women (*Journal of Social Service Research*) and When Clients Stay Away (*Social Service Review*, in press).

Nancy Van Ranst is a Postdoctoral Researcher at the Center for Developmental Psychology, Catholic University of Leuven (K. U. Leuven), Belgium. She completed her PhD in psychology at the same university. Her dissertation involved the topic of meaning in life in late adulthood and old age. Currently she is doing research on intergenerational relationships. Her interests include grandparenthood, and filial and parental maturity.

Gerben J. Westerhof is Associate Professor at the Department of Psychogerontology at the University of Nijmegen, The Netherlands. He is also a co-researcher in the interdisciplinary research project "The German Aging Survey" (financed by the German Ministry for Family Affairs, Senior Citizens, Women and Youth; carried out at the Department of Psychogerontology at the University of Nijmegen and the Research Group on Aging and the Life Course at the Free University of Berlin). In his research and teaching, he focuses on culture, meaning, self, and the life course, always working at the borders between psychology and other social sciences. He published on the work of the French sociologist Pierre Bourdieu, on cross-cultural differences in personal meaning systems, on the meaning of work, activities, and health in the second half of life as well as on well-being and meaning in relation to aging. He is interested in the epistemological grounds and the practical use of qualitative and quantitative methods, especially in large-scale survey research. On this topic, he wrote his PhD Thesis, *Statements and stories: Towards a new methodology of attitude research* (1994) as well as several articles. In the past, he worked at the Department of Cultural Psychology at the University of Nijmegen and spent one semester at the École des Hautes Études en Sciences Sociales in Paris.

Foreword

New doorways of the behavioral and social sciences are opening that are encouraging new traffic in ideas and research. Past defensiveness about qualifying as being "science" led to the exclusion of significant areas of life. Religion, for example was off limits and mankind's pursuit of religion was rarely addressed in research. Now students of religion, theology, and psychology can seek mutual perspectives on complex phenomena that have always accompanied mankind's existence.

Through the doorways between the sciences and humanities are blowing fresh breezes that encourage examination of some of the most intriguing questions. This book addresses the topic of the meaningfulness of life from different scholarly points of view. The various chapters are focused on concepts and theory, research, and the significance of how we attach meaning in life for the ways in which we transcend life's problems. How we interpret life or fit together our experiences is hardly a new topic. What is new is bringing into a shared discourse, concepts, theory, data, and outcomes of the search for meaning in life. The effort can only expand our knowledge and its use for human benefit.

Rather than looking solely at the meaning attributed to the experiences of life revealed through the insights of single talented philosophical or religious figures, in this book a broader net is thrown to embrace the processes used by everyday people. An attempt is made to characterize the process through which meaning is derived. The extent to which there are universal trends in the seeking of transcendent meaning is not yet clear.

Is the existentialist who shouts at me that "there is no meaning in life" solving the dilemmas of her quest for meaning in the very process of her denial? Is the street person who is taken into a residential facility but leaves after a short stay because he wants to return to the street showing a trend toward finding existential meaning in a lack of obligation? Christianity stresses the seeking of externally revealed meaning and Buddhism seeks meaning through inward meditation. What are the consequences of these orientations for what persons under what life conditions? Such questions come to my mind through stimulation by the contents of this book.

It is stimulating to see the mixture of previously separate domains of scholarly effort brought together in the human quest for understanding. Quantitative and qualitative methods stand side by side to show what they have to offer our understanding. It is expected that this work will provoke still broader inputs from anthropology and neuropsychology as to the avenues and the processes of deriving meaning in life.

James E. Birren, *Ph.D.*
UCLA Center on Aging
Los Angeles, California

Introduction

Gary T. Reker and Kerry Chamberlain

The construct of meaning can be conceptualized as consisting of two different, but interrelated aspects. The first, called *implicit* or *definitional meaning*, refers to the attachment of personal significance to objects or events in life. It involves the process of assigning or structuring meaning and addresses the *meaning of experience*, such as in the "meaning of growing old," the "meaning of leisure," or "cultural meanings." Since objects or events have implicit meanings, individuals undergoing an experience must strive to make sense of the experience. They must discover for themselves what "being a married person" or "growing older" or "having arthritis" means as an experience. Understanding the processes of implicit meaning is facilitated by the explication of diverse personal meanings of human experiences, obtained largely through qualitative research approaches.

The second, called *existential meaning* or *meaningfulness*, refers to attempts to understand how events in life fit into a larger context. It involves the process of creating and discovering meaning, which is facilitated by a sense of coherence (order, reason for existence) and a sense of purpose (mission in life, direction). It addresses the *experience of meaning* and asks questions about "What is worth living for?" "What is the purpose in life?" The will to meaning and the search for meaning are core processes in existential meaning-making (Reker & Wong, 1988).

Both implicit and existential meaning are important constructs in fully understanding human experience. They can be interrelated insofar as experiences requiring the realization of implicit meaning can often initiate and enhance the search for existential meaning. However, time and space do not allow for detailed consideration of both aspects in this volume. The interested reader is directed to the recent work of Wong and Fry (1998) who emphasize the "implicit" aspects of meaning. The broader context of existential meaning is the focus of our interest here.

Our own research in the last decade has indicated that existential meaning plays a crucial role in moderating the effects of stress on physical health and psychological well-being, and in enhancing feelings of well-being generally (Chamberlain & Rowsell, 1998; Chamberlain & Zika, 1988; Reker, 1994, 1997; Reker, Peacock, & Wong, 1987; Zika & Chamberlain, 1992). From a life-span perspective, the will to meaning is a continuous process, triggered by changing circumstances, shifting value orientations, and renewed aspirations. While themes and sources of meaning may change throughout the life span, the central feature of the will to meaning in preserving one's identity and promoting one's sense of coherence remains unchanged (O'Connor & Chamberlain, 1996; Reker, 1991). Indeed, the role of existential meaning at different stages of life and at points of transition between stages has much to teach us about optimal human development across the life span.

In the past, the study of biological, psychological, and social processes has relied primarily on the use of quantitative methods consistent with a positivistic orientation. While such an emphasis has contributed substantially to our knowledge, it has not given us a complete picture of the complexities of human development. Missing is an emphasis on the ordinary experiences of people as they advance through time, studied by methods consistent with an interpretive perspective. We are encouraged by the fact that qualitative research is becoming much more valued in the social sciences. It is our conviction that both quantitative and qualitative methods are necessary to achieve the goals of good science, those of theory creation and theory verification (see Reker, 1995). This book brings together the findings of quantitative and qualitative research on existential meaning in life.

We see this volume as having several interrelated purposes: to present some of the exciting recent developments in theorizing and researching existential meaning and to draw this together in one volume; to provide some insight into the role of existential meaning in human development across the life span; to address the need to incorporate the ordinary experiences of real people into meaning research; to illustrate the importance of quantitative and qualitative methods and the complementary contributions they can make toward understanding the complexities of existential meaning; and to highlight the human potential for physical, psychological, emotional, social, and spiritual growth.

The book is organized into four sections. Part One focuses on theoretical and conceptual issues underlying the construct of existential meaning. In Chapter 1, Gary Kenyon provides the philosophical foundations of existential meaning through an elaboration of the concept of personal existence. In Chapter 2, Hubert Hermans presents a theoretical model for understanding the processes of meaning construction and reconstruction and describes a methodology for explicating meaning-making at the individual level. In Chapter 3, Gary Reker introduces the existential paradigm, describes a model of how meaning is experienced, and reviews a number of available instruments to assess various facets of existential meaning.

Part Two focuses on major areas of research involving the construct of existential meaning. In Chapter 4, Nancy Van Ranst and Alfons Marcoen describe an empirical study of the cognitive, motivational, and affective components of meaning in life and link it conceptually and empirically to the existential issues of death attitudes and coping with aging. In Chapter 5, Kay O'Connor and Kerry Chamberlain highlight the importance of qualitative methods in engendering a deeper understanding of how meaning is experienced at midlife. In Chapter 6, Dominique Debats expands on this understanding through an examination of the construct of existential meaning from theoretical, clinical, and phenomenological perspectives and discusses the implications of this for clinical practice. In Chapter 7, Freya Dittmann-Kohli and Gerben Westerhof combine quantitative and qualitative analyses to chart developmental changes in the construction of various domains of meaning across the life span. In Chapter 8, attention is directed toward measurement issues. Edward Prager, Riki Savaya, and Liora Bar-Tur describe the development of a culturally sensitive measure of sources of meaning in life using a combination of qualitative and quantitative test construction methods.

Part Three focuses on the role of existential meaning in applied areas including geriatric nursing, coping with chronic illnesses, religiosity, and psychotherapy. In Chapter 9, Carol Farran, Karen Lowe Graham, and Dimitra Loukissa consider the positive aspects of caregiving and documents how broader ethnic and cultural issues inform and shape the search for meaning in caregivers of persons suffering from Alzheimer's disease. Doris Coward, in Chapter 10, explores the manner in which persons with illnesses, such as AIDS and breast cancer, discover and/or create meaning through the human capacity for self-transcendence. In Chapter 11, Susan McFadden examines the problems of meaning in late life and the solutions offered by religion, with particular emphasis on how the existential meaning model can be used to examine the function of religion in older people's lives. In Chapter 12, David Guttmann provides an overview of logotherapeutic and depth psychology approaches to meaning and to psychotherapy. In particular, the approaches of Szondi and Frankl are compared and contrasted and the implications for therapeutic intervention are discussed.

In Part Four, Gary Reker and Kerry Chamberlain review the contributions to the volume and offer future directions in the conceptualization, research, and applications of existential meaning.

REFERENCES

Chamberlain, K., & Zika, S. (1988). Measuring meaning in life: An examination of three scales. *Personality and Individual Differences, 9*, 589-596.

Chamberlain, K., & Rowsell, B. (1998, February). *Personal meaning in chronic illness: The experience of cancer.* Paper presented to the Fifth New Zealand Health Psychology Conference, Okoroire, New Zealand.

O'Connor, K., & Chamberlain, K. (1996). Dimensions of life meaning: A qualitative exploration at midlife. *British Journal of Psychology, 87,* 461-477.

Reker, G. T. (1991, July). *Contextual and thematic analyses of sources of provisional meaning: A life-span perspective.* Paper presented at the Biennial Meeting of the International Society for the Study of Behavioral Development, Minneapolis, MN.

Reker, G. T. (1994). Logotheory and logotherapy: Challenges, opportunities, and some empirical findings. *The International Forum for Logotherapy, 17,* 47-55.

Reker, G. T. (1995). Quantitative and qualitative methods. In M. Kimble, S. McFadden, J. W. Ellor, & J. Seeber (Eds.), *Aging, spirituality, and religion: A handbook* (pp. 568-588), Minneapolis, MN: Fortress Press.

Reker, G. T. (1997). Personal meaning, optimism, and choice: Existential predictors of depression in community and institutional elderly. *The Gerontologist, 37,* 709-716.

Reker, G. T., Peacock, E. J., & Wong, P. T. P. (1987). Meaning and purpose in life and well-being: A lifespan perspective. *Journal of Gerontology, 42,* 44-49.

Reker, G. T., & Wong, P. T. P. (1988). Aging as an individual process: Toward a theory of personal meaning. In J. E. Birren & V. L. Bengtson (Eds.), *Emergent theories of aging* (pp. 214-246). New York: Springer.

Wong, P. T. P., & Fry, P. S. (Eds.). (1998). *The human quest for meaning: A handbook of psychological research and clinical applications.* Mahwah, NJ: Lawrence Erlbaum.

Zika, S., & Chamberlain, K. (1992). On the relation between meaning in life and psychological well-being. *British Journal of Psychology, 83,* 133-145.

PART I

THEORETICAL AND CONCEPTUAL ISSUES

CHAPTER 1

Philosophical Foundations of Existential Meaning

Gary M. Kenyon

The notion of existential meaning has its roots in the literature and insights of existentialist philosophy and existential phenomenology. In what follows, these insights will be explored by means of the concept of personal existence (Kenyon, 1988). Personal existence is best characterized as a metaphor or ontological image of human nature. As such, it is a lens through which the philosophical foundations of existential meaning can be made visible. The notion of personal existence is inspired by the work of such central existentialist thinkers as Martin Heidegger, Jean-Paul Sartre, Maurice Merleau-Ponty, and Gabriel Marcel (references to specific works of these authors will appear throughout the chapter).

The focus of this chapter will be on the aspect of personal existence that constitutes the necessary condition for existential meaning, namely, human beings as searchers for meaning. This objective will be carried out through a discussion of the following four themes, which form the main sections of the chapter. First, the personal-interpersonal dimensions of human nature will be considered; that is, existential meaning manifests itself in the paradox of living an inner life or *inside story* (Kenyon & Randall, 1997), while we simultaneously live with other persons in a culture and a society.

The second and third themes central to existential meaning are death and time. When viewed from the perspective of personal existence, these phenomena also contain both outer and inner dimensions, outer and inner meanings, a feature that has significant implications for the way that we 'live them'. The fourth important theme concerns the way in which existential meaning works; it is something that we seek naturally and yet it often involves a relinquishing of control, an ability to be receptive. In narrative terms, the experience of existential meaning, again paradoxically, involves the loss or letting go of an old story, as part of our becoming a new story, or experiencing new meaning. The chapter will conclude with a discussion of an optimistic and hopeful image of the human *journey* that arises from an exploration of the philosophical foundations of existential meaning.

CHARACTERISTICS OF PERSONAL EXISTENCE

There are three fundamental characteristics of the personal existence metaphor. First, as biological organisms, human beings are *embodied*, we have physical bodies, and those bodies are finite. Thus, as is the case with any organism, we are born, grow, and eventually die. As biologists remind us, our probability of survival decreases with age. However, the distinctive aspect of "human" nature is that we are aware that we have bodies (Heidegger, 1962; Merleau-Ponty, 1962, 1963). As Merleau-Ponty (1963, p. 204) points out: "For a being who has acquired the consciousness of self and his body, who has reached the dialectic of subject and object, the body is no longer the cause of the structure of consciousness; it has become the object of consciousness." This means that to be human is to *have a perspective* on our bodies; that they have meaning for us. This quality of self-awareness is the ground of existential meaning, the necessary condition for the notion to have any cognitive content. (The discussion of whether other sentient beings are also aware to a greater or lesser degree will not be explored here; however, one can speculate that such a discussion may eventually shed further light on our understanding of human nature.)

The second characteristic of the personal existence metaphor is that human beings, as embodied and self-aware, or as "being-in-the-world" (Dasein) are *situated* (Heidegger, 1962). In Heidegger's (1962) terms, we are *thrown* into the world and *find* ourselves in a particular situation. Human beings are, therefore, fundamentally relational entities, who are by their very nature involved with other persons and with a physical and social environment. Merleau-Ponty (1962) explains this idea by referring to the human being as an *opening through perception*.

The essential idea here is that we are aware of ourselves and of the world around us, but being in a body in this place and not another means that this awareness is contextualized, it is awareness from a particular perspective. From this point of view, the very process of perception establishes us in a world that becomes a field of practice for reflective activity (Carr, 1986). Another way to say this is that our lives, like our life stories, are lived before they are told (Bruner, 1987). To illustrate these qualities of situatedness and relatedness, consider that, even at the physical level, there are aspects of my body, such as the back of my head, that are accessible to others but that are normally not accessible to me. In this basic sense, the human body is both a physical and a social object that, as Gadow (1986, p. 240) points out, "belongs to the world as well as to the self."

The third important aspect of personal existence, which has been alluded to in the foregoing discussion, concerns the nature of human perceptual activity. That is, as authors, including importantly, Merleau-Ponty (1962, 1963) argue, human perceptual activity is both creative and active; it is *intentional*. We do not simply receive sense impressions and stimuli, as, for example, in the strict behaviorist sense, but we do something with what we see and hear. In other words, our bodies, the world, and other persons are *structures of signification*, they have meaning for us, and we place meaning on them. The two parts of this activity result in a paradox in which human beings actively constitute or create their worlds, while at the same time, they are created by that world, and that includes other persons. The phenomenon of existential meaning, then, involves both action or creation, and receptivity or discovery. As we will consider later, this paradox is highlighted in the discussion of existential meaning and death.

EXISTENTIAL MEANING AND THE STORIES WE LIVE WITHIN

The ontological image of human nature contained in the personal existence perspective is that of an interpersonal entity. As the word implies, there are two aspects to be considered here; the personal and the interpersonal. The personal dimension concerns the inviolable and unique center out of which each of us creates and discovers meaning. Aristotle is among those authors who say that the singular cannot be known exhaustively. Each person brings to his or her journey a unique set of past experiences, present perceptions, and future expectations (Kenyon, 1991).

However, we have also said that our bodies themselves belong only partly to us and partly to the world. An important implication of this interpretation is that part of what "I am" is constituted by another person. As Plank (1989) explains:

> It is important to understand that the contribution of the other to our being is not merely on the order of the psychological, but that it has the impact of the ontological, that is, in a very straightforward way it constitutes an aspect of our self, and creates an integral part of that self. (p. 21)

The point here is that the journey of life is simultaneously individual and social. The development and aging of each person takes place in a world with other persons, and existential meaning gets manifested in this paradoxical situation. Borrowing from Luborsky (1993), in narrative terms, the biographical unit is not to be equated with the biological body. Finally, Jean-Paul Sartre's (1956) way of expressing this insight is to argue that there is an aspect of our selves that is unique and in process, namely, being-for-itself, and an aspect that is derived from our being-for-the-other (être-pour autrui).

The statement that people are not, in the final analysis, separate from one another sometimes assumes either a mystical connotation, or becomes a cliché.

However, in the present context, it means that we are dealing with a fundamental paradox of human nature. That is, we create our world personally, idiosyncratically, and dynamically; yet, to a significant extent, we are also influenced and created by a world that is larger than ourselves, individually speaking. Following Sartre (1956), as a self-aware being, I am aware of the other person's activity in creating part of my being, and I am also engaged in creating their being. There is a dynamic, ongoing interplay of, borrowing from Randall (1995), our inside-out stories (expression), with our outside-in stories (impression). Therefore, the existential situation that we "find" ourselves in, is already a "we" situation. To have a self, then, we must maintain a viable being-for-itself and being-for-the-other relationship.

It follows from the foregoing that relatedness is a primary human phenomenon. Conversely, modes of being-in-the-world such as separation, isolation, and solipsism, some of which are masterfully represented in Sartre's (1956) *L'Homme au Café*, for example, are to be understood as responses to an underlying connectedness of human beings. To repeat, there is an aspect of being human that is intensely personal and unique; however, we are not by nature set off entirely from the rest of humanity. Nevertheless, there are many forms or styles of human relatedness, as examples, from the early Sartre's (1955) notion that "Hell is other people," to Marcel's rendering of "presence" and "participation" (Kenyon, 1991; Marcel, 1962). There is a broad range of possibilities; from trust, love, and acceptance, to betrayal, hate, and rejection, as well as disillusionment, resentment, and indifference.

This is not to suggest that ways of life based on separation and closure, which are associated with existential meaninglessness, are not common; however, it is to suggest that they may not always be necessary, or at least that other forms of being-in-the-world are possible. The elements of contingency, risk, and opacity are also basic to the human journey (Kenyon, 1991), and negative and unexpected experiences create separation, anxiety, and even despair, sometimes temporarily and sometimes apparently permanently, in the case of people who are thoroughly hardened by life. However, it is a basic aspect of the discussion of existential meaning that human life also offers the possibility of hope and communion (Marcel, 1962), personal meaning (Reker & Wong, 1988), compassion, openness, and even wisdom (Randall & Kenyon, forthcoming).

In considering the context out of which the human search for meaning takes place, or the larger story we live within, it is important to include such things as the family dimension of our lives, the community, a person's ethnic story, gender story, and professional story. Further, we need also to consider the society in which we live. The expression of existential meaning can be either facilitated or constrained depending on the quality of these aspects of personal existence. "Voices" can be silenced or enhanced by racism, sexism, ageism, as well as by particular types of paternalistic social policies and/or institutional arrangements (see, for example, Gubrium, 1993). Finally, there is also the cosmic story and our connection to the universe that forms a dimension of existential meaning.

To sum up by way of a statement about philosophical foundations, from the point of view being outlined here, human beings are subject to biological, social structural, and cultural influences; however, within this context, human beings also engage in creating meaning as an integral part of their being. There is an important paradigm shift involved here for some people in that personal existence suggests that we are not egoistic or solipsistic beings living in our own world; alternatively, nor are we exclusively socially or genetically determined or constructed beings.

People do make choices. This statement has important implications for understanding and theorizing about, for example, human aging, where we need to ensure that this process, on the one hand, is not reduced to biological or social determinism, and, on the other hand, that existential meaning be included in that theorizing (Kenyon, 1988; Kenyon, Ruth, & Mader, 1999; Reker & Wong, 1988). In the next section we will consider further the creating-created process that is an integral aspect of existential meaning.

CREATING, DISCOVERING, AND FINDING EXISTENTIAL MEANING

The characteristic of intentional relatedness has important implications for an understanding of the way that existential meaning functions in our lives. That is, while we possess what Frankl (1962) calls a *will to meaning*, we do not create that meaning in a vacuum. As we have discussed, there is an opaque quality to the human journey, we cannot and do not see all; neither all aspects of ourselves, nor of other persons. Moreover, there is the fact that we are, in effect, coauthors (Randall, 1995) of our lives and our life stories in that we are partly created by the larger story that we live within.

Following Jean-Paul Sartre, our lives and our life stories are made up of two elements, *facticity* and *possibility* (Maddi, 1988; Sartre, 1956). The term *facticity* refers to those aspects of our lives that make us who we are at any point in time. These elements include the stories we tell (and live) about ourselves, which constitute our sources of meaning (Reker & Wong, 1988), as well as the biological, social, structural, interpersonal (Kenyon & Randall, 1997), and even basic emotional (Mader, 1996) dimensions or themes that characterize our present existential situation.

The term *possibility* refers to those aspects of our lives wherein new meaning can be created. What is perhaps the most crucial of the philosophical foundations of existential meaning is the claim that we do not know, a priori, which aspect of a particular person's life, at any particular time, belongs to his or her facticity set or to his or her possibility set. As Maddi (1988, p. 183) notes, "Our sense of what is possible is intertwined with what we perceive as given and the dynamic balance between the two gives our lives its particular flavor." From this point of view, then, we are free to create other stories or new meaning for ourselves. However, we do this within the context and limitations of our facticity. In other words, things are open-ended, but they are not arbitrary.

New or changed sources of existential meaning are not achieved by simply enrolling in a course on autobiography, wherein the effort is being made to make up a convenient new individual life story to last a few months. Changes in meaning involve not only ideas, but also feelings and actions. In other words, it is less a matter of *having* a new story and more a matter of *being* a new story. It is this characteristic that gives significance to the term *existential* in existential meaning, in that it involves our entire being. Another important issue in this context concerns the question whether it is more appropriate to claim that meaning is created or discovered. From the personal existence perspective, it is both. Further, it is this dual quality of the process that also makes it resemble a spiritual process. That is, it is our nature to seek meaning, and yet this often involves a letting go, an ability to be vulnerable and receptive, and giving up control. As with falling in love, or middle-of-the-night insights, we may find meaning when we least expect it.

Existential meaning makes itself known or arises in silence and rest, as well as in action. These are qualities of the creative process as applied to anything, including creating meaning, but with ourselves we often have difficulty or even deny the "receiving" aspect of the process and believe that we can find a technique or solution to any problem or dilemma. Nevertheless, it is the first step in finding new meaning, or in any *restorying* (Kenyon & Randall, 1997) process, whether learning or therapy, that we be able to "read" and see the present story as part of our facticity in order for it to become part of our sense of possibility. In this way, as the foregoing statement implies, it is possible for us to cultivate our sense of possibility by using our imagination and perhaps developing journey-like qualities in our lives such as wonder, curiosity, and anticipation, perhaps even play (Kenyon, 1991).

Nevertheless, it is important to emphasize that finding new meaning is not accomplished by a quick fix. While this perspective generates hope and possibility within virtually any human situation, compassion and charity are the order of the day in working with existential meaning in other's lives as well as in our own. The power of facticity and resistance to restorying should not be underestimated. We will consider further topics related to this issue in the final section of the chapter.

EXISTENTIAL MEANING AND TIME

Time is a central aspect of existential meaning. Further, human beings experience at least two different kinds of time. These two kinds of time are captured in a statement attributed to Martin Heidegger by Victor Frankl, that what *has* passed is gone and what *is* past is yet to come. Following Achenbaum (1991), there is a physical, outer time and a psychological, inner time, or what Kenyon and Randall (1997) call *clock time* and *story time*. In one sense, human nature is being-in-time (Heidegger, 1962), but not being-of-time, objectively speaking, in that there are individual experiences of and perspectives on time; moreover, those personal time perspectives can change over the life span.

Our experience of time is subject to the same tension or dialectic as the rest of our being, namely, the tension between our inside story and the larger story we live within. It is part of existential meaning to develop a relationship with outer time, or social time and social clocks. For example, human beings often judge themselves to be on-time or off-time with respect to such important activities as career development or starting a family (Neugarten & Hagestad, 1976). This experience of clock time can sometimes be crucial to persons who are, say, looking at what sort of pension they have compared to the threat of retirement or downsizing.

However, the crucial issue concerning time is the analysis of the creative ways that people interact, and can be helped to interact, with this outer clock. Outer or clock time must be dealt with as it is part of our nature as interpersonal beings, as Sartre (1956) would say, part of my being-for-the-other. The important point is that it is only part of it. It is the inner experience of time, which is highly personal, that may in the end tell us more about the nature of time. Further, it is a focus on existential meaning that could give us this insight.

Research into the aging process is instructive in further clarifying this issue. Simone de Beauvoir (1973, p. 420), the existentialist writer, for example, has noted that, "Our private inward experience does not tell us the number of our years, no fresh perception comes into being to show us the decline of years." In the same vein, Sharon Kaufman (1986), in her often cited study of older persons, found that people did not identify with aging as a significant part of their identity or inside story; rather they felt that they were themselves only older. These observations point us to the importance of examining the meaning of time as it is experienced by human beings.

Time from the outside has a discrete past, present, and future. It is linear and unidirectional (Heidegger's what *has* passed is gone), and is the commonly accepted measure of our finitude. As we discussed at the outset of the chapter, we are born, we grow, and we die. However, it is possible that this very definition or meaning of time, wherein people often feel that they are locked in by their past, is a construction. As Plank (1989) explains:

> We commonly accept this essentialistic view of the past as a thing or a series of events which happened once and for all in a specific way and which we, as historians, as witnesses in court, or merely as ordinary men who must live with what they have done, can grasp by a careful perusal of our memories or appropriate archives and documents. (p. 33)

The point here is that the deterministic assumptions contained in this view of time may themselves be only one story of time, and may be partly our own creation, or even possibly a cohort phenomenon when one thinks of, for example, predicted and actual career and family life courses in a postmodern society.

It is interesting to note that the consideration of these issues calls into question the basic assumptions of a number of scientific theories in gerontology. One can ask, for example, whether continuity theory is about aging per se, or whether it reflects a cohort, or cultural, period effect that is based on a widespread belief in a linear view of time that has created a "bondage to the past" (Plank, 1989). There are significant differences in an understanding of aging based on, on the one hand, clock time, and, on the other hand, story time.

In fact, it is recent research on aging, in particular studies that focus on narratives and life stories, which are sensitive to existential meaning or the inside of aging (Ruth & Kenyon, 1996), that is providing one of the sources of these insights into the nature of human time. From this point of view, while it is true that the stories of older persons do involve a considerable past dimension, a past life, and include patterns of meaning created earlier on, this past is being reconstructed or restoried creatively in serving the present. People ascribe present meaning or express present metaphors of past events. This is what is meant by the second part of Heidegger's remark, namely, that what *is* past is yet to come; it is very much available and open to new meaning.

From this view, life stories are a storehouse of experiences and become very important from an existential meaning perspective because, in one sense, the past exists *only* as it is remembered and created and re-created in the interaction with present and future experiences and the meaning, interpretations, and metaphors ascribed to those experiences. Human existence and action therefore consist, in agreement with Carr (1986), not in overcoming time, not in escaping it or arresting its flow, but in shaping and forming it. Human time is configured time.

Nevertheless, the time that is configured is not arbitrary. The future that is projected is not simply a picture of what might be, but our very being. It is a future that we are already, that is based on this present and a past (Heidegger, 1962; Sartre, 1956). This conclusion follows from the discussion that our personal meaning of time is subject to the dynamic between our facticity and our sense of possibility. That is, while change is always possible, like a story, our lives come from somewhere, are something now, and are going somewhere.

EXISTENTIAL MEANING AND DEATH

An existentialist dictum states that human nature is characterized by the search for love and meaning in the face of death. The just discussed subject of inner time-aging suggests that, from the inside, time is not what it appears to be from the outside, that existentially it means more than clock time. A similar point can be made about death. While there are clinical and legal definitions of death, which are themselves sometimes complicated, death is, along with love and meaning itself, the quintessential existential phenomenon. There are at least three main points to be made about death and existential meaning.

First, from a clock time point of view, we might expect that everyone who gets older would be expecting death and want to review their lives before that eventuality arrives. Further, it has been argued that the awareness of approaching death makes one lose a sense of the future (see Schroots & Birren, 1988). It turns out that neither of these claims is necessarily true, and the implication is that the meaning of death may require a closer look.

For example, a number of recent studies have shown that age is not a significant predictor of reminiscence frequency (Webster, 1994). As Webster (1994) points out in his review of these studies, if lifespan samples are employed, the expected triggers of advanced age and approaching death are not evident. Following Agren (1992), even the oldest old, although they must adjust to the limited number of years left, are still *living* time with a present, past, and future. And further, these dimensions are continuously interlocking and have meaning. Finally, Jaber Gubrium (1993) captures the essence of this argument in the following statement, which forms part of the findings of his work with nursing home residents.

> The longitudinal material gathered from residents interviewed more than once indicates that the very idea of a course of adjustment at the end of life shortchanges its variety, complexity, improvisations. There is little overall evidence that affairs are ultimately settled, sundered ties finally repaired, transgressions at last righted or accounted for, or preparations for the future or afterlife completed. While some residents, of course, do speak of waiting for heaven, buying cemetery plots, and making funeral arrangements--points of information that indeed may hold considerable value for them--these do not necessarily signify terminal horizons. (p. 188)

The first important point about death, then, is that it must be distinguished from the aging process. Second, in terms of its existential meaning, death is not something solid, like an object that one can face directly, or that we automatically do face once we reach a particular age. In Heideggerian terms, death is a *possibility*, it is, in a sense, a concept with no specific meaning content, and yet, it is very real (Heidegger, 1962). As Pablo, who is sentenced to die in Sartre's (1969, p. 8) play *The Wall*, puts it, "I can feel the wounds already; I've had pains in my head and in my neck for the past hour. Not real pains. Worse. That is what I'm going to feel tomorrow morning. And then what?" The other character, Tom, responds: "We aren't made to think that Pablo. Believe me; I've already stayed up a whole night waiting for something. But this isn't the same; this will creep up behind us, Pablo, and we won't be able to prepare for it."

Third, I cannot represent my death to myself, since I am not an object to myself. Returning to the basic characteristics of personal existence, we said that not even my body belongs completely to me. I *am* only partly my body, as an opening through perception. Therefore, I cannot say exactly who I am, and I cannot say exactly what my death "is the death of." From this perspective, death has the dual character of immediacy and indefiniteness, that is, I know I will die and yet I can neither predict when, nor know what my death will be like.

As with time, death is open to the same dynamic of facticity and possibility.

This is, in fact, what it means to speak about existential meaning. Again, our ontological situation is such that the basis of our lives and our deaths is open-ended, we have choices that we make, whether we like to think that we have them or not. And further, since we coauthor our lives as interpersonal beings, we can help each other to trade in and trade up our personal metaphors about, in this case, death.

It is interesting to consider that, from this point of view, death as the annihilation of my being, which follows from my view of myself as a body only, and as an egoistic being, is a choice. I can choose to think of myself and my death in this way. In fact, along with denial, this is the most common North American story of death. As Marcel (1952, p. 202) notes, from this point of view, "Death at first sight looks like a permanent invitation to despair." Moreover, it is possible for this despair to be virtually complete, in that I may see nothing else. For authors such as Marcel (1964), this ultimate point of despair is manifested in suicide as the ultimate negation or closing in on oneself.

The contemplation of human death can provide an excellent opportunity to experience existential meaninglessness, as just outlined. However, the very qualities of our being human that provide this opportunity also give rise to a very different possible story of death, one that is imbued with hope and existential meaning. Moreover, as we will discuss in the next section, it is this other story of death and life acceptance that appears to show itself, and that many people live, as they get older and/or if they experience extreme life circumstances.

The fact of death is a fundamental aspect of the human journey. Human life is not complete without the inclusion of death. Yet, since it is part of the opaqueness or indeterminacy of the journey that the nature of death is unknown to us, at least experientially, it is possible to view death as part of the voyage. That is, one can consider death as another aspect of the path, as an open question (Kenyon, 1990). In this important sense, human life can be viewed both as a journey and as one that does not necessarily end as a fait accompli.

Death also becomes a powerful source of existential meaning in so far as we are able to live a more interpersonal story of ourselves. That is, death ends a life, but it does not necessarily end a relationship. The death of another may provide one of the most potent opportunities or catalysts for wonder, openness, or a search for meaning (Frankl, 1962) on the part of the survivor. Moreover, the loss of a loved one or a fellow traveller does not remove the experience of what the person meant to the traveller. In an important way, the fellow traveller may still be present and may continue to share the journey. Gabriel Marcel (1956, 1973) provides a sensitive treatment of this notion through his discussion of the phenomenon of "presence." Beginning with the fact that we are larger than our individual selves, Marcel argues that we can be present and open to each other in life and love, and that there is no reason why a loved one's life story cannot go on after he or she has died.

The phenomenon of presence is a mystery for Marcel, and does not refer to the survival of a person after death in a parapsychological manner. As such, it is something that can be spoken about, that is meaningful, but cannot be known exhaustively. In Marcel's (1956, p. 39) own words to a deceased loved one, "Even if I cannot see you, if I cannot touch you, I feel that you are with me."

EXISTENTIAL MEANING, ORDINARY WISDOM, AND THE JOURNEY OF LIFE

Two further important and interrelated issues that have to do with philosophical foundations need to be considered. The first issue pertains to the characteristics or conditions of an authentic (Heidegger, 1962; Marcel, 1962; Sartre, 1956) or meaningful life. An important question here is whether the "examined life" of Socrates is indeed worth living, if it leads to the emergence of existential meaning and perhaps everyday or *ordinary wisdom* (Randall & Kenyon, forthcoming). The second issue concerns the purpose or directionality of human lives, that is, where the journey is going. The detailed analysis of these issues is far beyond the spatial constraints of this chapter; however, the following remarks could form the basis of that larger discourse.

The Directionality of Human Life

Taking the second issue concerning purpose and teleology first, one question that can be asked is whether there is a transition in aging that brings with it an increase in such things as existential meaning, wisdom, and acceptance. A further question is whether there is a relationship between the suffering, loss, and disillusionment that the human traveller faces, and a movement from *having* to *being* in life. It is this relationship that Florida Scott-Maxwell (1968, p. 47) seems to be referring to in her autobiography, written well into her eighties: "The hardness of life I deplore creates the qualities I admire."

While more research that focuses on existential meaning as a phenomenon worthy of serious investigation needs to be carried out, such as the other chapters in this volume, the list of observations supporting the claim that existential meaning is both possible to experience and central to human development and aging continues to grow. Manheimer (1992, p. 431), for example, captures this insight in a review of studies that "give dramatic form to retelling the story of late-life transformation in which disability, frailty, limitation, dependency, and despair undergo an inversion, becoming qualities such as capability, strength, possibility, autonomy, and wisdom."

In addition to studies of older persons, other sources of the observation of existential meaning and what Kenyon and Randall (1997) call *radical restorying* include studies of victims of abuse, incest, cancer, widowhood, terminal illness, and near-death experiences. Finally, researchers have begun to look specifically at the spiritual dimensions of aging as sources of existential meaning (see Kenyon &

Randall, 1997, for an expanded discussion of this literature).

These systematic findings, as well as other more anecdotal and personal observations, invite philosophical speculation regarding our ontological roots and destiny. However, they invite very practical speculation, as well, that has a direct bearing on ourselves as meaning-seekers personally and interpersonally. That is, if our lives truly are open to both existential meaning and the sharing of that meaning, then we are presented with a potentially positive and hopeful direction for the human journey. That optimism stems from the basic assumption that our lives and our life stories are never, in principle, locked in, that they are made up of facticity *and* possibility, and that what is possible is not known in advance. Nevertheless, not everything is possible for any person at any particular time.

Existential Meaning and Authenticity

It is a basic assumption of this inquiry that there is an aspect of openness and creativity built into the very fabric of human life. However, there are philosophical and ethical issues that follow from a focus on existential meaning concerning, in narrative terms, the nature of the relationship between storyteller and storylistener, and what to expect or assume in a *biographical encounter*, whether that encounter is with our self or another (Kenyon, 1996a, 1996b).

As Aldous Huxley (1944/1962) eloquently pointed out some 50 years ago, it is possible for just about any human characteristic to go with any other characteristic in a particular human being. And yet, within the virtually infinite set of possible characteristics, we all have, following Sartre (1956), a *fundamental project* made up of our predispositions and basic attitudes, which form part of our facticity and which could be called the raw material for our sense of possibility, for increasing existential meaning in our lives. The question at this point becomes that of what is an authentic human life given the human situation as portrayed by personal existence; what are the conditions of a good life (see also Cole, 1992; Kenyon, 1991).

The key to the understanding of an authentic or meaningful life from the personal existence perspective is the situation wherein I am a self-aware being who exists in an interpersonal setting. My story and my life as a person are already larger than my individuality. Yet, although I find myself in a larger situation, I am still responsible for my belonging there (Heidegger, 1962; Sartre, 1956). What is important is whether I am participating in the unfolding of my story or only drifting along, having it written for me. Many people, when they hear about such things as existentialism, existential meaning, and authenticity, become anxious and concerned about how they should live and what to expect from themselves. This may also be a concern of those who are interventionists who wish to include more aspects of existential meaning in their practice. In this spirit, the following four aspects of the human journey are offered as general outcomes of the foregoing inquiry into existential meaning.

First, it does not seem to matter ultimately what has happened in a life so long as one can say that one did and is doing one's best under the circumstances or facticity of the journey. That is, mistakes are made, the wrong path is taken, unexpected crises and catastrophes occur. Nevertheless, as long as the voyage of life continues, and so long as it can be viewed as a voyage, there is movement onward. The studies referred to earlier regarding radical restorying and increased meaning and acceptance in later life, along with the philosophical analysis of the characteristics of personal existence, support the view that, over time, there can be a realization that there is a transitoriness to all experience. It is as though the experiences and events of life are counterposed with a fundamental contingency, a void aspect, as a Buddhist would put it. This radical contingency, while possibly creating an opportunity for existential dizziness, can also enable continuing opportunities for the creation/discovery of new meaning, and for the acknowledgment and appreciation of what has already been experienced on our personal journey.

Second, as human beings, we need to develop a healthy respect for the necessary opaqueness of the traveller's perspective. We understand certain things, accept others, and perhaps wonder about many things. Human life cannot be totally controlled or mastered, either our own or another's. It follows from this statement that it is not appropriate to hold ourselves responsible for all that occurs in life. Again relying on a Buddhist perspective, which has much in common with the existentialist perspective being outlined here, we need to make friends with ourselves. Authenticity implies both ownership and forgiveness or compassion in relation to our shared voyage (see also Randall & Kenyon, forthcoming).

Third, the indefiniteness of the pilgrimage suggests that there may be, in one sense, no final destination of the human journey. The real purpose of human life and human aging becomes the journey itself, or more precisely, the quality of the journey and not the destination. It is possible that there are no better or worse paths in life; the real significance is in what one does with one's path and if one can keep the journey going, not cut it off. The best that one can hope for and work for is that the quality of one's voyage will be informed by wonder, love, curiosity, openness, and perhaps even enthusiasm even in the face of loss, suffering, and disillusionment. The literature reviewed earlier strongly supports the plausibility of this interpretation.

Fourth, an authentic or meaningful life or journey expresses itself in creative, dynamic, and idiosyncratic ways. While we can discuss lives from an aggregate point of view, since the station-stops for human beings are similar, existential meaning originates, in the end, in our inside story, our existential-spiritual center. Thus, on the one hand, we can learn a great deal from sharing the stories of our journey, but each of our stories is, in the final analysis, unlike any other. Moreover, from an ethical perspective, we should never assume that the story we are listening to is the same as another story or fits exactly into a particular theoretical or therapeutic category, a process that silences the personal voice. For example, the required degree of coherence in a life story is a function of my experience of existential meaning and not necessarily the degree of coherence demanded by another to understand my life (Kenyon, 1996a).

CONCLUSION

It may be the case that there is a vital role for such a phenomenon as existential meaning to play in a postmodern Western society as we enter the 21st century. Many lives are currently characterized by modes of being-in-the-world that reflect isolation, separatedness, or existential meaninglessness. Perhaps we need to learn to move from an overemphasis on our outside story to our inside story as important sources of meaning, since many of the "grand narratives" associated with religion, work, and family are, to say the least, in a state of flux. It is not a case of dismissing these necessary aspects of our being-for-the-other, but of imbuing them with authenticity and inner meaning, and not just relying on outside authority or the 'experts'. As the existentialist philosopher Miquel de Unamuno (1954) has said, perhaps it is a matter of "personalizing our universe."

Finally, an interesting question is whether the stories of older persons, with their lessons of meaning, acceptance, and "ordinary wisdom," could be of great value if we are disposed to storylisten as the first step in our experiencing increased existential meaning.

REFERENCES

Achenbaum, A. (1991). Time is the messenger of the gods: A gerontologic metaphor. In G. Kenyon, J. Birren, & J. J. F. Schroots (Eds.), *Metaphors of aging in science and the humanities* (pp. 83-101). New York: Springer.

Agren, M. (1992). *Life at 85: A study of life experiences and adjustment of the oldest old.* Gothenberg, Sweden: University of Gothenberg.

Bruner, J. (1987). Life as narrative. *Social Research, 4(1)*, 11-32.

Carr, D. (1986). *Time, narrative, and history.* Bloomington: University of Indiana Press.

Cole, T. (1992). *The journey of life: A cultural history of aging in America.* Cambridge, UK: Cambridge University Press.

De Beauvoir, S. (1973). *The coming of age.* New York: Warner.

Frankl, V. (1962). *Man's search for meaning.* New York: Simon & Schuster.

Gadow, S. (1986). Frailty and strength: The dialectic of aging. In T. Cole & S. Gadow (Eds.), *What does it mean to grow old: Reflections from the humanities.* Durham, NC: Duke University Press.

Gubrium, J. (1993). *Speaking of life: Horizons of meaning for nursing home residents.* Hawthorne, NY: Aldine de Gruyter.

Heidegger, M. (1962). *Being and time.* New York: Harper & Row.

Huxley, A. (1962). *The perennial philosophy.* Cleveland, OH: Meridian. (Original work published 1944.)

Kaufman, S. (1986). *The ageless self.* New York: New American Library.

Kenyon, G. (1988). Basic assumptions in theories of human aging. In J. Birren & V. Bengtson (Eds.), *Emergent theories of aging* (pp. 3-18). New York: Springer.

Kenyon, G. (1990). Dealing with human death: The floating perspective. *Omega, 22,* 59-69.

Kenyon, G. (1991). Homo viator: Metaphors of aging, authenticity and meaning. In G. Kenyon, J. Birren, & J. J. F. Schroots (Eds.), *Metaphors of aging in science and the humanities* (pp. 17-35). New York: Springer.

Kenyon, G. (1996a). Ethical issues in aging and biography. *Ageing and Society, 16(6),* 659-675.

Kenyon, G. (1996b). The meaning-value of personal storytelling. In J. Birren, G. Kenyon, J. E. Ruth, J. J. F. Schroots, & T. Svensson (Eds.), *Aging and biography: Explorations in adult development* (pp. 21-38). New York: Springer.

Kenyon, G., & Randall, W. (1997). *Restorying our lives: Personal growth through autobiographical reflection.* Westport, CT: Praeger.

Kenyon, G., Ruth, J. E., & Mader, W. (1999). Elements of a narrative gerontology. In V. Bengtson & K. W. Schaie (Eds.), *Handbook of theories of aging* (pp. 40-58). New York: Springer.

Luborsky, M. (1993). The romance with personal meaning in gerontology: Cultural aspects of life themes. *The Gerontologist, 33(4),* 442-452.

Maddi, S. (1988). On the problem of accepting facticity and pursuing possibility. In S. Messer, L. Sass, & R. Woolfolk (Eds.), *Hermeneutics and psychological theory* (pp. 182-200). New Brunswick, NJ: Rutgers University Press.

Mader, W. (1996). Emotionality and continuity in biographical contexts. In J. Birren, G. Kenyon, J. E. Ruth, J. J. F. Schroots, & T. Svensson (Eds.), *Aging and biography: Explorations in adult development* (pp. 39-60). New York: Springer.

Manheimer, R. (1992). Wisdom and method: Philosophical contributions to gerontology. In T. Cole, D. van Tassel, & R. Kastenbaum (Eds.), *Handbook of the humanities and aging* (pp. 426-440). New York: Springer.

Marcel, G. (1952). *Metaphysical journal.* Chicago: Henry Regnery.

Marcel, G. (1956). *The philosophy of existentialism.* Secaucus, NJ: Citadel Press.

Marcel, G. (1962). *Homo viator.* New York: Harper & Row.

Marcel, G. (1964). *Creative fidelity.* New York: Noonday Press.

Marcel, G. (1973). *Tragic wisdom and beyond.* Evanston: Northwestern University Press.

Merleau-Ponty, M. (1962). *Phenomenology of perception.* London: Routledge & Kegan Paul.

Merleau-Ponty, M. (1963). *The structure of behavior* Boston: Beacon.

Neugarten, B., & Hagestad, G. (1976). Age and the lifecourse. In R. Binstock & E. Shanas (Eds.), *Handbook of aging and the social sciences* (pp. 35-55). New York: Van Nostrand Reinhold.

Plank, W. (1989). *Gulag 65: A humanist looks at aging.* New York: Peter Lang.

Randall, W. (1995). *The stories we are: An essay on self-creation.* Toronto: University of Toronto Press.

Randall, W., & Kenyon, G. (Forthcoming). *Ordinary wisdom: Biographical aging and the journey of life.* Westport, CT: Praeger.

Reker, G. T., & Wong, P. T. P. (1988). Aging as an individual process: Toward a theory of personal meaning. In J. Birren & V. Bengtson (Eds.), *Emergent theories of aging* (pp. 214-246). New York: Springer.

Ruth, J. E., & Kenyon, G. (1996). Biography in adult development and aging. In J. Birren, G. Kenyon, J. E. Ruth, J. J. F. Schroots, & T. Svensson (Eds.), *Aging and biography: Explorations in adult development* (pp. 1-20). New York: Springer.

Sartre, J. P. (1956). *Being and nothingness.* New York: Simon & Schuster.

Sartre, J. P. (1955). *No exit.* New York: Vintage.

Sartre, J. P. (1969). *The wall.* New York: New Directions.

Schroots, J. J. F., & Birren, J. (1988). The nature of time: Implications for research on aging. *Comprehensive Gerontology, 2,* 1-29.

Scott-Maxwell, F. (1968). *The measure of my days.* New York: Penguin.

Unamuno de, M. (1954). *Tragic sense of life.* New York: Dover Publications.

Webster, J. (1994). Predictors of reminiscence: A life-span perspective. *Canadian Journal on Aging, 13(1),* 66-78.

CHAPTER 2

Meaning as Movement:
The Relativity of the Mind

Hubert J. M. Hermans

> *We are all framed of flappes and patches, and of so shapelesse and*
> *diverse a contexture, that everie piece, and everie moment playeth his*
> *part. And there is as much difference found betweene us and our selves,*
> *as there is betweene our selves and others.*
> — De Montaigne, 1580/1603, pp. 196-197

> *They that be whole need not a physician.*
> — Matthew, 9:12

The polar contrast between unity and fragmentation is central to many discussions and publications on the functioning of the self in general, and on the process of meaning construction in particular. In these discussions unity is typically considered as a desirable end-state, whereas its opposite, fragmentation, is perceived as an aberration. The implicit or explicit purpose is often to avoid fragmentation and to foster unity. In marked contrast to this view, it is my central thesis that it is not the opposition between *unity* and *fragmentation*, but the opposition between *unity* and *multiplicity* that is particularly important to understanding the process of meaning construction. Whereas the former opposition implies a strong evaluative difference (unity is good, fragmentation is bad), the latter is based on the assumption that the two principles are equivalent and even presuppose one another as complementary perspectives in the study of meaning.

When we consider meaning construction as originating from a self functioning as a unity-in-multiplicity or as multiplicity-in-unity, we avoid two pitfalls; I will label here the first as "premature unity," and the other as "unintegrated multiplicity." By the first term I mean that an overemphasis on the unity of the self as a desirable end-state may have the unintended implication that the diversity of the self and its manifold possibilities are insufficiently explored or even foreclosed. Premature unity may be a risk in those views that consider the self as *basically* striving for unity, or fundamentally oriented toward integration, with multiplicity and diversity considered as accidental or secondary in the formation and development of the self. This view implies that every deviation from the main road, in its direction toward unity, should be corrected as being a distraction or disorientation from the central purpose. The other pitfall, unintegrated multiplicity, may be found in those conceptions in which the self is considered as increasingly diversified and, under the influence of historical and cultural changes, as not being able to integrate or unite at all. This view, underlying some postmodern views of the self, emphasizes the multiplicity and changeability of the self to such a degree that unity and integration acquire the status of out-of-date concepts, reflecting a past era in the history of the human mind.

In this chapter I will consider the process of meaning construction as emanating from the dialogical nature of the self, a view inspired by the literary scholar Michael Bakhtin. As I will argue, Bakhtin has exposed a view of the human mind in which both multiplicity and unity (better: dialogicality) are equivalent forms of organization. In his intriguing metaphor, the polyphonic novel, a multiplicity of voices is supposed to exist not only between several people, but also within one and the same person. In this metaphor, the different voices are not reducible to one another and not subsumed under any superordinate form of integration. At the same time, however, the notion of dialogue is elaborated in such a way that the different voices are not isolated or separated in any definitive way. I will argue that the coexistence of unity and multiplicity is central to the multivoiced, dialogical self, and offers a balanced and compelling view on the process of meaning construction. I will illustrate this perspective with an actual case of a 40-year-old man, who, involved in a process of self-exploration across time, discovered that his self was composed of three very different, even opposing, parts, from which equally different structures of personal meaning emerged. At the same time, the case shows that these different structures contribute, each in their own ways, and in varying degrees, to the person's subjective experience of unity and his experience of meaningfulness of his life as a whole.

BAKHTIN'S POLYPHONIC NOVEL: OPPOSING VOICES

The literary scholar Michael Bakhtin introduced his concept of the polyphonic novel in his book *Problems of Dostoevsky's Poetics*, originally published in Russian in 1929. The principal feature of the polyphonic novel is that it is composed of a number of independent and mutually opposing viewpoints embodied by characters involved in dialogical relationships. Bakhtin proposed this metaphor in an attempt to capture a particular feature in the works of Dostoyevsky. This feature concerns the specific relationship between the author, Dostoyevsky himself, and the variety of characters in his novels. As a great innovation at the end of the 19th century, Dostoyevsky introduced "the retreat of the omniscient author." On the stage of mutually interacting characters, the author, Dostoyevsky himself, is no longer "above" his characters, but only one of many. The characters are not "obedient slaves," in the service of Dostoyevsky's intentions, but are capable of standing beside their creator, disagreeing with the author, even rebelling against him. Each character is "ideologically authoritative and independent," that is, each character is perceived as the author of his or her own legitimate ideological position, not as an object of Dostoyevsky's all-encompassing artistic vision. In his novels there is not one single author, but several authors or thinkers, Raskolnikov, Myshkin, Stavogin, Ivan Karamazov, the Grand Inquisitor, each having his own voice and telling his own story. There is not a multitude of characters within a unified objective world, subordinated to Dostoyevsky's individual vision, but "a plurality of consciousnesses," represented by voices who give vent to their own ideas. As in a polyphonic composition, moreover, the several voices or instruments have different spatial positions and accompany and oppose each other in a dialogical fashion.

Logical Versus Dialogical Relationships

In order to understand the nature of the polyphonic novel it is necessary to distinguish between logical and dialogical relationships. Bakhtin gives the following example (see also Vasil'eva, 1988). Take two phrases that are completely identical, "life is good" and "life is good." They are, in fact, one and the same statement and, therefore, they are, according to Aristotelian logic, related in terms of *identity*. From a dialogical perspective, however, they are different, because they are remarks expressed by the voices of two spatially separated people in communication, who in this case entertain a relationship of *agreement*. Here we have two phrases that are identical from a logical point of view, but different as utterances: the first is a statement, the second a confirmation. From a dialogical perspective, the spatial opposition of different voices is of more concern than the fact that these voices express similar or even identical views. Along the same lines, the phrases "life is good" and "life is not good" can be analyzed. In terms of logic, one is a *negation* of the other. However, as utterances from two different speakers, a dialogical relation of *disagreement* exists. In Bakhtin's view, the relationship of agreement and disagreement are, like question and answer, basic dialogical forms. For a good understanding of Bakhtin's position it must be added that he certainly does not reject the rules of logic: "Dialogical relationships are totally impossible without logical and concrete semantic relationships, but they are not reducible to them; they have their own specificity" (Bakhtin, 1929/1973, p. 152).

Logical relationships are "closed," or "finalized" in so far as they do not permit any conclusion beyond the limits of the rules that govern the relationship. Once an identity or negation thesis has been applied to a set of statements, there is nothing left to be said, nor is an opening created to the domain of the unexpected. In

Bakhtin's view, however, "consciousness is never self-sufficient; it always finds itself in an intense relationship with another consciousness. The hero's every experience and his every thought is internally dialogical, polemically colored and filled with opposing forces ... *open to inspiration from outside itself ...*" (p. 26, emphasis added).

Bakhtin's conception of dialogue is not only open, and "unfinalized," but also highly *personal*. He observes that Dostoyevsky's world is "profoundly personalized" and that each character is a "concrete consciousness, embodied in the living voice of an integral person" (p. 7). A particular utterance is never isolated from the consciousness of a particular character. And because one particular character is always implicitly or explicitly responding to another character, "a dialogical reaction personifies every utterance to which it reacts" (p. 152). In this view a particular utterance is always personalized, and not reducible to any general principle or abstract ideology.

Spatialization of Characters

Bakhtin's notion of dialogue and spatialization of the mind allows a differentiation between the inner world of one and the same individual in the form of an interpersonal relationship. The transformation of an "inner" thought of a particular character into an utterance engenders dialogical relations spontaneously occurring between this utterance and the utterance of imaginal others. Dostoyevsky's novel *The Double*, for example, is based on the spatial opposition between the first hero (Golyadkin) and the second hero (the Double), the latter being introduced as a personification of the interior voice of the first. The externalization of the interior voice of the first hero instigates a fully fledged dialogue between two independent parties. In Bakhtin's terms: "This persistent urge to see all things as being coexistent and to perceive and depict all things side by side and simultaneously, *as if in space rather than time*, leads him [Dostoyevsky] to dramatize in space even the inner contradictions and stages of development of a single person ..." (p. 23, emphasis added). As a manifold variety of this narrative construction, Dostoyevsky portrays characters conversing with the devil (Ivan and the Devil), with their alter egos (Ivan and Smerdyakov), and even with caricatures of themselves (Raskolnikov and Svidrigailov). In this way Dostoyevsky constructs a plurality of voices representing a plurality of worlds that are not identical, but rather heterogeneous and even opposed.

With the polyphonic novel Bakhtin has introduced a metaphor in which we observe the coexistence of multiplicity and unity. Given his ideas on spatial differentiation, Bakhtin would oppose a premature unification of the mind. At the same time, he elaborated on dialogical relations in such a way that the different characters are not depicted as isolated voices in a hollow space. In acknowledging both the distinctness and originality of the voices and their dialogical interconnection, the proposed metaphor provides a view on the mind in which multiplicity and unity are considered as equivalent principles.

THE DIALOGICAL SELF: MOVING BETWEEN *I* POSITIONS

Drawing on the polyphonic metaphor and its implication of spatialized dialogue, Hermans, Kempen, and Van Loon (1992) conceptualize the self in terms of a dynamic multiplicity of relatively autonomous *I* positions in an imaginal landscape. In this conception, the *I* has the ability to move, as in a space, from one position to the other in accordance with changes in situation and time. The *I* fluctuates among different and even opposed positions, and has the capacity imaginatively to endow each position with a voice so that dialogical relations between positions can be established. The voices function like interacting characters in a story, involved in a process of question and answer, agreement and disagreement. Each of them has a story to tell about their own experiences from their own standpoint. As different voices, these characters exchange information about their respective *Me*'s, resulting in a complex, narratively structured self. (For a more detailed discussion of the relationships between *I* positions, including James's and Mead's theories, see Hermans & Kempen, 1993.)

A defining feature of the dialogical self is its combination of temporal and spatial characteristics. Sarbin (1986), Bruner (1986), Gergen and Gergen (1988), and McAdams (1993), main advocates of a narrative approach, have emphasized the temporal dimension of narratives. Bruner's (1986) sentence "The king died, and then the queen," nicely illustrates this emphasis. The dialogical self certainly acknowledges the temporal dimension as a constitutive feature of stories or narratives. Without time and temporal organization there can be no story. However, in agreement with Bakhtin's emphasis on the spatial dimension, time and space are of equal importance for the narrative structure of the dialogical self. The spatial nature of the self is expressed in the terms *position* and *positioning*, terms that are, moreover, more dynamic and flexible than the traditional term *role* (cf. Harré & Van Langenhove, 1991).

The Pervasive Influence of Imaginal Dialogues

In her book, *Invisible Guests*, Watkins (1986) argues that imaginal dialogues play a central role in our daily lives: they exist beside actual dialogues with real others, and interwoven with actual interactions they contribute to the narrative construction of the world. Even when we are outwardly silent, we find ourselves communicating with our critics, with our parents, our consciences, our gods, our reflection in the mirror, with the photograph of someone we miss, with a figure from a movie or a dream, with our babies, with our pets, or even with the flowers we care for.

Watkins is critical of most psychological theories in which imaginal phenomena are approached from the perspective of the real. These theories give clear ontological priority to the real and the existence of actual and real others, with imaginal others seen as derivative from and subordinate to them. Nevertheless, imaginal others and the dialogical relations with them cannot be separated from actual interactions. A simple example may clarify this point of view. Participating in a meeting involves much more than actual interactions with actual people. These interactions are embedded in preparing the meeting, during which the person may have a vivid imagination of the people involved. They also entail memories in which rehearsals of parts of the conversations take place, followed by imaginations of future conversations ("Next time I should not forget to say ..."). Even during the meeting, the person has imaginations about the actual meaning *behind* the spoken words and about the intentions and possible responses of the people who are *not* speaking at a particular moment. In fact, meaningful interactions are unthinkable without the constitutive role of imaginations and imaginal interactions.

When imaginal others are not actually present in a particular situation they are, despite their invisible quality, typically perceived as having spatially separated positions. This applies not only to our own culture (e.g., imaginal contact with an ideal lover, a wise advisor, or a deceased parent or friend), but also to non-Western cultures. Watkins, referring to the work of Warneck (1909), gives the example of the Bataks of Sumatra who hold the belief that the spirit, who determines the character and fortune of a person, is like a person within a person. Such a spirit does not simply coincide with the personality of the host and can even be in conflict with his *I*. The spirit is experienced as a special being within a person, with its own will and desires. As Cassirer (1955) emphasizes, in mythical consciousness a tutelary spirit is *not* conceived as the "subject" of someone's inner life but as something objective, "which dwells in man, which is spatially connected with him and hence can also be spatially separated from him ..." (Cassirer, 1955. p. 168).

Caughey (1984), a social anthropologist, also emphasized the role of imaginal social worlds, both in Western and in non-Western cultures. Caughey, who did field work on Fáánakker, a Pacific island in Micronesia and in the Margalla Hills of Pakistan, compared these cultures to North American culture and concluded that imaginal interactions are in no way restricted to non-Western cultures. Besides the "real" social world of most North Americans (e.g., family, friends, acquaintances, colleagues), a host of individuals may exist in imaginal social worlds and invite a person to enter this world. Caughey divides imaginal figures into three groups: (a) media figures with whom the individual engages in imaginal interactions (e.g., pop heroes in the fantasy of adolescents); (b) purely imaginary figures produced in dreams and fantasies; and (c) imaginal replicas of parents, friends, or lovers who are treated as if they were really present. Caughey demonstrates, as did Watkins (1986), that imaginal dialogues and interactions exist side by side with real interactions (e.g., "If my mother could see me now ...") and may or may not have a direct link with reality.

Caughey (1984), like Watkins (1986), is critical about the identification of "social relationships" with only "actual social relationships." He qualifies this conception as incomplete and actually representing "an ethnocentric projection of certain narrow assumptions in Western science" (p. 17). For the same reason, he prefers to speak of an (imaginal) "social world" rather than a purely "inner world" in order to emphasize the interaction with somebody who is felt to be "there." Both authors are opposed to a sharp distinction between a private self and a public self, because the so-called private self is populated by imaginal others and imaginal interactions with real others.

The Simultaneity of Internal and External Dialogical Relationships

It would be a misunderstanding to restrict the dialogical self to "internal conversations" or to "self-talk." The concept takes into account the close interdependence of internal and external dialogical relationships. The following example, borrowed from Baldwin's (1992) research on relational schemas, may illustrate this point of view. A teenage boy asks his mother if he may borrow the keys to her car. The goal of the boy is to borrow the car. He expects, moreover, that the goal of his mother is to make sure that both he and the car are returned safely. If he suspects that she is reluctant, he knows that the required behavior is to convince his mother that he will act in a responsible way. So he comes up with phrases that have been successful in the past, such as, "I'll drive carefully" and "I'll be home before 1!" In proceeding in this way, he expects that his mother will give him the keys. If not, he may use different routines, such as emphasizing his urgent need for transport, complaining about her unfair behavior, and so on. Finally, his mother gives him the keys. At first sight, the mother proceeds as an individual, that is, as an undivided person she takes the decision from *one* (her own) point of view. When we take a closer look at the mother, however, we find out that there are different "I positions" emerging from the interaction with her son. What happens in the mind of the mother before she decides to give the keys? As a mother concerned with the welfare of her son, she is hesitant and perhaps fearful to lend the car. At the same time she takes the position of her son, who wants a fine day, and she can imagine that he needs the car. In fact, she vacillates between two positions, the fearful mother and the helpful mother. From the first position she would say: "I am afraid that ..."; from the second: "I can imagine that ...." After moving to and fro between the two positions, and after a process of negotiation between them, she finally decides to give the keys.

The above example exemplifies a specific feature of the dialogical self: *both* positions are part of the mother's self. According to this view, the son's point of view is not only an external position, that is, outside the mother's self, but at the same time represented as an intrinsic part of the mother's self. The mother's self is, as Bruner (1990) would say, "distributed" between two positions located in a field of tension and her decision results from dialogical movements between them. The mother's second position ("I can imagine that ...") is, during the process of interchange, continuously influenced and fed by the remarks from her son, on the one hand, and interrogated and even criticized by her first position ("I am afraid that ..."). Her final decision is the result of a process of negotiation between two actively contributing voices corresponding with the two positions in the mother's self with an increasing dominance of one voice over the other. A similar analysis could be given for the son, because he can only be successful in getting the keys when he effectively negotiates between two positions: "I want the keys" and "I can imagine that she ...."

In summary, the notion of the dialogical self is an attempt to transcend the restrictive boundaries so typical of individualized and rationalized Western conceptions of the person. The dialogical self represents a highly active process of positioning and repositioning, expressed in the dynamics of self-negotiations, self-oppositions, and self-integrations. The self is not conceived as an a priori unified individual, but as a diversity of contrasting and opposing voices involved in a process of interchange. In fact, this conception denies the existence of sharp boundaries between the (internal) subject and the (external) object so characteristic of traditional neo-Cartesian psychological theories.

TRAITS AS CHARACTERS: A CASE STUDY

In the many handbooks on personality psychology the notion of trait is a common ingredient. The trait theories formulated by Cattell, Eysenck, Guilford, and many others are well-known examples and, more recently, the "Big Five" (e.g., Goldberg, 1990) are attractive to many students in the field. Despite their central position in personality psychology and their far-reaching influence in psychology as a whole, some criticisms can be heard. First, little mention is made of personality development, growth, and change. Usually, trait theories emphasize the relatively stable and enduring aspects of personality. Second, these theories generally fail to take situations into account. Typically, they focus on those aspects that have a certain degree of transsituational consistency, that is, they assume that the behavior covered by a trait is expressed in overt behavior across a variety of situations (for other criticisms of trait theories, see McAdams, 1994). Within the context of this chapter, a third criticism is of particular importance: traits as such do not say very much about the personal meaning of a trait for a particular individual in a particular period of his or her life. This neglect of personal meaning is closely related to the objectifying nature of attributing trait categories to persons. In essence, there is no difference between attributing traits to an object (e.g., an object is long, heavy, and black) and to a person (who may also be long, heavy, and black). As long as one adheres to an objectifying description of a person in terms of traits categories, one sticks to a reification of the person, with a shallowing of the personal meaning of traits as a consequence.

As a response to the three criticisms mentioned above (temporal stability, transsituational consistency, and reification), I devised a procedure, inspired by the dialogical self, in which traits are not considered as something a person *has*, but as something a person *is*; that is, as characters or *I* positions in a self-narrative. Suppose you are the client and I put to you the following question: "When you consider your own personality, can you see two opposite sides, one of which is more dominant than the other?" In our research, different people answer with different trait pairs: open versus closed, playful versus serious, active versus passive, rational versus emotional, ordinary versus spiritual, sociable versus

authoritarian, and many others. The purpose of this exercise is that a personal pair
of opposites is constructed, that is, one that is most significant to you in your daily
life. The next step is to invite you to tell, from your dominant side, a self-narrative
about your past, present, and future (e.g., you tell about your life from the
perspective of yourself as, say, a rational person). After completion of this
narrative, you are invited to take your opposite side, say, your emotional side, and
tell your self-narrative from that position, in turn. The third and final step is that
you follow your two self-narratives and the implied personal meanings across some
weeks or months following this investigation, by keeping a diary for example, so
that the development of your two self-narratives and the implied personal meanings
through time can be compared.

Rick's Three Positions:
Enthusiastic, Vulnerable, and Being Close to Myself

Let me illustrate this procedure with an actual case. Rick, a 40-year-old manager,
asked for therapeutic assistance in a period in which he, a married man with two
adolescent children, had a relationship with a girlfriend. He was criticized by other
people and by himself for having left his family and often suffered from feelings
of guilt and regret. When his therapist (Els Hermans-Jansen) proposed that he
describe two opposite sides of his personality, he explained to her that he had an
"enthusiastic side" but at the same time a "vulnerable side," seeing the former as
more dominant than the latter. Rick had the feeling that he was able to fire other
people with his own enthusiasm, particularly in his work situation, and that he
could easily make friends. About his "vulnerable side" he said that this aspect was
not so much associated with his work situation, but more with the relationships he
had with significant others. He saw this side as the "hidden side" of his personality
and, therefore, he considered it "less dominant."

Next, Rick was invited to describe from his enthusiastic position and vulnerable
position separately a number of "valuations." The term *valuation*, the central term
in valuation theory (Hermans & Hermans-Jansen, 1995), is an active process of
meaning construction. It is an open concept and includes anything people find to
be of importance when telling their life story. A valuation is any unit of meaning
that has a positive (pleasant), negative (unpleasant), or ambivalent (both pleasant
and unpleasant) value in the eyes of the individual. It includes a broad range of
phenomena: a dear memory, an impressive event, a difficult problem, a beloved
person, an unreachable goal, the anticipated death of a significant other, and so
forth. Through the process of self-reflection, valuations become organized into a
system and, depending on the individual's position in time and space, different
valuations may emerge. The questions which are used to elicit valuations as part of
a self-investigation are listed in Table 2.1. The psychotherapist proposed to Rick
that he phrase two valuations referring to his past, two to his present, and two to his
future, and to do so successively from the perspective of his enthusiastic *I* position

TABLE 2.1 Questions of the Self-Confrontation Method

Set 1: The Past
These questions are intended to guide you in reviewing one or more aspects of your life that may have been of great importance to you.
   Has there been anything of major significance in your past life that still continues to exert a strong influence on you?
   Was there in the past any person or persons, experience, or circumstance that greatly influenced your life and still appreciably affects your present existence?

Set 2: The Present
This set again consists of two questions that will lead you, after a certain amount of reflection, to formulate a response.
   Is there anything in your present existence that is of major importance to you or exerts a significant influence on you?
   Is there in your present existence any person, persons, or circumstance that exerts a significant influence on you?

Set 3: The Future
The following questions will again guide you to a response. You are free to look as far ahead as you wish.
   Do you foresee anything that will be of great importance for, or exert a major influence on, your future life?
   Do you feel that a certain person, persons, or circumstance will exert a significant influence on your future life?
   Is there any future goal or object that you expect to play an important role in your life?

---

and his vulnerable *I* position (see Table 2.2).

   In the next session, two weeks after his self-investigation, he presented to the therapist, quite unexpectedly, an additional list of six new valuations (see Table 2.2). He explained that in his eyes these valuations represented a very important aspect of his personality about which he had not been aware during the preceding self-investigation. He had left the preceding session with the supposition that the trait-pair enthusiastic versus vulnerable was the main opposition playing a central role in his present life. After about a week he quite suddenly realized that the two opposites were not opposites at all, but were, instead, intimately related. He even admitted: "Sometimes I have the feeling that they are the same," and added: "I am becoming aware that I am continuously trying to make other people enthusiastic because I want them to like me ...." In other words, he discovered that his second position (vulnerable) was the driving force behind the first position (enthusiastic). He discovered that his enthusiastic side, instead of being dominant, was rather in the service of his vulnerable side and, in fact, subordinate to it. He continuously and

TABLE 2.2 Rick's Valuations Referring to His Past, Present, and Future From the Perspective of Three Positions (Enthusiastic, Vulnerable, and Being Close to Myself)

Enthusiastic Position

Past

1. I could always convince people and fire them with my enthusiasm.
2. I could always make friends easily.

Present

3. With Ruth [girlfriend] I am used to taking initiatives and generating ideas.
4. In my work I have many ideas to present to different levels in the organization, and I try to make people enthusiastic.

Future

5. In the future I want to buy, together with Ruth, a beautiful, cosy, old house.
6. In my work I want to see results and try to score.

Vulnerable Position

Past

7. Sitting on the bike behind my mother, I went with her to her work place; she used to ask the name of the statue that we passed; I always answered: Spinoza.
8. I want to be seen as nice, and humorous, and I want to be understood.

Present

9. I want to be physically caressed.
10. I am ashamed and feel very vulnerable when I say what I have done and the choice I have made [leaving his wife].

Future

11. I will ask love, warmth, and much attention from Ruth.
12. I will do those things in my work for which I will earn credit.

Being Close to Myself Position

Past

13. I once had the experience that I was the sun: I was shining for everybody, was giving warmth, wanted to give without desiring something in return.
14. I felt very peaceful, totally myself and very encompassing when I decided to break with Ruth [for a short time he broke off the relationship with his girlfriend].

Present

15. In a discussion with John and Francis [friends] I remained calm, myself, not self-opinionated, on my own stance, because *I* felt it this way.
16. It feels good that nothing is gnawing inside, no regret, when I think back to the choice I have made [leaving his wife].

Future

17. I anticipate with enjoyment the philosophy course, which will help me to know myself better and to be at peace with myself.
18. I do not want to become overdemanding of myself in the future, but to accept who I am and even love myself.

often successfully tried to arouse other people with his ideas in order to reduce his own vulnerability. After having elucidated this, he introduced, to the surprise of his therapist, an entirely new element in the process of self-investigation: "I discovered that there is something in myself which is quite different than what I have mentioned before . . . and it strongly contrasts with it." He described this aspect as "being close to myself." The six valuations he had formulated from the perspective of this position had in common that in all of them he felt very close to himself, at a deeper level than he usually felt in his daily life. Sometimes the valuations refer to brief, but highly significant moments (nos. 13-15 in Table 2.2), at other times he described a general attitude (no. 16) or goals that he saw as relevant to his personality development in the future (nos. 17-18).

So far Rick's process of self-investigation can be summarized from a theoretical point of view as follows:

- Rick is able to formulate two oppositional traits (enthusiastic versus vulnerable), which function as two *I* positions in a *multivoiced* self.
- From each position Rick is able to tell a *specific* story about himself resulting in specific units of meanings (valuations) referring to past, present, and future. In these meanings, Rick refers many times to significant others: traits as characters are not separated from the situation but, instead, interactively relate to other characters (see the formulation of the valuations).
- Rick's meaning construction is highly *dynamic* and is more *emerging* than given: after his initial self-investigation he finds out that there is a third position ("being close to myself") that he feels as being even more important than the initial ones, and becomes part of a new opposition (3 versus 1+2).
- The valuations from the different positions are *not* formulated as if they are from different, unrelated people. Although the relationships are not always clear, there are clear signs of *disagreement* among positions (e.g., compare valuations 10 and 16 in Table 2.2). In the present theoretical context, such disagreements or conflictual relationships between positions should not be removed in the manner of "tension reduction," but function as constructive constituents of a dialogical self in process.
- Note that the valuations from the three positions are not entirely separated. Sometimes there are overlapping valuations (e.g., valuations 6 and 12 in Table 2.2). Multiplicity does not coincide with separation.

Unity in Multiplicity

In the theoretical part of this chapter I proposed that the opposition between unity and multiplicity is a more fertile starting point for the study of meaning than the opposition between unity and fragmentation. However, how do we know if there is any unity in the multivoiced self? In Rick's case: How do we know that his meaning system, as "distributed" in a variety of positions and valuations, has any unity at all? In order to answer this question I decided to pose this question to Rick himself. In collaboration with his therapist, I presented his valuations in a random order and proposed that he rate each valuation on a 9-point scale as an answer to the following question: "To what extent do you feel yourself as a unit with this valuation?"

In order to arrive at more certainty about the validity of the unity question, I decided to ask Rick a convergent question: "To what extent in this valuation do you feel that you approach the center in yourself?" (a question that he understood) and to rate all valuations again on a 9-point scale. Calculation of the means for the three positions revealed that the unity question and the center question give similar results: the valuations from the position "being close to myself" are associated with the highest level of unity and the highest degree of centeredness, whereas the valuations from the vulnerable position are associated with the lowest degree of unity and centeredness, with the enthusiastic position being in the middle. These results suggest that the positions clearly differ in the extent of bringing unity into the self, with one position contributing more than another position to its felt integration. In other words, the fact that the self is multivoiced and distributed does not exclude the existence of unity, although one position is more unifying than another.

After Eight Months: Stability and Change

Eight months after the initial self-investigation and a series of sessions every three weeks, Rick and his therapist decided to perform a brief and final investigation in which they checked the main changes. In this investigation, Rick summarized the changes by formulating only one valuation for each of the three positions that expressed most directly the specific quality of the particular position (see Table 2.3).

TABLE 2.3 Second Self-Investigation After Eight Months: Valuations for Three Positions

Position	Valuation
1. Enthusiastic	I radiate warmth and enthusiasm toward my environment and also receive this back.
2. Vulnerable	The small boy who calls for his mother is afraid of being alone and is not very firm.
3. Being close to myself	I do not want to become overdemanding of myself but love and accept who I am.

The valuation under position 1 suggests that there has been a merging of elements of positions 1 and 3. The original valuation "I was the sun . . ." (Table 2.2) and the valuations referring to his enthusiasm (Table 2.2) go together in "I radiate warmth and enthusiasm toward my environment and also receive this back." The initial controlling and manipulative quality of his enthusiasm has been changed into a give-and-take quality, expressed in a new and integrative meaning unit. This is an indication of the movement of the *I* between positions and the dialogical nature of this movement.

On the other hand, Rick did not succeed in changing his experience of being vulnerable, and there remains a strong opposition between this experience and his experience of "being close to myself." These two positions, which initially showed the strongest opposition and the greatest differences in unity and centeredness, were perhaps too different to be reconciled. Contrasting experiences are at the very heart of Rick's self and require a constant struggle between mutually opposing forces. Unity can be reached but opposition and contradiction persist simultaneously.

THE LOGICAL ARISTOTLE VERSUS THE DIALOGICAL HERACLITUS

The theme of this chapter is an invitation to go back to the original Latin word *individuum* meaning "undivided" or "indivisible." More specifically, the question can be raised as to what extent the present contribution is doing justice to the indivisible nature of the individual. This question can best be answered by taking into consideration the fact that, as psychologists, we are used to defining individuality on the basis of Aristotelian logic. In an elucidating paper Marková (1987) discusses the influence of Aristotle's *law of noncontradiction* in Western thinking, stating that the same attribute cannot at the same time belong and not belong to the same subject and in the same respect. An important implication of this law is that, when an object is attributed a certain feature (e.g., "this object is hot"), it can *not* at the same time and in the same respect have the opposite feature ("this object is cold"), a state of affairs that we experience as obvious. There is, however, a fundamental difference, Marková argues, between Aristotle's conception of opposites and that of the earlier, pre-Socratic philosopher Heraclitus. The philosophy of Heraclitus was founded on the belief that the world is in a state of constant change, and he reasoned that, when things appear to be stable, it is only because the opposites are present together in a state of dynamic balance. It is, however, the tension between opposites that keeps the world in this state of constant change. In other words, *opposites always coexist*. Aristotle's law of noncontradiction, however, clearly specifies that opposites cannot be present in a thing at the same time, and therefore a thing in Aristotle's system of thought is defined by the presence of *one opposite only* of a pair of opposites. As far as we deal with static phenomena, Marková continues, the law of noncontradiction is certainly applicable (e.g., when we define a hot object as cold, we could burn our hands). However, the law runs into problems when we apply it to dynamic phenomena (e.g., the movement of something can only be understood when we assume that at one and the same moment it is both *here* and *not here*). As Hegel has said: "Contradiction is at the root of all movement and vitality" (quoted by Marková, 1987, p. 280).

The polyphonic metaphor and the concept of the multivoiced self assume that the *I*, in its dialogical orientation to its counterpart, is at the same time *in* this counterpart, and consequently a continuous tension between the two positions is assumed. We have adopted the term *I* position to express that the *I* is in a flux in such a way that when it is in its first position, the second, opposite position is present at the same time like an accompanying and opposing voice in a polyphonic composition. This flux implies an enlargement of the boundaries of the usual self-definition because the *I* is conceived of as "indivisible" from its opposite (Hermans, 1993).

I have presented Rick's case as demonstrating this movement among opposites. According to the instruction, he was able to point to two "sides of his personality" (enthusiastic versus vulnerable) that were then treated as opposite *I* positions in the self, suggesting that he felt a strong distance and contrast between these two sides. Shortly after this formulation, however, and perhaps stimulated by it, he became aware that the two sides, which he initially saw as strongly different and even opposed, were apparently intimately related. He discovered that his enthusiastic attitude and concomitant attempts to fire other people with his ideas, functioned as a shield against threats to his vulnerability. At the same time, he discovered that there was a new opposite ("being close to myself") that stood out sharply against the initial ones (enthusiastic and vulnerable). On the basis of this new opposition, Rick made attempts to influence and alter the initial positions from the perspective of the new one, resulting 8 months later in a clear integration of the "being close to myself" position and the enthusiastic position. This integration provided a more interactive quality to the latter position than it initially had. Despite all these changes, a basic conflict (between the "small boy who calls for his mother" and his positive attitude of self-acceptance and self-love) remained across time and revealed a basic and stable opposition that seemed to form a more fundamental structure for Rick's self-organization. It should, however, be added that the polar opposites of this stable structure, irreconcilable as they may seem from a personal or therapeutic point of view, are as meaningfully related to one another as all the other polarities in his self-system. The small boy functions as a constant challenge and even as a threat to Rick's unity and integrity, and, therefore, he needs the precious moments in which he feels close to himself so that he can be vulnerable as an integrative person.

I have stressed in this chapter the process of meaning construction as movement in an imaginal space. I have argued that this movement assumes an active process of positioning and repositioning in a self that can be understood as multivoiced and dialogical. When Montaigne said, four hundred years preceding our postmodernist era, that "we are all framed of flappes and patches," he was certainly right. Equally right, however, is a person's continuous struggle for unity, a unity that sucks its energy and strength from the mind's inherent multiplicity.

NOTE

I thank Els Hermans-Jansen for putting the case study material at my disposal.

REFERENCES

Bakhtin, M. (1973). *Problems of Dostoevsky's poetics* (2nd ed.). Trans. R. W. Rotsel. U.S.A.: Ardis. First ed. published in 1929 under the title *Problemy tvorchestva Dostoevskogo* [*Problems of Dostoevsky's art*].

Baldwin, M. W. (1992). Relational schemas and the processing of social information. *Psychological Bulletin, 112*, 461-484.

Bruner, J. S. (1986). *Actual minds, possible worlds.* Cambridge, MA: Harvard University Press.

Bruner, J. S. (1990). *Acts of meaning.* Cambridge, MA: Harvard University Press.

Cassirer, E. (1955). *The philosophy of symbolic forms: Vol. 2: Mythical thought.* New Haven, CT: Yale University Press.

Caughey, J. L. (1984). *Imaginary social worlds: A cultural approach.* Lincoln: University of Nebraska Press.

Gergen, K. J., & Gergen, M. M. (1988). Narrative and the self as relationship. *Advances in Experimental Social Psychology, 21*, 17-56.

Goldberg, L. R. (1990). An alternative "description of personality": The Big Five factor structure. *Journal of Personality and Social Psychology, 59*, 1216-1229.

Harré, R., & Van Langenhove, L. (1991). Varieties of positioning. *Journal for the Theory of Social Behaviour, 21*, 393-407.

Hermans, H. J. M. (1993). Moving opposites in the self: A Heraclitean approach. *Journal of Analytical Psychology, 38*, 437-462.

Hermans, H. J. M., & Hermans-Jansen, E. (1995). *Self-narratives: The construction of meaning in psychotherapy.* New York: Guilford.

Hermans, H. J. M., & Kempen, H. J. G. (1993). *The dialogical self: Meaning as movement.* San Diego: Academic Press.

Hermans, H. J. M., Kempen, H. J. G., & Van Loon, R. J. P. (1992). The dialogical self: Beyond individualism and rationalism. *American Psychologist, 47*, 23-33.

Marková, I. (1987). On the interaction of opposites in psychological processes. *Journal for the Theory of Social Behavior, 17*, 279-299.

McAdams, D. P. (1993). *The stories we live by: Personal myths and the making of the self.* New York: William Morrow.

McAdams, D. P. (1994). *The person: An introduction to personality psychology* (2nd ed.). New York: Harcourt Brace.

Montaigne, M. de. (1603). *The essayes: Or morall, politike and millitarie discourses* (J. Florio, Trans.). London: Blount. (Original work published 1580.)

Sarbin, T. R. (1986). The narrative as a root metaphor for psychology. In T. R. Sarbin (Ed.), *Narrative psychology: The storied nature of human conduct* (pp. 3-21). New York: Praeger.

Vasil'eva, I. I. (1988). The importance of M. M. Bakhtin's idea of dialogue and dialogic relations for the psychology of communication. *Soviet Psychology, 26*, 17-31.

Warneck, M. (1909). *Der Religion der Batak* [*The religion of the Batak*]. Leipzig: T. Weicher.

Watkins, M. (1986). *Invisible guests: The development of imaginal dialogues.* Hillsdale, NJ: Lawrence Erlbaum.

CHAPTER 3

Theoretical Perspective, Dimensions, and Measurement of Existential Meaning

Gary T. Reker

Existential meaning refers to attempts to understand how events in life fit into a larger context. It involves the process of creating and/or discovering meaning, which is facilitated by a sense of coherence (sense of order, reason for existence, understanding) and a sense of purpose in life (mission in life, direction, goal orientation). It addresses the *experience of meaning* and seeks answers to questions about, "What is worth living for?", "What is the purpose of my life?", "Is there meaning in my life?" Searching for meaning and finding meaning are core processes in existential meaning-making.

Existential meaning in life has received increased attention in recent years. This welcomed change can be attributed to a number of factors, including a shift away from a pathological orientation of the human condition toward the human potential for growth, renewed interest by psychologists in the "inner" development of the whole person, more precise conceptualization and operationalization of existential meaning, and an increasing acceptance of qualitative methods as a legitimate form of scientific inquiry.

Contemporary psychological and gerontological research has shown that existential meaning is an important psychological construct in the prevention of illness, the promotion of wellness, and successful adaptation to life's changing circumstances (Emmonds & Hooker, 1992; Reker, 1994, 1997; Reker, Peacock, & Wong, 1987; Reker & Wong, 1988; Shek, 1992; Ulmer, Range, & Smith, 1991;

Zika & Chamberlain, 1987, 1992). Meaninglessness or existential vacuum, on the other hand, lies at the very root of psychopathology including neurosis (Maddi, 1967; Ruffin, 1984), depression (Phillips, 1980), suicidal behavior (Harlow, Newcomb, & Bentler, 1986), drug abuse (Harlow et al., 1986; Newcomb & Harlow, 1986), and alcohol dependence (Nicholson et al., 1994; Waisberg & Porter, 1994).

The purpose of this chapter is threefold. First, an attempt is made to provide an overall theoretical framework that places the construct of meaning within an existential paradigm. Next, a particular conceptualization of existential meaning is presented in which the structural components and dimensions of meaning are described and evaluated. Finally, a number of existing measures of existential meaning are described, compared, and assessed in terms of their reliability, validity, and sensitivity.

THEORETICAL PERSPECTIVE

In recent years, we have witnessed a shift from traditional ways of doing science toward a perspective that also takes into account the lived experiences of the individual. A central tenet of this human science perspective is that humans are self-interpreting animals who are conscious, active, purposive, self-regulating organisms capable of symbolization and symbol manipulation. Moreover, detailed descriptions of subjective life experiences, as expressed through personal documents and related qualitative methods, are accepted as legitimate sources of data for further scientific analyses. The human science orientation is reflected in a theoretical perspective known as existentialism, whose assumptions comprise the existential paradigm.

The Existential Paradigm

Existentialism is a philosophy that focuses on people's attempts to make sense of their existence by assigning meaning to it and taking responsibility to act accordingly. While existentialism cannot claim to be a systematic and unified philosophy, its followers share a common set of beliefs. First, existentialists are concerned with the nature of being or becoming. Existentialists take the person as the starting point, bringing the person's inner world of experiences into our view of science. Existentialists pose fundamental questions about existence: Who am I? Is there meaning in life? Is life worth living? Second, to be human means to exercise free will, to make choices, to pursue goals, to act authentically. Third, existentialists focus on the immediate experiences of a person's daily existence, on what is called being-in-the-world. There are three modes of being-in-the-world: natural, personal, and social. A person's conscious experience incorporates all three modes at once. Fourth, human existence is seen as a continuous struggle as individuals cope with the problems of life and as they move toward the realization of their potential. The search for meaning is a central feature of that struggle.

Existentialists recognize that the human condition is characterized by paradox and by dialectical thought and reasoning. Humans often experience multiple truths that can appear to be contradictory. A person can be at the center of his/her world, yet at the same time, feel totally insignificant in the grand scheme of things. We are both responsible for our existence and victims of being born at a particular time in history. In the struggle to come to terms with such existential paradoxes, new possibilities arise that lead to deeper understanding and invite one to find new ways of being-in-the-world.

New ways of being-in-the-world are achieved through two existential processes: transcendence and transformation. Transcendence is the process of making sense of and rising above one's circumstances or situations. Transformation is the dynamic process of transforming a given reality into a new potentiality. As the new potentiality becomes actualized, the stage is set for other potentialities. In essence, the human potential for growth is unlimited, extending upward and outward to higher plateaus and broader horizons. Existential meaning is discovered and created through the processes of transcendence and transformation, respectively.

The existential paradigm represents an intuitive and interpretive philosophy of science. It addresses the uniqueness of the human experience, which can only be understood in the context of a life lived and from the perspective of the individual viewer. Themes are identified that relate to human conflicts or "ultimate concerns" with the givens of existence such as life, death, freedom, isolation, and meaninglessness. Emphasis is also placed on the capacity of humans to choose, to be responsible for their choices, to hope, and to find meaning in adversity (Frankl, 1963; Yalom, 1980).

Existential Meaning

Existential meaning is defined as the cognizance of order, coherence, and purpose in one's existence, the pursuit and attainment of worthwhile goals, and an accompanying sense of fulfillment. A person with a high degree of existential meaning has a clear life purpose, a sense of directedness, strives for goals consistent with life purpose, feels satisfied with past achievements, and is determined to make the future meaningful.

Reker and Wong (1988) are of the conviction that a complete and proper understanding of existential meaning requires both a bottom-up or *elemental* and a top-down or *holistic* view of life. At the elemental level, life as a whole has no meaning; life only *contains* meaning – a series of meaningful activities, quests, and goals. Individuals create meaning from specific encounters through making choices, taking actions, and entering into relationships. However, specific encounters need to be integrated into a larger and higher purpose, as expressed through philosophical understanding and spiritual connectedness, from which meaning can be discovered. In effect, an enduring type of existential meaning can only be achieved through the dual processes of creating and discovering meaning.

DIMENSIONS OF EXISTENTIAL MEANING

Reker and Wong (1988) proposed four different dimensional features of existential meaning. The four dimensions relate to how meaning is experienced (structural components), the contents of the experience (the sources of meaning), the diversity with which meaning is experienced (breadth), and the quality of the experience of meaning (depth).

Structural Components

Existential meaning is a multidimensional construct consisting of cognitive, motivational, and affective components. The cognitive component pertains to making sense of one's experiences in life. Individuals not only construct a belief system or worldview to address existential concerns, but also seek existential understanding of the value and purpose of various life events, circumstances, or encounters.

The motivational component of existential meaning refers to the value system constructed by each individual. Values are essentially guides for living, dictating what goals individuals pursue and how they actualize their goals. Values are determined by individual needs, beliefs, and society. Both the process of pursuing selected goals and their attainment give rise to a sense of purpose and meaning to one's existence. It is the worthwhile ends that keep one going in spite of obstacles, setbacks, and extremely traumatic experiences.

The affective component comprises the feelings of satisfaction and fulfillment individuals get from their experiences and from achieving their goals. Although the pursuit of individual happiness may not result in meaningfulness, whatever is meaningful must also provide satisfaction to the pursuer.

Reker and Wong (1988) have proposed that the three structural components of existential meaning are interrelated and are common to an individual's experience of meaning (see Chapter 4, this volume, for an empirical assessment of these components). In a recent study, O'Connor and Chamberlain (1996) explored middle-aged people's accounts of their experiences of life meaning. Using qualitative in-depth interviews, they found, among other things, that each source of meaning revealed cognitive, motivational, and affective components. Moreover, all three components were necessary, forming an integral part of the experience of meaning, confirming Reker and Wong's structural components model.

Sources of Meaning

Sources of meaning refers to the different content areas or personal themes from which meaning is experienced. Where does meaning come from? Values and beliefs are the bedrock for sources of meaning. Values have been defined as constructs that transcend specific situations and that are personally and socially preferable. Values incorporate modes of conduct (instrumental values) and goals in life (terminal values), and impel one to action (Rokeach, 1973). Values are reflected in the answers individuals provide when questioned about the areas of their lives from which meaning is derived.

For Frankl (1963), meaning stems from three broad sources: (1) creative, or what one accomplishes in terms of creative work, (2) experiential, or what one derives from beauty, truth, or love, and (3) attitudinal, or what one derives from reflections on negative aspects of life such as pain and suffering.

Research based on case studies, cross-sectional samples, and general surveys, using either qualitative or quantitative methods, suggest that meaning can be derived from a wide variety of specific sources that vary according to cultural and ethnic background, socio-demographics, and developmental stage (DeVogler & Ebersole, 1980; Kaufman, 1986; Klinger, 1977; O'Connor & Chamberlain, 1996; Yalom, 1980). Recently, Reker (1991) summarized the most common sources of meaning cited in the literature. His list includes personal relationships, altruism, religious activities, creative activities, personal growth, meeting basic needs, financial security, leisure activities, personal achievement, leaving a legacy, enduring values or ideals, traditions and culture, social/political causes, humanistic concerns, hedonistic activities, material possessions, and relationship with nature. Individually and collectively, these sources contribute to an overall sense of existential meaning (Reker, 1991).

Do sources of meaning change or do they remain stable over the life span? Continuity theory would predict that individuals will continue to derive meaning from the same sources throughout the life course. Kaufman (1986) refers to these sources as "themes," defined as organizational and explanatory markers created by individuals to "explain, unify, and give substance to their perceptions of who they are and how they see themselves participating in social life" (p. 25). Life-span theorists, on the other hand, postulate changes in values and beliefs and shifts in orientations toward greater introspection (Jung, 1971), increasing interiority (Neugarten & Associates, 1964), higher integration (Erikson, 1963), and deeper levels of faith (Fowler, 1983). The empirical evidence suggests that while an overall sense of meaning remains high and relatively stable, the sources from which meaning is derived show both stability and change over the life course, depending on one's developmental stage and points of transition between stages (Prager, 1996; Reker, 1991).

Breadth of Meaning

Breadth of meaning refers to the tendency for an individual to experience meaning from a number of different sources. Do individuals experience meaning from only one central source or do they derive meaning from a broader sampling of diverse sources of meaning? Does a larger network of meaningful sources contribute to a higher or lower sense of fulfillment in life? The findings of DeVogler-Ebersole and Ebersole (1985) suggest that most individuals derive meaning from a variety of valued sources and only a few rely on a single, central source. Reker and Wong (1988) proposed that an individual (1) will experience meaning from several different valued sources and (2) that a greater variety of these will lead to a greater sense of fulfillment.

In a direct test of the first component of the breadth postulate, Reker (1994) found that young, middle-aged, and elderly participants reported, on average, between 6 and 7 highly meaningful sources out of a possible 13. No differences were found across the age groups in number of sources. Regarding the second component, Reker (1994) found that greater breadth culminated in a heightened sense of meaning fulfillment and psychological well-being.

Depth of Meaning

Depth of meaning refers to the *quality* of a person's experience of meaning. Is the experience of meaning shallow, fragmented, and superficial or is it deep, integrated, and complex? We need to be able to differentiate between these seemingly different levels of meaning and to assess the extent to which they contribute to an overall sense of fulfillment. But how is depth of meaning to be conceptualized and operationalized?

Based on Frankl's (1963) conviction that the full meaning of life can only be achieved by transcending self-interests and on Rokeach's hierarchical nature of values in which certain values hold greater significance than others, Reker and Wong (1988) defined depth as the degree of self-transcendence that is realized. Four levels of depth were proposed into which experiences of meaning could be classified: self-preoccupation with hedonistic pleasure and comfort (level 1); devotion of time and energy to the realization of personal potential (level 2); service to others and commitment to a larger societal or political cause (level 3); and entertaining values that transcend individuals and encompass cosmic meaning and ultimate purpose (level 4). When viewed in three-dimensional space, each level provides a horizon or background against which meaning is created/discovered. The implication of such an analysis of depth is that individuals will be able to integrate the contradictions, conflicts, and absurdities of life by rising above them and viewing them in the context of more comprehensive horizons.

Empirical evidence supports Reker and Wong's conceptualization of depth. For example, Reker (1991) demonstrated that individuals who experience meaning from sources at levels 3 and 4 are more fulfilled and satisfied with life compared to individuals who experience meaning at levels 1 and 2. In a qualitative study of sources of meaning at midlife, O'Connor and Chamberlain (1996) found clear evidence of differences in depth of meaning ranging from self-preoccupation to the highest level. Bolt (1975) found that an intrinsic religious orientation, a belief system based on transcendent meaning, correlated positively with scores on purpose in life. Crandall and Rasmussen (1975) found that pleasure, excitement, and comfort correlated negatively with purpose in life.

In summary, the structural components and dimensions of existential meaning provide a useful framework for understanding the experience of meaning. The model of existential meaning has been supported by empirical investigations using both quantitative and qualitative approaches. While additional empirical research is warranted, the model presented here can serve as a springboard for future investigations of existential meaning.

MEASUREMENT OF EXISTENTIAL MEANING

Empirical investigations of existential meaning can only proceed when reliable and valid operational measures of meaning and purpose in life have been developed. Following Frankl's inspirational writings of the early 1960s, a number of instruments were developed to measure facets of the existential meaning construct. Most of these are quantitative instruments of a self-report nature. In this section, a number of widely used measurement instruments are described and assessed in terms of their psychometric properties and their level of sensitivity in the measurement of existential meaning. For organizational clarity, the instruments are presented under three headings: general measures of meaning in life, domain-specific measures of meaning in life, and context-specific measures of meaning.

General Measures of Meaning in Life

General measures of meaning in life assess the existential meaning construct in a general or global way. Such measures reflect an individual's understanding of how events in life fit into a larger context as facilitated by a sense of coherence (order, reason for existence) and a sense of purpose (mission in life, direction). These are measures that assess meaning or purpose in one's personal existence and involve an approach to life that transcends events. The measurement approach tends to be primarily quantitative using self-report questionnaires.

Purpose in Life Test (PIL). In 1969, Crumbaugh and Maholick developed the Purpose in Life (PIL) test, a 20-item unidimensional attitude scale constructed from the orientation of logotherapy, to measure Frankl's basic concept of "existential vacuum." Each item is rated on its own separately labeled 7-point semantic differential type scale with different labels across items for endpoints. Scores can range from 20 to 140, representing very low to extremely high meaning and purpose in life.

The psychometric properties of the PIL, both as reported in the manual (Crumbaugh & Maholick, 1969) and in a large number of research studies conducted across a variety of settings and among diverse populations, are very favorable. Internal consistency and temporal stability reliabilities ranging from the high .70s to the low .90s are routinely reported (e.g., Crumbaugh & Maholick, 1969; Reker, 1977; Shek, 1986; Zika & Chamberlain, 1992), and both construct and concurrent validity studies attest to the suitability of the PIL as a measure of meaning and purpose in life (Crumbaugh & Maholick, 1969; Reker, 1992; Zika & Chamberlain, 1992). Positive relationships have also been reported between the PIL and measures of extroversion, positive attitude toward life, life satisfaction, self-acceptance, psychological mindedness, self-control, emotional stability, and responsibleness; negative relationships have been reported between PIL scores and depression, anxiety, anomie, neuroticism, and psychoticism (Crumbaugh & Maholick, 1964, 1969; Chamberlain & Zika, 1988; Garfield, 1973; Pearson & Sheffield, 1989; Phillips, 1980; Reker, 1977; Reker & Cousins, 1979; Zika & Chamberlain, 1992).

While the PIL has been the most popular quantitative measure of meaning and purpose in life, a number of concerns pertaining to its format and factorial validity have been raised. For example, the format of the PIL is considered to be "somewhat awkward and bulky," which may be "confusing to the test taker and makes it difficult to display the test compactly" (Harlow, Newcomb, & Bentler, 1987, p. 235). A number of factor analytic studies have shown the underlying structure of the PIL to be multidimensional (Chamberlain & Zika, 1988; Harlow et al., 1987; Reker & Cousins, 1979; Shek, 1986), not unidimensional as proposed by its developers. Dyck (1987) has been most critical of the PIL, arguing that it is mainly an indirect measure of depression and consequently not an appropriate measure of the "existential vacuum" construct.

In spite of these shortcomings, the PIL continues to be one of the most widely used instruments in the measurement of meaning and purpose in life. In a recent comparison study of three meaning scales, Chamberlain and Zika (1988) concluded that the PIL was the most useful general measure of meaning in life.

Life Regard Index (LRI). In 1973, Battista and Almond introduced a multidimensional measure of meaning in life called The Life Regard Index (LRI). Meaning in life was defined by the concept of positive life regard, referring to an individual's belief that he/she is fulfilling his/her positively valued life-framework or life-goals. The LRI consists of 28 items with a 5-point scale, divided equally into two subscales, Framework and Fulfillment. The Framework scale assesses the degree to which an individual has a life-view, a set of life-goals or a purpose in life. The Fulfillment scale assesses the degree to which life-goals are fulfilled, or are in process of being fulfilled. High scores on the LRI reflect the attainment of a meaningful life.

In a preliminary evaluation of the LRI, Battista and Almond (1973) reported an extremely high temporal stability coefficient of .94 for the index. However, the time interval between testings was not stated and no reliability coefficients were provided for the separate subscales. Validity studies showed that the LRI related in predicted ways to several criteria, including meaning in life as measured by the PIL, the Self-Actualizing Value scale of the Personal Orientation Inventory, observer ratings of meaningfulness, number and duration of visits to a psychiatrist, and self-esteem. In addition, scores on the LRI were not influenced to any significant degree by the tendency to respond in a socially desirable way, degree of openness, and defensiveness (Battista & Almond, 1973).

Two recent studies provide further evidence in support of the reliability, construct, and factorial validity of the LRI (Debats, 1990; Zika & Chamberlain, 1992). Using principal component factor analyses, Debats (1990) extracted two factors corresponding to the Framework and Fulfillment theoretical subscales. The internal consistency estimate of reliability was .80 for Fulfillment, .79 for Framework, and .86 for the LRI. The LRI was negatively related to anxiety, hostility, and depression and positively related to a clear philosophy of life, elation, happiness, and life satisfaction (Debats, 1990). Zika and Chamberlain (1992) also found the LRI to correlate positively with meaning in life as measured by the PIL, life satisfaction, psychological well-being, and positive affect. Negative correlations were found between the LRI and psychological distress and negative affect.

While the inclusion of the Fulfillment subscale appears to make the LRI a more appropriate operational measure of the multidimensional concept of meaning in life, there remains a great deal of overlap between the two LRI dimensions. For example, Battista and Almond (1973) reported a substantial correlation of .76 between Framework and Fulfillment, while Debats (1990) reported a lower but still sizeable correlation of .54. Thus, the status of the LRI as a multidimensional measure of meaning in life remains questionable. Overall, the LRI appears promising but more empirical studies are needed to clarify the underlying structure (see Chapter 6, this volume, for more details on the LRI).

Life Purpose Questionnaire (LPQ). The Life Purpose Questionnaire (LPQ), developed by Hablas and Hutzell (1982), was designed to be an uncomplicated, easily administered, self-report measure of the degree of life-meaning experienced by older individuals living in institutional environments. It was structured to measure the same concept as the PIL. Each item of the 20-item scale requires only an "agree" or a "disagree" response. A high score reflects a strong sense of life-meaning.

The psychometric properties of the LPQ have not been extensively investigated. Hutzell (1986) reported a one-week test-retest reliability of .90 among a small group of geriatric, neuropsychiatric patients. Across several validational studies of geriatric patients and alcoholics conducted by the authors, the LPQ correlations with the PIL ranged from .60 to .84. The LPQ also correlated negatively with depression and positively with life satisfaction, a pattern of relationships very similar to that of the PIL.

While the LPQ is not as psychometrically robust as the PIL, it may have advantages over the PIL under certain situations and for certain populations. Due to the simplicity of its format, the LPQ is less demanding and less time-consuming. It may thus be more appropriate for hospice/palliative care patients and patients with terminal illness. Hablas and Hutzell (1982) report that, in situations were the LPQ and the PIL were administered in written form to the same geriatric patients, almost 50% more geriatric patients could complete the LPQ than could complete the PIL. However, the LPQ has not been researched widely enough to warrant its use as an alternate measure to the more established PIL.

Life Attitude Profile-Revised (LAP-R). The Life Attitude Profile-Revised (LAP-R), developed by Reker (1992), is a 48-item multidimensional measure of discovered meaning and purpose in life and the motivation to find meaning and purpose in life. The LAP-R is an operational measure of Frankl's logotherapeutic constructs of will to meaning, existential vacuum, personal choice and responsibleness, realities and potentialities, and death transcendence. Each item on the LAP-R is rated on a 7-point Likert scale of agreement, ranging from "strongly agree" to "strongly disagree." The LAP-R is scored and profiled in terms of six dimensions and two composite scales. The six dimensions are Purpose, Coherence, Choice/Responsibleness, Death Acceptance, Existential Vacuum, and Goal Seeking. The Personal Meaning Index is a composite scale, derived by summing the Purpose and Coherence dimensions. Existential Transcendence is a composite scale derived by summing the scores on the dimensions of Purpose, Coherence, Choice/Responsibleness, and Death Acceptance and subtracting the scores on Existential Vacuum and Goal Seeking.

The psychometric properties of the LAP-R have been extensively investigated in samples of males and females across the entire life span from young adults to the old-old (Reker, 1992). Internal consistency reliabilities of the LAP-R dimensions range from .77 to .87; one-month test-retest reliabilities also range from .77 to .87. The internal consistency and temporal stability coefficients of the Personal Meaning Index and the Existential Transcendence composite scales are all in the low .90s. Principal components factor analyses with varimax rotation to simple structure revealed a five-factor model in which Purpose and Coherence loaded on the same factor. The five-factor structure was found to be invariant across three different age groups and between men and women, attesting to the factorial validity of the LAP-R (Reker, 1992).

Of particular interest, within the current context, is the composite Personal Meaning Index. Personal meaning is a dual-component construct defined as having life goals, having a mission in life, having a sense of direction, and having a logically integrated and consistent understanding of self, others, and life in general. The Personal Meaning Index was found to correlate substantially with the PIL, the Framework subscale of the LRI, and ratings of meaningfulness. Moreover, the Personal Meaning Index is predictive of a large number of outcome variables including psychological and physical well-being, physical health, ego integrity, internal locus of control, life satisfaction, self-transcendent values, and the absence of feelings of depression and alienation (Reker, 1992). The Personal Meaning Index of the LAP-R appears to be a very reliable and valid measure of general meaning in life. In addition, the LAP-R offers the advantage of a multidimensional measure through which other facets of Frankl's logotheory can be assessed in a single scale.

Domain-Specific Measures of Meaning in Life

Domain-specific measures of meaning in life assess the contents, categories, or sources that give rise to a general sense of meaning and purpose in life. Both quantitative and qualitative measures have been developed, making use of multiple data collection techniques including self-report scales, open-ended questionnaires, life journals, interviews, and personal documents.

Meaning Essay Document (MED). The Meaning Essay Document (MED), developed by DeVogler and Ebersole (1980), is based on the use of personal documents. It consists of a single sheet of paper containing two questions: "What is the strongest meaning in your life right now? If you feel you have no meaning right now, check in the following space and tell how you either lost your meaning or why you think you do not have one." The second question is, "Write about an example in your life that will help me better understand your meaning in life (or lack of it)." Responses are either tape-recorded or written verbatim. Preestablished categories of life-orientation identified by Battista and Almond (1973) were modified and expanded and used to code the essays into nine categories or *types* of meaning in life: relationships, service, belief, obtaining, growth, health, life work, pleasure, and miscellaneous. The lack of meaning in life can also be assessed. In a later extension of the MED procedure, DeVogler-Ebersole and Ebersole (1985) introduced a measure of *depth* of meaning in life. Independent judges rate essays on a 5-point scale anchored by five predetermined criteria of depth of meaning. Meanings that are discussed with more complexity and more specificity are considered to be deep; meanings that are new, relatively untried, and underdeveloped are considered to be shallow.

Inter-rater reliability for types of meaning have been consistently high across several studies, ranging from a low of 80% in the elderly (DePaola & Ebersole, 1995) to a high of 93% among adolescents (DeVogler & Ebersole, 1983). Inter-rater reliability coefficients for depth of meaning appear to be more variable, ranging from a low of .43 to a high of .84. Unfortunately, other than face validity, DeVogler and Ebersole (1980) provide very little evidence to support the empirical validity of types and depth of meaning in life.

In addition to the lack of validational evidence, the developers of the MED do not provide a conceptual definition of meaning in life, nor is their approach guided by theory. Also problematic is the fact that their approach is sensitive to only one major source of meaning – the strongest source of meaning – and fails to document other potential sources of meaning that coexist in the same individual. The number of categories required to accommodate the descriptions of meaning seems to vary, depending on the age of the respondent. For example, among 13 to 14 year olds, three new categories had to be added to the list (DeVogler & Ebersole, 1983). In the absence of an invariant measuring tool, it is very difficult to investigate differences in meaning across age cohorts and over time.

Sources of Meaning Profile-Revised (SOMP-R). The Sources of Meaning Profile-Revised (SOMP-R), developed by Reker (1996), is a 17-item measure of specific domains of a person's life from which meaning is derived. It is based on the premise that individuals create meaning through making choices, taking actions, and entering into relationships. The development of the SOMP-R was based on a thorough review of the available literature through which the most commonly cited sources of meaning were identified. Each source is rated on a 7-point "not at all meaningful (1)" to "extremely meaningful (7)" response scale. Thus, a high total score reflects the existence of a large network of meaningful sources in the present life of the respondent.

The total score on the SOMP-R can be further divided to yield four meaning orientations (identified through principal components factor analysis): self-preoccupation, individualism, collectivism, and self-transcendence. Self-preoccupation refers to sources that meet and satisfy the immediate needs of the respondent; individualism refers to sources that focus on self-improvement, self-development, self-growth, and the realization of one's potential; collectivism refers to sources that focus on the betterment of the group, on areas that involve service to others and dedication to a larger societal or political cause; and self-transcendence refers to sources that transcend the self, that go beyond self-boundaries to encompass cosmic or ultimate meaning.

The psychometric properties of the SOMP-R have been investigated in a number of studies in Canada, Australia, and Israel (Prager, 1996, 1997, 1998; Reker, 1996). Internal consistency reliabilities range from .71 to .80, with a median of .77. A 3-month stability coefficient was reported to be .70 (Prager, 1996). Regarding validity, total SOMP-R scores correlate positively with measures of self-transcendence and personal meaning, and negatively with depression (Reker, 1996). In his study of Australians and Canadians, Prager (1996) suggested that the SOMP-R may lack sensitivity to differences in the cultural and linguistic backgrounds of respondents. In response to this limitation, Prager and associates have begun to develop a measure of sources of life meaning that is more culturally sensitive (see Chapter 8, this volume, for details).

Context-Specific Measures of Meaning

Context-specific measures of meaning assess meaning within the context of a specific experience, such as unavoidable suffering or a life-threatening illness. These are largely measures of how meaning is constructed, searched for, or found in the experience.

Meaning in Suffering Test (MIST). In the mid-eighties, a logotherapeutically oriented research instrument, the Meaning in Suffering Test (MIST), was developed by Starck (1985). The MIST was designed to measure the extent to which an individual has found meaning in unavoidable suffering experiences. In Part 1 (20 items), respondents rate items such as, "I believe suffering can teach valuable lessons about life," on a 7-point scale ranging from "never" to "constantly." In Part 2, respondents are encouraged to respond to 17 questions asking them to elaborate on their experiences of suffering (e.g., "What does suffering teach you?"; "How do you cope with suffering?"; "What good/bad has resulted from your suffering?"; etc.) by choosing from a list of preselected options. Part 1 can be readily quantified; a high score reflects the extent to which an individual has found meaning in suffering experiences. Part 2 has potential as a qualitative measure of the meaning of suffering; however, the predetermined nature of the options limits its usefulness.

Although demonstrating an acceptable level of internal consistency reliability of .81, the MIST suffers from a lack of evidence pertaining to validity. The format is excessively repetitious; every statement begins with the phrase, "I believe ..." and the word *suffering* appears in almost every item. The scope of the MIST is narrow, tapping only the cognitive aspect of finding meaning in suffering. Respondents are asked to report the frequency of "feelings" to statements of belief. Some statements make reference to the person; other statements make reference to a person in general or to everyone. Although several definitions of suffering are presented in the manual, a common definition is not given on the test itself. Apart from Starck's (1985) paper, there are no other reports of studies in which the MIST was used. Unfortunately, the MIST, in its present format, does not appear to be a very useful measuring instrument for finding meaning in the experience of suffering.

Constructed Meaning Scale (ML). The Constructed Meaning Scale (ML), developed by Fife (1995), was designed to provide a measure of meaning that is formulated by individuals as they strive to adapt to the life-threatening illness of cancer. It is an 8-item, self-report 4-point Likert scale that assesses the impact of cancer on the individual's sense of identity, interpersonal relationships, and sense of what the future holds. A high score reflects a very positive sense of meaning that the illness holds for one's self and future life.

The psychometric properties of the ML, as reported by Fife (1995), appear to be good. The scale was found to have consistently high item-total correlations; the internal consistency reliability was .81. Content validity was established by the fact that items were generated from interviews with persons living with cancer. The ML was able to differentiate persons at different points in the illness trajectory (e.g., newly diagnosed, first recurrence, first remission) and was found to be predictive of personal control, body image, and psychological adjustment.

Fife (1995) is of the opinion that the ML is ready for further testing that includes participants with diagnoses other than cancer. While comparative studies of persons with other life-threatening and/or debilitating illnesses would be useful and helpful in understanding the construct of meaning, five of the eight statements on the ML refer explicitly to cancer. Given that scale construction relied heavily on the symbolic interactionist perspective, one would have to question the validity of substituting the names of other illnesses for cancer. In short, the ML appears to be sensitive to the assessment of meaning as it relates to cancer, but may not be generalizable to other health problems.

In this section, a number of general, domain-specific, and context-specific measures of meaning in life were reviewed. With few exceptions, the self-reported quantitative measures were found to be reliable, valid, and sensitive indicators of meaning in life. Whether these scales, as a collective, tap a unified, coherent construct of existential meaning needs to be demonstrated empirically through factor analytic investigations. The measurement review has also highlighted the need for more domain- and context-specific measures to clarify the contents and contexts that give rise to an overall sense of meaning and purpose. In addition, new measures sensitive to culturally specific sources of meaning in life are needed. Finally, more emphasis and effort should be placed on the development of qualitative measures that can complement and enrich our understanding of the existential meaning construct.

SUMMARY AND CONCLUSION

In this chapter, I offered a conceptual framework of existential meaning, grounded in the conviction that a complete understanding of meaning requires both an elemental and a holistic view of life. A model of how meaning is experienced was presented along four dimensions: the structural components of cognition, motivation, and affect; the sources from which meaning is experienced; the breadth of meaning; and the depth of meaning. A number of measuring instruments used to assess the holistic and the elemental facets of meaning were described and evaluated.

The existential perspective described in this chapter serves to complement and expand on the traditional stress/adaptation paradigm by taking into account the viewpoint of the experiencing person, by focusing on the human potential for growth, and by acknowledging the individual's ability to choose, to be responsible, and to act authentically. The model of existential meaning offers a useful framework for clarifying and understanding the experience of meaning, while the measures offer a variety of approaches to the measurement of meaning. Taken together, the existential perspective, the model, and the measures provide researchers with the necessary ingredients for conducting systematic, well-designed investigations into existential meaning.

In order to stimulate interest and to encourage more research into existential meaning, we must continue to strive toward greater conceptual clarity and toward the development of a diverse number of quantitative and qualitative measuring instruments. Only in this way will we come to understand fully the important role of existential meaning in optimizing human development across the life span.

REFERENCES

Battista, J., & Almond, R. (1973). The development of meaning in life. *Psychiatry, 36,* 409-427.

Bolt, M. (1975). Purpose in life and religious orientation. *Journal of Psychology and Theology, 3,* 116-118.

Chamberlain, K., & Zika, S. (1988). Measuring meaning in life: An examination of three scales. *Personality and Individual Differences, 9,* 589-596.

Crandall, J. E., & Rasmussen, R. D. (1975). Purpose in life as related to specific values. *Journal of Clinical Psychology, 31,* 483-485.

Crumbaugh, J. C., & Maholick, L. T. (1964). An experimental study in existentialism: The psychometric approach to Frankl's concept of nöogenic neurosis. *Journal of Clinical Psychology, 20,* 200-207.

Crumbaugh, J. C., & Maholick, L. T. (1969). *Manual of instruction for the Purpose in Life test.* Munster, IN: Psychometric Affiliates.

Debats, D. L. (1990). The Life Regard Index: Reliability and validity. *Psychological Reports, 67,* 27-34.

DePaola, S. J., & Ebersole, P. (1995). Meaning in life categories of elderly nursing home residents. *International Journal of Aging and Human Development, 40,* 227-236.

DeVogler, K. L., & Ebersole, P. (1980). Categorization of college students' meaning in life. *Journal of Psychology, 46,* 387-390.

DeVogler, K. L., & Ebersole, P. (1983). Young adolescents' meaning in life. *Psychological Reports, 52,* 427-431.

DeVogler-Ebersole, K., & Ebersole, P. (1985). Depth of meaning in life: Explicit rating criteria. *Psychological Reports, 56,* 303-310.

Dyck, M. J. (1987). Assessing logotherapeutic constructs: Conceptual and psychometric status of the Purpose in Life and Seeking of Noetic Goals tests. *Clinical Psychology Review, 7,* 439-447.

Emmonds, S., & Hooker, K. (1992). Perceived changes in life meaning following bereavement. *Omega: Journal of Death and Dying, 25,* 307-318.

Erikson, E. H. (1963). *Childhood and society.* New York: Norton.

Fife, B. L. (1995). The measurement of meaning in illness. *Social Science and Medicine, 40,* 1021-1028.

Fowler, J. W. (1983). Stages of faith: PT conversation with James Fowler. *Psychology Today, 17*(November), 56-62.

Frankl, V. E. (1963). *Man's search for meaning.* New York: Washington Square Press.

Garfield, C. A. (1973). A psychometric and clinical investigation of Frankl's concept of existential vacuum and of anomia. *Psychiatry, 36,* 396-408.

Hablas, R., & Hutzell, R. R. (1982). The Life Purpose Questionnaire: An alternative to the

Purpose-in-Life Test for geriatric, neuropsychiatric patients. In S. A. Wawrytko (Ed.), *Analecta Frankliana* (pp. 211-215). Berkeley, CA: Strawberry Hill.

Harlow, L. L., Newcomb, M. D., & Bentler, P. M. (1986). Depression, self-derogation, substance use, and suicide ideation: Lack of purpose in life as a mediational factor. *Journal of Clinical Psychology, 42,* 5-21.

Harlow, L. L., Newcomb, M. D., & Bentler, P. M. (1987). Purpose in Life test assessment using latent variable methods. *British Journal of Clinical Psychology, 26,* 235-236.

Hutzell, R. R. (1986). Meaning and purpose in life: Assessment techniques of logotherapy. *Hospice Journal, 2,* 37-50.

Jung, C. G. (1971). The stages of life. In R. F. C. Hill, *The portable Jung.* New York: Viking.

Kaufman, S. R. (1986). *The ageless self.* New York: Meridian.

Klinger, E. (1977). *Meaning and void.* Minneapolis: University of Minnesota Press.

Maddi, S. R. (1967). The existential neurosis. *Journal of Abnormal Psychology, 72,* 311-325.

Neugarten, B. L. & Associates. (1964). *Personality in middle and late life.* New York: Atherton.

Newcomb, M. D., & Harlow, L. L. (1986). Life events and substance use among adolescents: Moderating effects of powerlessness and meaninglessness in life. *Journal of Personality and Social Psychology, 51,* 564-577.

Nicholson, T., Higgins, W., Turner, P., James, S., Stickle, F., & Pruitt, T. (1994). The relation between meaning in life and the occurrence of drug abuse: A retrospective study. *Psychology of Addictive Behaviors, 8,* 24-28.

O'Connor, K., & Chamberlain, K. (1996). Dimensions of life meaning: A qualitative investigation at midlife. *British Journal of Psychology, 87,* 461-477.

Pearson, P. R., & Sheffield, B. F. (1989). Psychoticism and purpose in life. *Personality and Individual Differences, 10,* 1321-1322.

Phillips, W. M. (1980). Purpose in life, depression, and locus of control. *Journal of Clinical Psychology, 36,* 661-667.

Prager, E. (1996). Exploring personal meaning in an age-differentiated Australian sample: Another look at the Sources of Meaning Profile (SOMP). *Journal of Aging Studies, 10,* 117-136.

Prager, E. (1997). Sources of personal meaning for older and younger Australian and Israeli women: Profiles and comparisons. *Ageing and Society, 17,* 167-189.

Prager, E. (1998). Observations of personal meaning sources for Israeli age cohorts. *Aging and Mental Health, 2,* 128-136.

Reker, G. T. (1977). The Purpose-in-Life Test in an inmate population: An empirical investigation. *Journal of Clinical Psychology, 33,* 688-693.

Reker, G. T. (1991, July). *Contextual and thematic analyses of sources of provisional meaning: A life-span perspective.* Paper presented at the Biennial Meeting of the International Society for the Study of Behavioral Development, Minneapolis, MN.

Reker, G. T. (1992). *Manual of the Life Attitude Profile-Revised.* Peterborough, ON: Student Psychologists Press.

Reker, G. T. (1994). Logotheory and logotherapy: Challenges, opportunities, and some empirical findings. *The International Forum for Logotherapy, 17,* 47-55.

Reker, G. T. (1996). *Manual of the Sources of Meaning Profile-Revised (SOMP-R).* Peterborough, ON: Student Psychologists Press.

Reker, G. T. (1997). Personal meaning, optimism, and choice: Existential predictors of depression in community and institutional elderly. *The Gerontologist, 37,* 709-716.

Reker, G. T., & Cousins, J. B. (1979). Factor structure, construct validity and reliability of the Seeking of Noetic Goals (SONG) and Purpose in Life (PIL) tests. *Journal of Clinical Psychology, 35*, 85-91.

Reker, G. T., Peacock, E. J., & Wong, P. T. P. (1987). Meaning and purpose in life and well-being: A life-span perspective. *Journal of Gerontology, 42*, 44-49.

Reker, G. T., & Wong, P. T. P. (1988). Aging as an individual process: Toward a theory of personal meaning. In J. E. Birren & V. L. Bengtson (Eds.), *Emergent theories of aging* (pp. 214-246). New York: Springer.

Rokeach, M. (1973). *The nature of human values*. New York: Free Press.

Ruffin, J. E. (1984). The anxiety of meaninglessness. *Journal of Counseling and Development, 63*, 40-42.

Shek, D. T. L. (1986). The Purpose in Life questionnaire in a Chinese context: Some psychometric and normative data. *Chinese Journal of Psychology, 28*, 51-60.

Shek, D. T. L. (1992). Meaning in life and psychological well-being: An empirical study using the Chinese version of the Purpose-in-Life Questionnaire. *Journal of Genetic Psychology, 153*, 185-200.

Starck, P. L. (1985). *Guidelines – Meaning in Suffering Test*. Berkeley, CA: Institute of Logotherapy Press.

Ulmer, A., Range, L. M., & Smith, P. C. (1991). Purpose in life: A moderator of recovery from bereavement. *Omega: Journal of Death and Dying, 23*, 279-289.

Waisberg, J. L., & Porter, J. E. (1994). Purpose in life and outcome of treatment for alcohol dependence. *British Journal of Clinical Psychology, 33*, 49-63.

Yalom, I. D. (1980). *Existential psychotherapy*. New York: Basic Books.

Zika, S., & Chamberlain, K. (1987). Relation of hassles and personality to subjective well-being. *Journal of Personality and Social Psychology, 53*, 155-162.

Zika, S., & Chamberlain, K. (1992). On the relation between meaning in life and psychological well-being. *British Journal of Psychology, 83*, 133-145.

PART II

RESEARCH ON
EXISTENTIAL MEANING

Structural Components of Personal Meaning in Life and Their Relationship with Death Attitudes and Coping Mechanisms in Late Adulthood

Nancy Van Ranst and Alfons Marcoen

Preservation of Self in Late Adulthood

In the end phases of ontogenesis, aging is the more visible part of the global change process that constitutes the life course. Developmental processes become increasingly restricted to the aging person's higher mental functions (Birren & Schroots, 1984; Perlmutter, 1988). Many change processes and important events in advanced age are experienced as aversive and as more or less inevitable. Baltes (1987) indeed acknowledged that the ratio of gains and losses becomes increasingly negative in old age. One could expect that these inevitable experiences of loss should translate into reduced well-being. However, recent research results give testimony to a remarkable stability, resilience, and resourcefulness of the aging self (Brandtstädter & Greve, 1994). Most elderly people succeed in maintaining a positive identity and life perspective through reducing or avoiding "discrepancies between normative facets of self-representation and actual self-descriptive cognitions" (Brandtstädter & Greve, 1994, p. 57). They use so-called assimilative, accommodative, and immunization techniques. Assimilative activities aim at changing the situation in accordance with the person's normative self. Through the use of accommodative techniques the individual adjusts his or her self-evaluation standards in order to restore the fit between a given situation and the normative self. Immunizing mechanisms aim at mitigating experiences of discrepancy. Most aging people are not defenseless victims of their life circumstances and the inevitable processes of decline in their bodies. They continue to strive for congruence between their actual and expected self- and life-perceptions. Preservation of the self becomes the central motive in advanced old age (Tobin, 1991). This striving will go on as long as the elderly individual feels that his or her life is meaningful and valuable against an ultimate horizon of meaning.

Our culture does not provide clearly defined life tasks for elderly citizens. Aging people, especially the very old, must themselves find out how to make their lives meaningful. Eventually, elderly people have to learn simply to be there, to exist gracefully, notwithstanding illness, aloneness, and the inevitable nearness of death. The preservation of self in advanced old age becomes more and more a quest for meaning in life.

The Experience of Meaning in Life

Personal meaning has been conceptualized from a number of different perspectives, including the personal existence perspective (Kenyon, 1988), life themes (Thomae, 1968), life schemes (Thompson & Janigian, 1988), and needs for meaning (Baumeister, 1991). From these perspectives, it becomes clear that personal meaning has cognitive and motivational aspects. The experience of meaning in life implies views on self and life as coherent, and strivings for the realization of valuable goals. Reker and Wong (1988) rightly add a third component, the affective one, referring to the feelings of satisfaction that always accompanies the realization of personal meaning. They proposed to define personal meaning "as the cognizance of order, coherence, and purpose in one's existence, the pursuit and attainment of worthwhile goals, and an accompanying sense of fulfillment" (p. 221). It was this definition that served as a starting point for our research project in which personal meaning was explored in persons in their late adulthood.

Exploration of the Personal Meaning Structure in Older Adults

Indeed, the construct of personal meaning has recently been recognized as highly relevant to the study of successful aging. In this chapter we elaborate on the phenomenon of personal meaning in the lives of older adults and elderly persons. We consider personal meaning from the structural viewpoint introduced by Reker and Wong (1988). We explored the interrelationships between the different components of personal meaning and the connections of these components with death attitudes and coping mechanisms. We will illustrate our comments with findings from a study that we conducted with 376 community-dwelling older adults between the ages of 48 and 88 years (mean age = 65.90 years, 58.8 % of them were women). More than half of these participants lived together with a partner, mostly married. Most of them were retired. A great number had achieved a rather high professional status. Participants completed several paper-and-pencil questionnaires on the topics of meaning in life, death attitudes, and coping.

THREE STRUCTURAL COMPONENTS OF PERSONAL MEANING AND THEIR INTERRELATIONS

According to the above mentioned definition of personal meaning introduced by Reker and Wong (1988), personal meaning or meaning in life is a *multidimensional* phenomenon consisting of three interrelated components: cognitive, motivational, and affective. In the next section we elaborate on each of these components and their measures and report what we have found with respect to their interrelatedness.

Making Sense of Life and Looking for Purpose: The Cognitive Component

The cognitive component of meaning refers to one's life regard, one's beliefs and interpretations of the world as one sees it. This component contains the attempts to make sense of one's experiences and consists of ascriptions of meaning to events, activities, and life as a whole. Personal meaning from a cognitive perspective implies having a sense of meaning, an experience of purpose, and a framework.

In our survey we studied the cognitive component using two questionnaires: the Personal Meaning Index (PMI; Reker, 1989a) and the Life Regard Index (LRI; Battista & Almond, 1973). Two subscales were derived factorially from the PMI: (1) *Sense of Meaning*: referring to the expectation of a meaningful future and to the understanding of the meaning of life, and (2) *Life Purpose*: measuring the experience of life purpose. The subscale Framework of the LRI measured the ability to see life within some perspective or context, and to have derived a set of life goals or purpose in life. The scores on these three measures were all above the theoretical midpoint of the scales, indicating that most of our elderly participants felt that their life was meaningful. No gender differences nor correlations with age reached significance. This finding is in agreement with the results of Reker, Peacock, and Wong (1987), who also found high levels of life purpose and will to meaning among their oldest participants. Moreover, the zest for life and the search for ideals and values seem to become more important later in life.

Deriving Meaning From Different Sources or Goals: The Motivational Component

The motivational component of meaning refers to the pursuit and the attainment of personal goals that are consistent with one's values, needs, and wants. The achievement of personal goals is one of the cornerstones of a person's experience of meaning in life (Baumeister, 1991). People want their daily activities to have purpose. This purpose may be a goal to be achieved in a near or far future. Personal goals and values make it possible to direct and organize behavior.

Most of the studies on personal meaning in late adulthood and old age focus on personal goals of aging individuals. Research on personal goals of older adults showed that personal relationships with family members or friends are among the most important sources of meaning in later life; the preservation of health and rendering of services to others were also found to be meaningful goals (Burbank, 1992; DePaola & Ebersole, 1995; Ebersole & DePaola, 1987, 1989; McCarthy, 1983, 1985; Orbach, Iluz, & Rosenheim, 1987).

Lapierre, Bouffard, and Bastin (1992-1993) stated that older adults expressed a broad variety of goals. An important proportion of these aspirations referred to keeping one's health and autonomy and improving one's personality. Aspirations of contact were also found to be important, showing the participants' interest in meeting and helping other people. The results of this study revealed that the importance of transcendental aspirations increased with age and that desires for self-realization and exploration decreased with age.

Reker and Wong (1988) conceptualized the motivational component as being of a hierarchical nature, and they distinguished different levels of personal goals: some goals indicate a rather self-centered interest, others have a self-transcendent nature. At the lowest level of the hierarchy, they set self-preoccupation with pleasure and comfort. Devoting time and energy to the realization of one's potential is situated at a higher level. When the individual moves beyond the realm of self-interest, self-transcendent goals become important. This conceptualization was operationalized in a measure called the Sources of Meaning Profile (SOMP; Reker, 1988, 1989a). The SOMP contains 16 different sources of meaning in life. Each of these sources of meaning can be classified under one of the hierarchical levels of personal goals. In a life-span study with participants ranging in age from 18 to 98 years old, Reker (1991) found that personal relationships, enduring values and ideals, leisure activities, and meeting basic needs were the most important sources of meaning in the oldest group.

Our participants also completed the SOMP. However, the principal-components factor analysis we performed revealed only three levels of life goal orientations: *Self-Preoccupation* (containing the sources meeting basic needs, legacy, financial security, pleasurable activities, and possessions), *Individualism* (containing leisure activities, creative activities, personal achievements, and personal growth), and *Self-Transcendence* (containing personal relationships, religious activities, societal causes, and altruism). Three sources of meaning did not fit in any of the three subscales. These were enduring values and ideals, traditions and culture, and humanistic concerns. Our results show that material and self-preservation goals, grouped in the scale Self-Preoccupation, were rated as least important. The second set of goals, Individualism, indicating that the individual devotes time and energy to the realization of his or her potential, was the most important. So leisure activities, creative activities, personal achievements, and personal growth were on an average considered as the most important goals in life by our elderly adults. The mean score on the subscale Self-Transcendence was nearly as high as the mean score on Individualism. Self-transcendent sources of meaning were rated as very important as well. Women were found to derive more meaning from self-transcendent goals such as personal relationships, altruism, religious activities, and societal causes. This differential pattern in sources of meaning seems to reflect somewhat the traditional female sex-role stereotype of expressiveness, affiliation, and nurturance.

Feeling Good and Happy: The Affective Component

The affective component of meaning refers to the feelings of fulfillment, satisfaction, and happiness that accompany the conviction that life is worth living. This component has to do with well-being. Studies on the structure of well-being have revealed that several dimensions can be distinguished. Headey, Kelley, and Wearing (1993) considered four dimensions: life satisfaction, positive affect, depression, and anxiety. While life satisfaction is a rather cognitive aspect of well-being, positive affect, depression, and anxiety are purely affective dimensions.

In the study we conducted, we tried to measure those four different dimensions of well-being using the following scales. A principal-components factor analysis on the Life Satisfaction Index A (LSIA; Neugarten, Havighurst, & Tobin, 1961) revealed two factors that became two subscales: (1) *Positive State of Mind*: measuring positive mood and enthusiasm, and (2) *Satisfaction With the Past*: measuring the degree of satisfaction with life in the past and the degree of congruence between desired and attained goals. The subscale Fulfillment of the earlier mentioned Life Regard Index, which is a rather cognitive measure of well-being, gives an indication of the degree to which one sees oneself as having fulfilled the framework or life goals. The subscale Psychological Well-Being of the Perceived Well-Being scale (PWB; Reker & Wong, 1984) measures the presence of positive emotions and the absence of negative emotions. Feelings of depression were assessed by the Self-Rating Depression Scale (SRDS; Zung, 1965) and feelings of anxiety by the subscale Trait Anxiety of the State-Trait Anxiety Inventory (STAI; Spielberger, Gorsuch, & Lushene, 1970).

In the sample we studied, the scores on the positive measures of the affective component were rather high and those on the negative measures were low. These results demonstrate that our participants reported rather high levels of well-being. Gender differences emerged on four of the six measures. The older men were less depressed, less anxious, and more satisfied about their present and past life than the aged women. So men seem to experience higher levels of well-being. Both Trait Anxiety and Positive State of Mind correlated negatively with age.

How Are These Three Structural Components of Personal Meaning Related?

In the description of their structural model of personal meaning Reker and Wong (1988) hypothesized the three components to be interrelated in a specific way. The cognitive component is supposed to influence the motivational and the affective components, the motivational component should influence the affective component. The model also implies that the influencing component in each case receives feedback from the affected component.

Several studies provide some empirical evidence for the interrelatedness of the different aspects of the personal meaning experience. In Reker's (1991) life-span study, individuals who created meaning by transcending self-interests were found to experience a greater degree of ultimate meaning in life. The availability of a greater diversity of sources of meaning contributed to a global sense of meaning and to a higher level of psychological well-being. Lapierre, Bouffard and Bastin (1998) studied the relationship between the content of goals on the one hand and experienced meaning and well-being of participants on the other hand. Aspirations centered on health preservation were negatively associated with life satisfaction and experienced meaning in life. Life satisfaction and experienced meaning in life were positively related to goals of self-realization, maintaining contact with others, and wishes for others. Rapkin and Fischer (1992) also found that older individuals with different personal goals reported different levels of life satisfaction. In their study, satisfied elders were most concerned with maintenance, whereas dissatisfied persons wanted to make active improvements or to disengage.

A general tendency for happiness seems to be associated with finding life meaningful. In the group of older adults in the life-span study of Reker et al. (1987), psychological well-being was positively correlated with future meaning, life purpose, and life control, and negatively with lack of meaning in life. Zika and Chamberlain (1992) also found a strong association between meaning in life and well-being in a group of elderly.

In our own study we tried to shed light on the interrelatedness of the cognitive, motivational, and affective components of personal meaning. To evaluate a model of structural relationships between these three components, we used LISREL8 (Jöreskog & Sörbom, 1993). Two alternative models were investigated. In the first path model that was tested, the cognitive component of personal meaning affected the motivational and the affective component. The motivational component also influenced the affective component. This was the direction of influences that was originally suggested by Reker and Wong (1988). These authors also suggested several feedback mechanisms in their model of personal meaning. These were tested in a second alternative model in which the affective component influenced the cognitive and the motivational component and in which the motivational component had an influence on the cognitive component. Fit indices indicated that the second model of personal meaning had a better fit than the first one.

Figure 4.1 shows the final model on the relationships between the cognitive, motivational, and affective component of personal meaning. There were paths from the three different life goal orientations – Self-Preoccupation, Individualism, and Self-Transcendence – to the three measures of the cognitive component. The purely affective indices of the affective component – Psychological Well-Being, Depression, and Trait Anxiety – had both a direct and an indirect effect on the cognitive component. The more cognitive measures of the affective component – Fulfillment, Positive State of Mind, and Satisfaction with the Past – also influenced Sense of Meaning, Life Purpose, and Framework. There were no paths between the affective and the motivational components.

Contrary to the original hypothesis of Reker and Wong (1988), the best fitting model of personal meaning was one in which experiencing a sense of meaning, having a purpose in life, and a certain framework to look at life resulted from the presence of positive feelings, such as fulfillment, satisfaction, and the absence of negative emotions such as depression and anxiety, on the one hand, and valuing different personal goals, on the other hand. Striving for personal goals that are self-centered, for example, meeting materialistic and financial needs, resulted in a stronger experience of life purpose. Self-transcendent life goals on the other hand had a negative effect on life purpose. A possible explanation for these contradictory results is the fact that it is easier to determine if and when one has reached specific, materialistic goals than to realize fully self-transcendent goals. Self-transcendent sources of meaning do not constitute well-defined domains of possible goals. Rather, they form a continuously changing constellation of appealing situations in which the individual might engage in a spirit of availability. Deriving meaning from self-transcendent as well as from individualistic personal goals and tasks had a positive influence on the sense of meaning. It seems that working on one's own development as well as trying to build a better world for everybody, give meaning to life. Having a framework to look at life was positively affected by valuing individualistic sources of meaning. Our results do not confirm the findings of Reker (1991), who found that the strength of the association between experienced ultimate meaning in life and the different levels of personal goals increased in direct proportion to commitment to higher levels in the hierarchy of values.

The final path model provides some support for the distinction made between purely affective and rather cognitive aspects of well-being (Headey et al., 1993). The experience of fulfillment and satisfaction with life seem to bridge the purely affective aspects of well-being and the cognitive component. The absence of negative feelings and the presence of positive feelings were important determinants of considering life as meaningful. These results are in accordance with the definition of psychological well-being given by Ryff (1989). She even considers purpose and meaning in life as aspects of well-being. In contrast with the findings of Reker (1991), we found no relationship between the motivational and the affective component. However, Reker's operationalization of the motivational component was slightly different. He stated that a greater breadth of sources of meaning contributes to a higher level of psychological well-being, wherein breadth refers to both the number and the diversity of levels of sources of meaning.

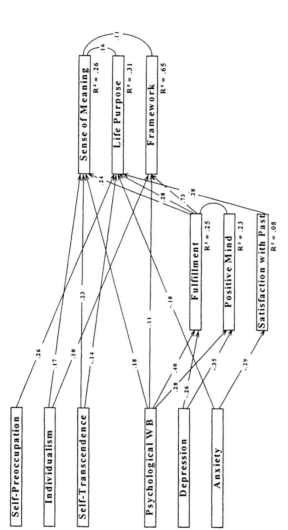

Figure 4.1: Interrelatedness of the Cognitive, Motivational and Affective Components of Meaning

PERSONAL MEANING AND DEATH ATTITUDES

In old age life's end is inevitably approaching. As older adults come closer to the end of their own life, they are also frequently confronted with the passing of familiar others and loved ones. Death and finitude are important themes of life in late adulthood and old age. Wong, Reker, and Gesser (1994) gave attention to the multidimensionality of death attitudes as they distinguished two negative attitudes toward death, death *avoidance* and *fear* of death, as well as three types of death acceptance. They define death acceptance as "being psychologically prepared for the final exit" (Wong et al., 1994, p. 124). This preparedness includes cognitive awareness of one's own finitude and a positive or neutral emotional reaction to this cognizance. The three types of death acceptance attitudes are a neutral, an approach, and an escape variant of acceptance. Considering death as an integral part of life is testimony of an attitude of *neutral acceptance*. In this case, one neither fears nor welcomes death. One simply accepts death as an unchangeable fact of life. An attitude of *approach acceptance* implies belief in a happy afterlife. Belief in an afterlife is often related to religious beliefs and practices. Finally, *escape acceptance* frequently occurs in people whose life is full of misery and pain. When individuals are overwhelmed by suffering and pain, death may become a welcome alternative that seems to offer the only escape. The authors developed an instrument to measure the different dimensions of death attitudes, the Death Attitude Profile-Revised (DAP-R).

The participants in our study also completed the DAP-R. An attitude of neutral acceptance prevailed in our sample. Most of the elderly seemed to accept death as a natural, undeniable, and unavoidable part of the course of life. This finding is in line with the results of Wong et al. (1994), who found that an attitude of acceptance of death was dominantly present in their elderly sample. To a certain extent our results also support the findings of Munnichs (1966), who found that an attitude of death acceptance characterized the largest group of elderly in his study. Respondents moderately agreed with the statements in the scales Approach Acceptance and Escape Acceptance. The mean scores on the scales Death Avoidance and Fear of Death were the lowest. On average, the participants moderately disagreed with the items in these subscales. Since we found no gender differences whatsoever regarding death attitudes, we could not confirm the general finding that women tend to report more fear of death than men (Neimeyer, 1988). We did find two effects of age on death attitudes: age correlated positively with Approach Acceptance and Escape Acceptance. In his review of the literature, Neimeyer (1988) also concluded that relatively healthy respondents show an increased comfort with mortality in later life. A possible explanation for the effect of age on Approach Acceptance is the greater religiosity of older people. The increase in Escape Acceptance could be traced to the diminished quality of health in late old age.

From an *existential* point of view, attitudes toward death cannot be separated from the search for meaning. The manner in which individuals look at life affects their attitudes toward death. But the converse is also true: the manner in which people look at death affects how they see life. The existential viewpoint is consistent with Erikson's (1963) view that individuals in their last stage of development have to come to terms with death by resolving the tension of integrity versus despair. Individuals who do not succeed in accepting their own life course as unique, as good the way it has been, are threatened with despair and have to contend with fear of death. Coupled with Erikson's last psychosocial crisis is the process of life review. Butler (1968) stated that the realization of impending death brings on the process of life reviewing. Older persons who have engaged in this process should have resolved many existential questions, come to terms with them to a certain degree, and, as a result, have fewer death anxieties. Studies on the relationship between life review and death attitudes tend to support Butler's view (Wong et al., 1994). In a study by Munnichs (1966) it was confirmed that elderly persons' attitudes toward finitude were linked with their outlook on life or philosophy. Having an explicit or implicit religious or humanistic sense of significance of life went together with a death attitude of acceptance or acquiescence.

In five different regression analyses we tried to predict the death attitudes of our elderly participants by using measures of the cognitive, the motivational, and the affective component of meaning as predictors. These regression analyses made it clear that all three components of personal meaning had some effect on the death attitudes. Older adults who stated that they understand the meaning of life and who could see life within some perspective had more positive death attitudes as they reported higher levels of Approach Acceptance and less Death Avoidance and Fear of Death. Striving strongly for life purpose, on the other hand, involved a more negative attitude toward death, given the positive effect of Life Purpose on Death Avoidance and Fear of Death. These results are in contrast with those of Rappaport, Fossler, Bross, and Gilden (1993), who found a negative relationship between purpose in life and death anxiety in a sample of older adults.

The three types of life goal orientations or sources of meaning were differently connected with the death attitudes. Valuing self-preoccupied sources of meaning was negatively associated with neutrally accepting and positively with avoiding and fearing death. It is understandable that a more materialistic life-goal orientation is associated with fear of death for death means leaving all possessions behind. Deriving meaning from personal growth as measured by the scale Individualism was positively related to Neutral Acceptance but negatively to Approach Acceptance. At the same time, elderly adults who strongly valued self-development did not avoid death. The rather strong effect of Self-Transcendence on Approach Acceptance is probably due to the fact that deriving meaning from religious activities is part of this subscale. That religion can play an important role in having a positive attitude toward death was already found in earlier studies (Thorson & Powell, 1990; Wittkowski & Baumgartner, 1977).

Only three measures of the affective component had a significant effect on the death attitudes. Elderly who enjoyed high levels of Psychological Well-Being were more likely to accept death as an inevitable reality of life. This result is in line with the findings of Wong et al. (1994). However, they did not consider death as an escape from a painful life. The causes that bring about pain and misery in life seem to threaten the mental health of the aged individual and at the same time make him or her long for death. Depression affected Neutral Acceptance in a negative way while Trait Anxiety had a positive effect on both Escape Acceptance and Fear of Death. Several other studies also recorded a positive correlation between general anxiety and death anxiety (Neimeyer, 1988).

To summarize, the experience of meaning in life favors positive feelings towards death and represses both avoidance and fear of death. However, too much striving for purpose may induce avoidance and fear of death. Deriving meaning from self-preoccupation seems to lead to more death avoidance and fear, individualism favors neutral acceptance, and self-transcenders tend to welcome death as an ultimate state of well-being. Psychological well-being and neutral acceptance of death go hand in hand. Depressive feelings thwart neutral acceptance, and trait anxiety may lead to both escape acceptance and fear of death.

PERSONAL MEANING AND COPING WITH AGING

Even a normally passing old age is a taxing experience that involves a multitude of important life events and developmental changes like bereavement, role losses, chronic health problems, or declines in physiological and psychological functioning. All these changes require a lot of adaptational capacities of the older individuals who face them. According to Lazarus and DeLongis (1983), appraisal and coping are essential concepts in the analysis of how one reacts to the stress that accompanies the process of aging.

We examined the way in which the adults in our sample seemed to deal with the vicissitudes of aging. Therefore we used the Coping Orientations and Prototypes (COAP; Wong, Reker, & Peacock, 1993) instrument that measures different ways of coping. In our research we distinguished Tension Reduction and Active-Instrumental, Religious, Social, Emotional, and Existential coping. The participants made maximum use of existential coping strategies as they tried to accept what had happened to them, for example, by cognitive restructuring. Active, instrumental coping was also frequently used. Seeking comfort and support in religious beliefs and practices was popular, too. This result confirms earlier findings that religion can play an important adaptational role in late adulthood and old age (Koenig, 1994). However, the standard deviation of the scale Religious Coping was rather high, indicating that respondents clearly differed regarding relying on religious beliefs and practices. Seeking social support and expressing emotions, reducing tension, and generating negative emotions were less popular coping techniques. Gender differences emerged as women reported higher levels of religious and social coping, and of tension reduction. Age correlated positively with existential, religious, and negative emotional coping.

The link between coping and personal meaning is made by authors such as Wong (1993) and Lazarus and DeLongis (1983). In his resource-congruence model of stress and coping, Wong (1993) assumed that the availability of sufficient resources and the appropriate utilization of these resources are essential to effective coping. In his model he emphasizes the importance of proactive coping, which stands for developing a variety of resources and avoiding unnecessary risks. According to Wong (1993), personal meaning is a major psychological resource that can be drawn on in times of need. Lazarus and DeLongis (1983) claimed that stress and coping should be examined from the standpoint of a person's central storyline or sources of personal meaning. They believe the two following personality variables to be very important in shaping stress and coping over the life course: patterns of commitment and beliefs about self and the world. Patterns of commitment express people's valued ideals and goals and the choices they make or are prepared to make in order to bring them to fruition. These commitments fit in with the motivational component of personal meaning. Beliefs, on the other hand, belong to the cognitive component of personal meaning as they are personally formed or culturally shared notions about reality that organize people's perceptions and appraisals of situations.

In line with these authors we assumed that coping and the preceding process of appraisal are influenced by the personal meaning system of an individual. We tested this hypothesis by means of regression analyses in which the three components of meaning were considered as predictors of the ways of coping. Our results confirmed the assumptions of Wong (1993) and Lazarus and DeLongis (1983). The cognitive, as well as the motivational and affective components, turned out to be predictors of coping behavior. Elderly people who claimed to understand the meaning of life made use of several different coping strategies. Adults with a stronger self-centered life goal orientation reported using more active and instrumental coping strategies. The individualists had less trust in God, too, when facing old age problems. Adults with a self-transcendent orientation, on the other hand, sought comfort and support in their religious conviction while at the same time reporting higher levels of negative emotional coping. A lack of psychological well-being gave rise to the use of tension reduction strategies. Individuals who felt more depressed coped less in an existential or active way but rather put their trust in God. Anxious elderly also used less existential but more negative emotional coping strategies. The older adults who experienced higher levels of fulfillment used less negative emotional coping.

CONCLUSIONS

Empirical investigations into the experience of meaning in life are still scarce. Each piece of research may lead to some new insights and suggestions for further research. This is the case for the present investigation. Indeed, some interesting results emerged. First, the best fitting model of the interrelations between the three components of personal meaning does not correspond to the original hypothesized model of Reker and Wong. The analysis does not reveal a relationship between measures of the affective component, on the one side, and the motivational component, on the other side. Moreover, both components precede the cognitive component in the model. Well-being and life satisfaction, or feeling good about life, past and present, can be considered as the affective ground that gives rise to positive statements about life's meaning and purpose and the belief in a global framework in which life is embedded. Depressive feelings and a generalized tendency to feel anxious are not conducive to positive evaluations of one's life in the present and the past, and consequently diminish the sense of meaning and the conviction that one's life has a purpose. The presence of these negative emotions is also linked to a diminished use of existential and active-instrumental coping strategies and a tendency to use religious coping or emotional coping when facing the vicissitudes of old age. The centrality, in the personal meaning model, of enduring affective states as a base of positive cognitions about one's life and the world seems understandable in a developmental perspective. Are not positive and negative affective states, and perceptions and cognitions intertwined right from the beginning of the life course? Whatever the causes of the positive mood states may be, they favor a positive life regard. Positive affective states imply a felt sense of meaning that can occasionally become articulated or elaborated. This occurs when people are asked to fill out scales and questionnaires (Marcoen, 1993). At least to a certain extent the felt or latent meaning of life becomes manifest or articulated. Only a minority of persons have an elaborated life view or worldview.

A second interesting result of the model testing pertains to the relationship between the motivational component and the cognitive component. Whatever sources of meaning the elderly persons in the sample considered important, they articulated a sense of meaning and the awareness of a framework for their lives. This was especially the case for those respondents who stressed the importance of individualistic strivings. Participants with self-centered materialistic concerns had more articulated life purposes. Perhaps they knew exactly what they were missing and therefore also what they were striving for. Transcendent concerns focusing on other people's well-being, social causes, and religious activities generated less articulated purpose-related evaluations but did contribute to a sense of meaning. The self-transcenders less focused goal orientation may reveal an open idealistic attitude with a long-range time perspective. This interpretation is supported by a third main result regarding the connections between life-goal orientations, coping, and death attitudes. Indeed, self-transcendent goal orientations were positively related to the approach acceptance of death and a certain inclination to religious coping. This finding contrasts with the other finding that individualistic dimensions in the pattern of goal orientations are negatively related to religious coping and approach acceptance of finitude and death.

On the basis of the regression analyses with the coping with aging strategies as dependent variables and the personal meaning measures as predictors, a fourth conclusion can be formulated. Awareness of meaning in life – and not the other aspects of the cognitive component, life purpose and framework – has predictive value with regard to the avowed use of all coping mechanisms except negative emotional coping. The conviction that life has meaning may imply that late adulthood and old age are considered as any other stage of the life course and therefore worthy of the mobilization of all adequate coping mechanisms. Or the other way around, the availability of a rich repertoire of strategies for coping with aging may help aging people to maintain a sense of meaning even when experiences of loss and decline are beginning to abound.

REFERENCES

Baltes, P. B. (1987). Theoretical propositions of life-span developmental psychology: On the dynamics between growth and decline. *Developmental Psychology, 23*, 611-626.

Battista, J., & Almond, R. (1973). The development of meaning in life. *Psychiatry, 36*, 409-427.

Baumeister, R. F. (1991). *Meanings of life.* New York: Guilford.

Birren, J. E., & Schroots, J. J. F. (1984). Steps to an ontogenetic psychology. *Academic Psychology Bulletin, 6*, 177-190.

Brandtstädter, J., & Greve, W. (1994). The aging self: Stabilizing and protective processes. *Developmental Review, 14*, 52-80.

Burbank, P. M. (1992). An exploratory study: Assessing the meaning in life among older adult clients. *Journal of Gerontological Nursing, 18*, 19-28.

Butler, R. N. (1968). The life review: An interpretation of reminiscence in the aged. In B. L. Neugarten (Ed.), *Middle age and aging: A reader in social psychology* (pp. 486-496). Chicago: University of Chicago Press.

DePaola, S. J., & Ebersole, P. (1995). Meaning in life categories of elderly nursing home residents. *International Journal of Aging and Human Development, 40*, 227-236.

Ebersole, P., & DePaola, S. (1987). Meaning in life categories of later life couples. *Journal of Psychology, 121*, 185-191.

Ebersole, P., & DePaola, S. (1989). Meaning in life depth in the active married elderly. *Journal of Psychology, 123*, 171-178.

Erikson, E. H. (1963). *Childhood and society* (2nd Ed.). New York: Norton.

Headey, B. W., Kelley, J., & Wearing, A. J. (1993). Dimensions of mental health: Life satisfaction, positive affect, anxiety, and depression. *Social Indicators Research, 29*, 63-82.

Jöreskog, K., & Sörbom, D. (1993). *LISREL8: Structural equation modelling with the SIMPLIS command language.* Hillsdale, NJ: Lawrence Erlbaum.

Kenyon, G. M. (1988). Basic assumptions in theories of human aging. In J. E. Birren & V. L. Bengtson (Eds.), *Emergent theories of aging* (pp. 3-18). New York: Springer.

Koenig, H. G. (1994). *Aging and God: Spiritual pathways to mental health in middle and later years.* New York: Haworth Pastoral Press.

Lapierre, S., Bouffard, L., & Bastin, E. (1992-1993). Motivational goal objects in later life. *International Journal of Aging and Human Development, 36*, 279-292.

Lapierre, S., Bouffard, L., & Bastin, E. (1998). *Personal goals and subjective well-being in later life.* Manuscript submitted for publication.

Lazarus, R. S., & DeLongis, A. (1983). Psychological stress and coping in aging. *American*

Psychologist, 38, 245-254.

Marcoen, A. (1993). The search for meaning: Some reflections from a psychogerontological perspective. *Ultimate Reality and Meaning, 16*, 228-240.

McCarthy, S. V. (1983). Geropsychology: Meaning in life for adults over seventy. *Psychological Reports, 53*, 497-498.

McCarthy, S. V. (1985). Geropsychology: Meaning in life for elderhostelers. *Psychological Reports, 56*, 351-354.

Munnichs, J. M. A. (1966). *Old age and finitude: A contribution to psychogerontology.* Basel: Karger.

Neimeyer, R. A. (1988). Death anxiety. In H. Wass, F. M. Berardo, & R. A. Neimeyer (Eds.), *Dying: Facing the facts* (2nd ed.) (pp. 97-136). Washington, DC: Hemisphere Publishing Company.

Neugarten, B. L., Havighurst, R. J., & Tobin, S. S. (1961). The measurement of life satisfaction. *Journal of Gerontology, 16*, 134-143.

Orbach, I., Iluz, A., & Rosenheim, E. (1987). Value systems and commitment to goals as a function of age, integration of personality, and fear of death. *International Journal of Behavioral Development, 10*, 225-239.

Perlmutter, M. (1988). Cognitive potential throughout life. In J. E. Birren & V. L. Bengtson (Eds.), *Emergent theories of aging* (pp. 247-268). New York: Springer.

Rapkin, B. D., & Fischer, K. (1992). Framing the construct of life satisfaction in terms of older adults' personal goals. *Psychology and Aging, 7*, 138-149.

Rappaport, H., Fossler, R. J., Bross, L. S., & Gilden, D. (1993). Future time, death anxiety, and life purpose among older adults. *Death Studies, 17*, 369-379.

Reker, G. T. (November, 1988). *Sources of personal meaning among young, middle-aged and older adults: A replication.* Paper presented at the Annual Meeting of the Gerontological Society of America, San Francisco.

Reker, G. T. (1989a). *Measuring ultimate meaning in life: The Personal Meaning Index.* Paper submitted to Division 20, APA, New Orleans.

Reker, G. T. (March, 1989b). *Operationalizing Frankl's logotherapy: Multidimensional measurements of the sources of personal meaning.* Invited address at the Meeting of the American Society on Aging, Washington, DC.

Reker, G. T. (July, 1991). *Contextual and thematical analyses of sources of provisional meaning: A life-span perspective.* Paper presented at the Biennial Meetings of the International Society for the Study of Behavioral Development, Minneapolis, MN.

Reker, G. T., Peacock, E. J., & Wong, P. T. P. (1987). Meaning and purpose in life and well-being: A life-span perspective. *Journal of Gerontology, 42*, 44-49.

Reker, G. T., & Wong, P. T. P. (1984). Psychological and physical well-being in the elderly: The Perceived Well-Being Scale (PWB). *Canadian Journal on Aging, 3*, 23-32.

Reker, G. T., & Wong, P. T. P. (1988). Aging as an individual process: Toward a theory of personal meaning. In J. E. Birren & V. L. Bengtson (Eds.), *Emergent theories of aging* (pp. 214-246). New York: Springer.

Ryff, C. D. (1989). Happiness is everything or is it? Explorations on the meaning of psychological well-being. *Journal of Personality and Social Psychology, 57*, 1069-1081.

Spielberger, C. D., Gorsuch, R. L., & Lushene, R. E. (1970). *STAI manual.* Palo Alto, CA: Consulting Psychologists Press.

Thomae, H. (1968). *Das Individuum und seine Welt: Eine Persönlichkeitstheorie.* Göttingen: Verlag für Psychologie.

Thompson, S. C., & Janigian, A. S. (1988). Life schemes: A framework for understanding the search for meaning. *Journal of Social and Clinical Psychology, 7*, 260-280.

Thorson, J. A., & Powell, F. C. (1990). Meanings of death anxiety and intrinsic religiosity. *Journal of Clinical Psychology, 46*, 379-391.

Tobin, S. S. (1991). *Personhood in advanced old age: Implications for practice.* New York: Springer.

Wittkowski, J., & Baumgartner, I. (1977). Religiosity and attitude toward death and dying in old persons. *Zeitschrift für Gerontologie, 10*, 61-68.

Wong, P. T. P. (1993). Effective management of life stress: The resource-congruence model. *Stress Medicine, 9*, 51-60.

Wong, P. T. P., Reker, G. T., & Gesser, G. (1994). The Death Attitude Profile-Revised: A multidimensional measure of attitudes towards death. In R. A. Neimeyer (Ed.), *Death anxiety handbook: Research, instrumentation, and application* (pp. 121-148). Washington, DC: Taylor & Francis.

Wong, P. T. P., Reker, G. T., & Peacock, E. J. (1993). *Coping Orientations and Prototypes (COAP).* Unpublished manuscript, Trent University, Peterborough, ON.

Zika, S., & Chamberlain, K. (1992). On the relation between meaning in life and psychological well-being. *British Journal of Psychology, 83*, 133-145.

Zung, W. W. K. (1965). A self-rating depression scale. *Archives of General Psychiatry, 12*, 63-70.

CHAPTER 5

Dimensions and Discourses of Meaning in Life:
Approaching Meaning From Qualitative Perspectives[1]

Kay O'Connor and Kerry Chamberlain

As this volume attests, research and theory on meaning in life is receiving more prominent attention in social science research. A number of general (e.g., Frankl, 1963; Yalom, 1980) and specific (e.g., Fife, 1994; Harlow & Newcomb, 1990; Janoff-Bulman, 1989; Reker & Wong, 1988; Thompson & Janigian, 1988) theoretical accounts of meaning have been proposed, and a variety of empirical research has demonstrated that meaning has important psychological consequences for individuals. With limited exceptions, most of this research has adopted a positivist, quantitative perspective for the investigation of meaning.

Taking a qualitative perspective, however, provides several advantages for research into meaning in life, partly because of the nature of these methods and partly because of the nature of the topic. Qualitative perspectives have different objectives, and different ontological and epistemological premises from a quantitative perspective. Qualitative research values, and gives priority to, the participant's own experience and point of view and seeks to avoid the imposition of the researcher's viewpoint through the use of pre-determined theoretical frameworks or measures. Hence, qualitative research attempts to uncover the nature of meaning from the participants' own understandings, accounts, and frames of reference, using open-ended techniques such as interviews, life histories, and biographies rather than structured techniques like questionnaires and scales.

Qualitative researchers seek to provide rich descriptive accounts of phenomena and to promote understanding rather than seek prediction; to provide interpretations rather than "facts." A qualitative perspective also seeks to include the value systems and social contexts of individuals in any interpretation. Thus, qualitative approaches give salience to detailed descriptions of the person's world, viewpoint, and understandings.

We suggest that meaning in life is particularly suited to investigation through qualitative research methods. Meaning is constructed by the person reacting to life experiences within his or her historical and social context. Sources of meaning can be diverse, and the experience of meaning varies among people. Hence, we believe that meaning is ideally suited to investigation with methods that value experience and understanding, and attempt to provide interpretative accounts.

For these reasons we utilized a qualitative perspective in our work, and conducted detailed semi-structured interviews about meaning in life with 38 adults (25 women and 13 men). These were all chosen to be at the stage of mid-life (between 40 and 50 years old) because we reasoned that issues of meaning are highly salient at this time of life. Researchers have identified this period as a time for looking inward, for the destructuring and restructuring of experience, and for stock-taking and reorienting to time-left-to-live rather than time-since-birth (e.g., Levinson, 1986; Neugarten & Neugarten, 1987). Our participants were also chosen to represent a diversity of occupations and were from middle- and working-class settings. The interviews, after an initial conversation to establish rapport, began with the question, "What do you think of as an important source of meaning in your life?" Beyond this, the interview process encouraged participants to reveal as much as possible about the nature of this source and went on to explore all other sources that they felt were relevant to themselves. Clarifying questions were used when necessary, and interviews could develop in any direction. Interviews were tape-recorded and lasted for an average of 40 minutes.

When we came to analyze and interpret this information, we approached it from two different perspectives, each examining different issues, and using different qualitative approaches. These are addressed in turn below.

DIMENSIONS OF MEANING[2]

Reker and Wong (1988) proposed a theoretical account of meaning with four different structural dimensions, relating to where meaning comes from (sources), how it is experienced (source components), the diversity with which it is experienced (breadth), and the degree of self-transcendence involved (depth). (See Chapter 3, this volume, for a more detailed treatment.) Once the interviews were conducted and transcribed, we examined their content for indications of these dimensions. Essentially, our goal was to discover to what degree the dimensions of meaning proposed previously would be found when people were asked to give rich, detailed accounts of meaning in an open-ended interview.

Sources of Meaning

These people described a very wide diversity of specific sources when allowed to talk extensively about meaning in their lives. We obtained 222 different specific sources of meaning from the 38 people, which could be classified into six broad categories. The first, *relationships with people*, was mentioned in one form or another by every person.[3] For most, relationships with children and family were central sources of meaning:

> My family is the center of my life and always has been, not just my immediate family now, but my family in the past. Most things relate to my family ... it's the center and most things branch out from it. (18)

Intimate relationships and friendships were another important source of meaning in this category:

> Relationships with people in the widest sense with friends are the basis for my existence. I see myself as an individual and connected strongly as if I am roped to them, to hundreds of people. (12)

Creativity was the second most prominent source category, mentioned in some form by three quarters of the participants. Some spoke of this in very general terms:

> Life exists for us as people, and we are the creators. (26)

... and others were more specific:

> When I am working out my paintings and painting paintings, I am very much aware of the meaning I am putting into them, all the things that I feel about life. (24)

Personal development was also a prominent category, with themes of self-responsibility and independence being common specific sources of meaning here:

> One goal is independence, and being able to be independent if I choose to be, taking responsibility for the things I decide to do. (28)

A less common category of sources was *religious and spiritual*, although the specific sources mentioned here covered a diverse collection of ideas, values, and feelings. For some, it was a deeply important area of meaning:

> Recently, I have had a deeper and more significant understanding of faith and how it leads me through my personal life ... it is a source of nourishment and a source of guidance. (40)

For others, Christian dogma was rejected, but the existence of some form of ultimate power and a final accountability was still accepted:

I don't think there is Jesus and God and the devil and the angels standing on clouds playing their harps, but I certainly think that there is another level of existence, otherwise I can't see the point of being here. (4)

A further important category of meaning was *social and political*. Again, people's accounts of meaning in this area included a diverse set of specific sources, ranging from the interpersonal to the self-transcendent:

I think it is only by people making mutual sacrifices that will help to overcome the social problems, the racial tensions, the political differences between people. If one dies before the process is finished, we accept that. We know that individually we can achieve little. We must join with others. (37)

The sixth source category, *relationship with nature*, contained specific sources related in one form or another to the natural environment. For some, this involved notions of responsibility for the planet and the role of the human species:

Humans are only part of the universe. Though we are the dominant being in the physical world, what humans haven't yet learned is how to interact with the rest of the world, with our environment. (15)

For others, nature provided a connection with cosmic meaning:

When I look up at the visible universe at night, I feel an incredible peace in my insignificance. (5)

This analysis revealed that, when people are given the opportunity to provide detailed accounts of meaning in their own words, they present with a rich diversity of specific sources from which they derive meaning. These can be classified into the six major source categories of meaning presented above. Five of these categories have been represented in previous research, but we found it necessary to add the further category, relationship with nature, in order to classify adequately the responses we obtained.

Source Components of Meaning

Reker and Wong (1988) described the components of meaning as cognitive, motivational, and affective. Cognitively, people interpret their experiences and develop understanding and beliefs. Motivationally, they develop value systems that dictate the goals they set, and the pursuit and attainment of these goals leads to a sense of purpose. Affectively, they have feelings of satisfaction and fulfillment from their experiences and the attainment of their goals.

We examined each of the 222 specific sources of meaning for evidence of the presence of these source components of meaning, and were surprised to find how extensive this was. Almost every participant reported all three components for every specific source described. For example, in talking about interpersonal relationships, one participant gave the following cognitive material:

> We are social animals. To satisfy that we need some overall set of beliefs to incorporate other people into one's life. It makes that into something bigger than just individual relationships with individual people. (11)

This was followed by material with a motivational content:

> I have social interaction with people. I have intelligent discussion ... ideas exchanged. I have physical relationships with people, all those things. ... Valuing one's own contribution gives life meaning in the context of all the other contributions that are made as well.

And then, the description moved to the affective component of this source of meaning:

> It's a big adventure to see what happens and where it goes ... the rewards and satisfactions that come from going places with other people. It expands one's thinking and it's interesting, and it's fun and it's satisfying.

This type of account was very common in the reports we obtained, and our analysis strongly confirmed that people's accounts of the specific sources of meaning in their lives consistently contain cognitive, motivational, and affective components. This provides clear support for this feature of Reker and Wong's (1988) theoretical account of meaning.

Breadth of Meaning

This dimension refers to how diversely people experience meaning in their lives. Using the number of sources as a measure of breadth, we found that people did differ in this aspect of meaning, although not markedly. Our participants reported about six specific sources of meaning on average, which is quite similar to previous findings (DeVogler-Ebersole & Ebersole, 1985). When we considered the more general categories of sources, rather than the specific sources, we found that our participants reported specific sources within about four of these categories on average. This reveals that specific sources are, in practice, spread across categories, and that there is considerable diversification in sources of meaning. People appear to find meaning in a broad variety of domains of life.

Depth of Meaning

This dimension differentiates between accounts of meaning that are superficial and those that are deep. The accounts of meaning also clearly demonstrated differences in depth from the self-oriented to the more cosmic and transcendent, as illustrated by the following quotations:

> I wouldn't like to be in the world by myself ... without other people around then ... yeah, that gives meaning to life. (32)

> This little universe that we are on and ... the life that exists within it is mutually connected. Nothing is exclusive of anything else, and the pattern of our little planet in the universe that we are on is just one of many and they are all interrelated again like the interrelationships of people. (28)

We classified people's accounts for depth using the criteria proposed by Reker and Wong (1988), but we found some difficulties with this procedure. Different source categories were associated with different levels of depth; greater depth was found for the categories of relationship with nature, religious and spiritual, and social and political than for the other categories. Also, levels of depth were not equally represented in accounts, and differed in scope. The first level was relatively narrow, relating solely to pleasure and comfort, whereas the third level was relatively extensive, ranging from the private and interpersonal to awareness of broad social and international issues. Finally, depth rated in this manner did not produce an ordinal assessment: ratings for a specific source could move from the first (pleasurable) to the third (interpersonal and social) level without mention of material at the second (personal) level. Depth is clearly an important dimension of meaning present in people's accounts, but we suggest that its assessment requires better conceptualization.

Overview

This analysis examined whether the dimensions of meaning that had been proposed previously could be found in unstructured personal accounts of meaning. Our findings suggest that all four dimensions can be identified relatively readily, although their evaluation is sometimes problematic. Further, it became apparent that several of our participants integrated these specific dimensions into an overall framework of meaning. Frequently, these frameworks were associated with a specific and predominant category of meaning such as creativity or relationships with people. As an example, one participant referred to several different source categories (identified here) within a framework of creativity:

> I often think that the meaning of life is to be creative. You can be creative in lots of ways and dedicate the activity to either yourself (*personal development*), or a God (*religious and spiritual*), or society (*social and political*), or some other end. I think that having kids (*relationships with people*) is quite a creative thing to do and that's one of the things I really enjoyed. (12)

This notion of a framework has received little attention, although it supports the concept of a life framework proposed by Battista and Almond (1973), and deserves more attention. A framework of meaning enables people to reflect upon their experiences of meaning, to look forward to future meaning in new domains, and to process their experience in different ways.

DISCOURSES OF MEANING

When conducting the analysis above, we noted that the accounts of our participants contained considerable material that made explicit or implicit reference to religion, Christianity, and church-related issues in various forms. We became interested in where their explications of meaning were drawn from, and how their various accounts of meaning were legitimized. We began to question how the social and cultural contexts of people are involved in the availability of accounts of meaning, and in what way these provided resources for meaning. In this section we explore some of the historical and cultural contexts in which meaning in life is constituted, this time adopting a discourse approach.

In this approach, we considered language as social practice, and focused on the text rather than the person because discourses are constituted in and by language. Discourses enable and constrain subject positions (as Christians or humanists, for example), reinforce existing social structures (such as the church), and construct our social worlds (Parker, 1992). Different discourses are identified by reading and rereading texts, looking for patterns and inconsistencies in ways of speaking, and interpreting the connotations of the text. Interrelationships of discourses are also examined by contrasting the ways in which different discourses are used to speak about the same phenomena (Parker, 1992). Discourses position speakers by providing them with perspectives for viewing their world, enabling and constraining ways of speaking (being) relevant to that perspective (Davies & Harré, 1990). For example, for a member of a Christian church there are appropriate ways of speaking available, and these differ according to whether the person is male or female, a member of the clergy or not, and so on. Therefore, language, constituting social discourses and providing subject positions, has enormous power to shape the way that we experience and behave in the social world (Burman & Parker, 1993).

In this analysis, the data were the transcribed accounts previously obtained from our participants. We read and reread these texts, identifying discourses, exploring connotations, and discussing how our personal reactions and belief systems, past and present, influenced our reading (Parker, 1992). In reading these texts, we found a rich array of existential, humanistic, and Christian discourses informing the accounts of meaning. We might have expected that differing accounts of meaning would access separate and corresponding discourses: meaninglessness and existentialism; ultimate meaning and Christianity; terrestrial meaning and humanism. However, the texts demonstrated considerable complexity with multiple, inconsistent, and frequently overlapping discourses. We were particularly struck by the multiple uses of the language of Christianity. The language of religion and God was not only utilized in accounts of ultimate meaning but also in accounts of terrestrial meaning and meaninglessness. Further, language disclaiming religion and God was utilized in accounts of ultimate meaning. We present our reading of these texts discussing meaninglessness, ultimate meaning, and terrestrial meaning in turn.

Meaninglessness

Existentialist discourse produces meaninglessness as a challenge requiring a response. Because there is no external ultimate meaning to be discovered, we have the task of creating meaning for ourselves. In producing meaninglessness, participants constitute themselves as aware of the existential proposition:

> I think I believe that the world is not on about anything very much at all. ... What is essential about existence, is the complete unreliability and randomness. (14)

The discourses of existentialism position speakers as individuals who, functioning as free agents, create meaning from chaos:

> If life is meaningless, death is even more meaningless! It's kind of it's been as logical and rational as that. I've actually made the choice to survive. Because in fact I have to find meaning here if there isn't meaning after. (21)

Producing meaninglessness, in this way, is paradoxical in that it enables space for speakers to claim the search for meaning as valuable in its own right. Meaninglessness and meaning are co-produced and inform each other. Thus, existential dilemmas enable positions from which explicit questions can be asked about what life might mean and whether there is any ultimate meaning.

> I guess that that's the great, that's the biggest question of life. Why are we here, why are we being subjected to all this pain and joy and is there any truth in the things that were drummed into us in our youth or is it just a load of witchcraft and bullshit ... I can remember as a kid, actually, I used to sleep outside and look up at the stars, and besides whether there was a God up there, was there anyone else up there, and if so what were they doing. It's the big ... figure out the big question. (5)

Existential discourse is thus manifest in an interweave of multiple and overlapping discourses, of meaninglessness, of the search for meaning, and of the creation of meaning. However, these texts are also rich with talk about meaningfulness, drawn from a variety of other sources. In order to articulate meaning, speakers positioned themselves in theological, social, and biological contexts. We present and discuss these in the next two sections, relating to ultimate and terrestrial meaning, respectively.

Ultimate Meaning

Accounts of ultimate meaning are permeated with the rhetoric of religion, and the discourses here are also overlapping and inconsistent. God, institutionalized religion, and Christian values, both claimed and disclaimed, are all explicitly constituted in discourse throughout the texts. Some speakers disclaim institutionalized religion and God as sources of meaning, but invoke other nonspecific powerful entities or grander plans. In these texts, Christian discourses are intertwined with the discourses of humanism and existentialism, to co-produce beliefs, values, and social mores.

God Exists. One belief attested to in the accounts is the claim that God exists. By professing belief in God, speakers position themselves in historical and cultural systems that are resources of meaning for them. Invoking a credo in this way positions the speaker as 'believer' and signals a theological context for meaning. God is thus produced and reproduced by such Christian discourse.

> God exists, there is no need to question it ... God is, um, everywhere and in all things. In us and in everything. (25)

The Church. In Christian culture the primary institution of religion is the church. Christian discourses are formalized in ways that give churches authority over members, with explicit requirements such as church attendance. In talking about church attendance speakers position themselves variously, as obedient to and as resisting the authority of the institution.

> Can you really be – call yourself a Christian and not go to church as often as perhaps you should? (27)
>
> I don't like being made to feel guilty because I don't go to church or pray. (9)

In these fragments, using terms such as *should*, participants reproduce a moral Christian discourse serving to constrain actions. Church membership carries obligations and produces emotions such as 'guilt' for noncompliance. In these ways, speakers reproduce Christian discourse ratifying the Church as an institution with power over people's minds as well as over their behavior. This power is produced and reproduced as people are disciplined into self-surveillance, a practice that continues after church membership has ceased.

Although discourses constituting God and the institutions of religion are intertwined and mutually inform each other, God and church are produced separately in some texts, positioning speakers as believers and yet outside the institution:

> You don't necessarily have to join a club to experience what God is; there are lots of clubs around the place, they are called churches or whatever. (25)

Taking up humanistic discourses enables resistance to the authority of church and provides subject positions outside the confinement of institutionalized religion. Humanistic discourse gives space for the production of freedom and tolerance, and for church to be disclaimed as constraining.

> I see (churches) as narrowing and confining and condemning ... I see organized religion forces people to be very judgmental. (15)

In talk about ultimate meaning, Christian discourse constructs the Church, religion, and God, but also alternative sources of ultimate meaning. We see evidence of how institutionalized religion has constituted and continues to reconstitute God, and also how it co-opts 'not-God' alternatives in language that is formalized, repeated, and familiar both to those within churches and those without.

Christian Values. Christian values are co-articulated in discourses of Christianity and humanism. This occurs both from within and outside church membership, and with or without a profession of belief in God. Participants who identified as active members of a church and those who disclaimed the church as a source of meaning both talked about Christian values, and some who positioned themselves among church-going Christians invoked Christian values in preference to God as a source of meaning in life:

> I believe that the Christian attitudes in life are, um, are important and the Christian attitudes of course tie in to, ah, moral values and various other values that I have in life. (31)

Christian values are also produced in the talk of avowed nonbelievers, functioning to reproduce Christian discourse outside religious institutions. When belief in God and established church are removed, the religious metaphor persists.

> The religious people get it (serenity), I'm sure, out of the total conviction that, that, that, the total belief in Christianity and in a God, and they live according to the teachings that He has laid down, which are not bad. I mean, where would, where would you be without the basic principles of Christianity? (5)

This production of Christian values enables speaking positions outside the constraints of Christian institutional power. Christian values are relocated from inside the formal institution to 'free' spaces outside and are co-articulated among humanist constructs of individual choice and freedom to create 'personal' meaning. The values invoked are named as Christian, not humanistic, although the speakers position themselves outside Christianity. The interrelationship of these discourses is further complicated by Christian discourses co-opting humanistic discourse and reclaiming the objects produced by humanist discourses. These objects, in this example 'values', are produced by speakers who position themselves within church institutions, thus reproducing the humanistic discourse within religion. The production of Christian values outside and within the institution continues to intertwine the discourses of Christianity among those of humanism.

Not-God. Some texts refer to a nonspecific supernatural power and to externally produced plans for life, and echoes of God and established religion are also audible in these. The disclaiming of Christianity, 'Jesus' and 'God', and the location of meaning in an unspecified form of supernatural power produce a form of ultimate meaning that we label 'not-God'. This allows for alternative discourses of ultimate meaning that are outside the constraints of Christianity.

> Well, I am sure there is something else beyond this particular physical life we are in. I don't think there is Jesus and God and the devil and the angels standing on clouds playing their harps, but I certainly think that there is another level of existence, otherwise I can't see the point of being here. (4)

'Grand schemes', 'plans', or 'destiny' are located outside Christianity and formalized religion. Appropriate language is not available to articulate what is outside the institutional discourses of meaning, and the origin of this 'scheme' or 'plan' is not stated or is said to be unknown. It is not located in institutionalized religion or credited to a known deity, but the language used is very similar to that professing Christian belief, perhaps because no other language resources are available.

> Um, I guess it gives a point to the whole thing, because it says here I am, this is me, I'm important, and I am a part of all of this grand scheme of things. (20)

> If you think, well, be positive and then somehow things happen, I can't explain it. There's something that makes things happen. (4)

Things 'happen' and speakers position themselves as acted upon according to unspecified plans under the surveillance of unspecified agents. Speakers have difficulty in articulating sources of ultimate meaning outside religion. 'Schemes' and 'plans' are positioned outside Christianity, but utilize the same language of ultimate meaning; there is purpose in life that is a given, and that is to be discovered. The difficulty of rejecting institutionalized religion and at the same time locating ultimate meaning in externally preexisting 'schemes' was openly explored within some accounts:

> I think, yes, there is some overall meaning to life, but it's not necessarily a plan, it could be an accident as well, and it's not necessarily directed by God, or a supreme being any longer, um, although I still hang on to vestiges of that. I think there has got to be some point to it all. (20)

The Christian discourse is disclaimed by these speakers. The explanations they offer as alternatives are informed by the Christian discourse repositioned in humanism. God is no longer legitimated as the creator of meaning, and the social practices of religion have assimilated the language of humanism. At the same time, the discourses of humanism resonate with echoes of religion.

Terrestrial Meaning

The language of terrestrial meaning produces and reproduces humanistic discourses, locating sources of meaning within the observable universe rather than the supernatural. These discourses produce a 'self' who 'transcends the self', constituting meaning as part of a wider existence. The 'transcended self' is produced in two forms: through contribution, a spatial connectedness to others and to society; and through continuity, a temporal connectedness through a cultural and biological heritage, from the past through the present and into the future.

Contribution. The 'self' is produced and at the same time transcended by contributing to others or to society. The talk about 'contribution' enables subject positions that are embedded in social relations.

> I think that we all have the capacity to ... contribute in ways that are significant to us. Being in there, being part of the human condition. ... Pitching in and saying I'm a human being and what affects other people also affects me. ... Valuing one's own contribution gives life meaning in the context of all the other contributions that are made as well. (11)

While this humanist discourse prevails, cooperation with the status quo ensures that social institutions and social practice are supported and maintained. The valuing of 'contribution' acts as a form of social control because the reproduction of this humanist discourse ensures that people will continue to seek to contribute to society. People are "lucky" or "fortunate" to have "the chance" to contribute to the 'good' of others. Subject positions of 'self-transcendence' are not actively sought, because seeking the moral advantage of 'contribution' undermines the 'self-transcendence' of that position.

> Mmm, I gain meaning from – it's very hard to describe this – having a sense of purpose, having something to strive for, having a goal of some sort. Work as in my paid career type work is one source of that purpose. ... It gives me a chance to contribute something towards other people. (16)

Ironically 'social change' also maintains the status quo. Talk about 'social change' enables subject positions at the forefront of resistance and outside responsibility for the unjust power relations that are maintained by and also maintain dominant institutions. 'Social change' is reproduced in the discourses of humanism and Christianity in these texts. Meaning is constituted in working for 'social change' even though change may not result, at least in the short term:

> I guess that part of my value system is being able to make a contribution to society, the society I live in. And, um, particularly to be able to express my political beliefs, or the way I believe things should be going. ... I am involved in protest and activism

to get rid of the inequalities. ... I won't win the war, but I'll win some battles. (12)

Contribution is presented here as working for social change, and the work is not expected to bring results. This expectation of no change paradoxically supports the status quo. Dominant institutions maintain power by tolerating activity seeking change that is not expected to be effected. This is one way in which dominant discourses adapt to disempower discourses of resistance, and the reproduction of power is from the bottom up, in this case out of social action itself.

Continuity. Continuity is produced as a source of meaning where speakers are positioned in social and biological contexts. Social 'continuity' connects human beings through the ages and reproduces 'heritage' and 'civilization'. Appreciating the 'heritage' of past generations and passing it on to the next generation produces claims for 'continuity' of life itself as a context for meaning, and enables speakers to position themselves in social relations across time.

> I see myself as an individual, but very much as part of a culture, or part of a belief system, and I like the idea of passing that on, and I like the idea of having some influence in the way that what I'm part of will continue to go. (12)

Biological 'continuity' enables speakers to position themselves in a biological context that is wider than human. The 'world' is an organic whole that has 'direction', 'energy', and 'continuity'. Here, subjectivities are constituted as embedded in the greater whole.

> I think there is something inherent in me from my education from my – the religion I was brought up in and all the things that make up my life. This fact I've got kids, it makes me believe that there is something when this physical body is gone and buried, that there is something else that survives of me, somewhere in this universe. So, I, I, yeah, I have this innate belief that there is continuity, that I can't get away from. (21)

By claiming 'continuity' as terrestrial meaning, humanist discourses co-opt religious discourses that locate meaning in large-scale explanations of life. Human existence is meaningful within an overall pattern of things. This pattern is described as belonging to nature, enabling meaning to be located in the context of the biological world. Contemplation of nature is an object of traditional Christian discourse, in which the speaker is positioned as an observer of nature outside the observed, and the 'creator' is positioned outside both the observer and the observed.

> ... and there's nobody there but you. You really get the feeling of the meaning in life then, because you just – the majesty of the scenery and that – you can feel it, you can feel the power of whatever has created it. (4)

This traditional account of meaning experienced in contemplating nature has clearly discernible religious undertones. However, the texts also include ways of talking about nature that go beyond the discourses of Christianity, humanism, and existentialism. We label this as ecological discourse. Ecological discourses are more recent, and position humans within nature rather than as observers of it:

> ... it is a little universe that we are on, and um, it's, it and the life that exists within
> it is is is sort of mutually connected, nothing is exclusive of anything else, and um,
> so the, the pattern of our little planet within the universe that we are in is is just one
> of many and it's all, they are all interrelated. (28)

'Continuity' thus enables subject positions in a continuum of connections with other people and the world. 'Continuity' is produced alongside 'heritage,' 'culture', and 'life force' in the articulation of human meaning in the context of the cosmos. We interpret talk about biological continuity as resisting humanist and Christian discourses. Biological continuity challenges the production of individual rights and the individual/social dichotomy that is at the center of humanist and Christian discourses. Ecological discourses are discourses of resistance that position people as inextricably interwoven in the biology of the natural world.

The natural environment is a site for both ultimate and terrestrial meaning. In Christian and 'not-God' discourses of ultimate meaning, nature is the object of observation. Ecological discourses bring the context to the foreground, and position subjectivities in cosmology. In ecological discourses ultimate and terrestrial meaning are integrated, and the importance of the human perspective is eliminated. These shifts challenge and resist the constitutive power of dominant Christian and humanist discourses.

Overview

In this analysis, meaning in life is constituted through discourses of existentialism, humanism, and Christianity. Few texts reproduced meaninglessness, and those that did gave accounts of meaning drawing on Christian and humanist discourses in complex and intertwined ways. Christian discourses co-opt humanism, for example in talk of values, and humanist discourses co-opt the language of religion. We also find a resistant discourse in these accounts that we call ecological, which positions human beings and meaning in life in wider biological and cosmological contexts. These texts reproduce meaning in life constructed within the social contexts of competing and collaborating ideologies and social institutions.

CONCLUSION

The two sections of this chapter, both concerned with meaning in life and drawing on the same data, illustrate quite different understandings of meaning. These two sections seek to realize quite different objectives through the way they approach meaning, through the way they conduct their analyses, and more fundamentally, in the assumptions they make about the nature of knowledge.

In the first analysis, we adopted a post-positivist paradigm of enquiry (Guba &

Lincoln, 1994). In this critical realist approach, we assume that a reality exists and can be probabilistically, but not completely, apprehended. We assume that there is meaning in life, and that it is possible to approximate how much of it people experience (in terms of such things as breadth and depth) and what sources it is derived from. Further, we accept that participants' talk will express their version of that reality, and that it can be analyzed to reveal this. We then examined their talk for specific, predetermined content to determine how well it relates to and confirms a theoretical proposal about the nature of meaning (Reker & Wong, 1988). We assume that if Reker and Wong (1988) have the dimensions of meaning correct, this will be reflected in how people talk about meaning, particularly those people who are at a stage of life when issues of meaning are held to be highly salient. Having made these assumptions and conducted the analysis, we can conclude, as we did above, that we find support for the theory. Holding to a post-positivist paradigmatic view, we can now assert with more certainty that Reker and Wong's theory is 'correct'. We have confirmed it using different data, different participants, in a different cultural location, and with a different analysis technique. Although there were aspects of the theory that may require modification or further research, we have increased confidence in this theory of the dimensions of meaning.

In the second analysis, we recognized that our participants were located in a particular sociocultural context, and that this privileged and legitimated certain ways to talk about meaning. Their talk of meaning drew on discourses that were dominant in that context. Here, we adopted a different ontological and epistemological stance, located in a constructionist-interpretive paradigm of enquiry (Denzin & Lincoln, 1994). In contrast to the objectivist stance of the first section, this is a subjectivist position which assumes that reality is only subjectively apprehended, and that the researcher creates knowledge through constructing an interpretation of the phenomenon, in this case how meaning is created in talk. We assume that language is a social act, and we focus on the talk of participants rather than on the participants themselves. We do not assume there is any such thing as meaning in life, but only talk about meaning in life – ways of expressing meaning through available linguistic resources. The second analysis therefore provides us with an account, our interpretation, of how meaning is constructed. It presents a very different view of meaning, exposing how talk about meaning in this sociocultural context is drawn from discourses rooted in Christianity. In this analysis, meaning in life was construed as a product of wider social and ideological contentions. The analysis revealed how different discourses construct meaning in different ways, and how resistant discourses challenge and support dominant world views.

These two sets of findings contrast very different paradigms of research for understanding meaning. In the first we were interested in the individual and the nature of meaning; in the second the focus moved from the individual to the social context, and from experience as reported in interviews to the constitutive power of language itself. In presenting these two analyses of the same interview data, our intent was to illustrate how qualitative perspectives open opportunities to explore the psychological and social implications of personal meaning. The juxtaposition of the two analyses illustrates how these two very different qualitative approaches enabled different possibilities for exploring how life meaning is constructed and produced. These are only two of a variety of possibilities, and we look forward to further explorations of meaning taking other qualitative perspectives to provide further depth and breadth to our understanding of meaning in life.

NOTES

1. We would like to acknowledge support from the Laboratoire de Psychologie Génétique et Différentielle, Université Victor Segalen Bordeaux 2, and in particular from the Équipe de Psychologie de la Santé, to the second author during preparation of this chapter.

2. A more detailed account of the research in the first section of this chapter can be found in O'Connor, K., & Chamberlain, K. (1996). Dimensions of life meaning: A qualitative exploration at midlife. *British Journal of Psychology, 87*, 461-477.

3. Brief quotes, selected to capture the essence of an issue under discussion, are included throughout the chapter to illustrate specific points. Quotations were taken directly from the transcripts of the interviews, and all participants consented to the use of such quotations. A simple transcription of content was used and no attempt was made to include pauses and tone. Numbers are used to identify quotations from different individuals.

REFERENCES

Battista, J., & Almond, R. (1973). The development of meaning in life. *Psychiatry, 36*, 409-427.
Burman, E., & Parker, I. (Eds.). (1993). *Discourse analytic research: Repertoires and readings of texts in action.* London: Routledge.
Davies, B., & Harré, R. (1990). Positioning: The discursive production of selves. *Journal for the Theory of Social Behaviour, 20*, 43-63.
Denzin, N. K., & Lincoln, Y. S. (1994). Introduction – Entering the field of qualitative research. In N. K. Denzin & Y. S. Lincoln (Eds.), *Handbook of qualitative research* (pp. 1-17). Thousand Oaks, CA: Sage.
DeVogler-Ebersole, K., & Ebersole, P. (1985). Depth of meaning in life: Explicit rating criteria. *Psychological Reports, 56*, 303-310.
Fife, B. L. (1994). The conceptualization of meaning in illness. *Social Science and Medicine, 38*, 309-316.
Frankl, V. E. (1963). *Man's search for meaning.* New York: Washington Square Press.
Guba, E., & Lincoln, Y. S. (1994). Competing paradigms in qualitative research. In N. K. Denzin & Y. S. Lincoln (Eds.), *Handbook of qualitative research* (pp. 105-117). Thousand Oaks, CA: Sage.
Harlow, L. L., & Newcomb, M. D. (1990). Towards a general hierarchical model of meaning and satisfaction in life. *Multivariate Behavioral Research, 25*, 387-405.
Janoff-Bulman, R. (1989). Assumptive worlds and the stress of traumatic events:

Applications of the schema construct. *Social Cognition, 7*, 113-136.

Levinson, D. J. (1986). A conception of adult development. *American Psychologist, 41*, 3-13.

Neugarten, B. L., & Neugarten, D. A. (1987). The changing meanings of age. *Psychology Today, 21(5),* 29-33.

Parker, I. (1992). *Discourse dynamics: Critical analysis for social and individual psychology.* London: Routledge.

Reker, G. T., & Wong, P. T. P. (1988). Aging as an individual process: Toward a theory of personal meaning. In J. E. Birren & V. L. Bengtson (Eds.), *Emergent theories of aging* (pp. 214-246). New York: Springer.

Thompson, S. C., & Janigian, A. S. (1988). Life schemes: A framework for understanding the search for meaning. *Journal of Social and Clinical Psychology, 7*, 260-280.

Yalom, I. D. (1980). *Existential psychotherapy.* New York: Basic Books.

CHAPTER 6

An Inquiry Into Existential Meaning:
Theoretical, Clinical, and Phenomenal Perspectives

Dominique L. Debats

Over the past decades, an increasing number of publications have addressed the subject of existential meaning. This phenomenon is not accidental, because it coincides with the growing tension between existentialist thinking and traditional religion. Throughout history humans perceived life and the world as expressions of some ultimate design or cause. However, in modern times this perception has been disturbed by the statement that all existing things are born for no reason, continue through weakness, die by accident, and that it is meaningless that we are born and meaningless that we die (Sartre, cited in Hepburn, 1965). Since then various writers have addressed the issue of the meaninglessness or meaningfulness of existence (e.g., Frankl, 1976).

At the same time philosophers have cooled to the topic of existential meaning, social scientists have been warming to it and gradually recognizing that despite its vague and boundless nature, the topic can be seriously and fruitfully investigated. And while the initial work of psychologists and sociologists on existential meaning was mostly theoretical and based on clinical observations, there is a recent trend to approach the subject from a more research-oriented perspective in a variety of disciplines and problem areas, such as trauma (e.g., Janoff-Bulman, 1992) and psychological well-being (e.g., Zika & Chamberlain, 1992). These and other investigations have generally underlined that the need for a valued and meaningful life is a significant factor in human existence.

The issue of existential meaning has been ignored by empirically oriented social scientists until recently because of their preference for objective data rather than feelings and subjective experiences. It has also been neglected because of the prevailing notion that this subject relates primarily to the puzzling, philosophical question, "What is the meaning of life?" This "eternal quest," as old as mankind, is indeed ipso facto out of reach of modern objectivist scientific methodology. However, the existential and psychological significance of this most important of all questions is revealed when it is rephrased by any individual who asks, "What makes my life worth living?" In a similar way, the subject of meaning in life becomes accessible to empirical investigation when the focus is shifted toward the questions, "What are the components of individuals' experiences of their lives as meaningful?" and, "What are the conditions under which individuals will experience their lives as meaningful?"

This contribution presents the main findings of a research project that was conducted during the last decade. This research aimed to find relevant answers to the previous two guiding questions. The focus was on finding significant phenomena related to existential meaning from three different perspectives: theoretical, clinical, and phenomenal. The general purpose was to establish empirical evidence for the clinical significance of the existential meaning concept by means of both quantitative and qualitative research methods. On the one hand, patients and non-patients filled out questionnaires designed to measure psychological well-being and existential meaning. Based on the subjects' scores on these measures, various hypotheses derived from the literature about the relation between mental health and existential meaning were tested statistically. On the other hand, and in addition to this standard nomothetic approach, the focus was on analyzing by means of content analysis the most significant themes and structural elements in the answers of the subjects to relevant open questions. The advantage of this combined inductive-deductive research approach is that it both enables us to comprehend more of the inner world of the participants, and to analyze data in a numerical-mathematical way. This chapter concludes with an evaluation of the findings and their implications for clinical practice.

THEORETICAL PERSPECTIVE

At the beginning of this research project the available literature about existential meaning was screened for a suitable theoretical perspective. This concept appeared to be described in association with a variety of concepts such as self-transcendence (Frankl, 1973) and self-actualization (Maslow, 1962). In addition, the views of the various existentialist humanistic theorists regarding the postulated 'true' nature of existential meaning proved to vary substantially. Therefore the theories of Frankl (1973), Maslow (1962), and Yalom (1980), which have been most influential in psychology and psychiatry during the last decades, were considered as theoretical frameworks for the present inquiry.

Frankl conceived of existential meaning as a process of discovery within a world that is intrinsically meaningful. In his view, existential meanings are not invented and can only be found outside the person. Meanings are not arbitrary human creations, but possess an objective reality of their own. There is only one meaning to each situation and this is its true meaning. Individuals are intuitively guided by their conscience to find this true meaning. Existential meaning is to be attained through productive or creative activities, positive human experiences, and through taking a stance toward unavoidable, negative conditions. Frankl postulated that prolonged absence of meaning may lead to a "noögenic neurosis," a condition typified by boredom and apathy.

In contrast, Maslow conceived of existential meaning as an intrinsic property within the person. This emerges as a dominant motivational force in individuals when their lower needs are satisfied. Individuals are free to choose their existential meanings, but they will be healthier if they choose meanings that help them to fulfill their inner nature. Existential meanings are "metamotives" that require fulfillment for healthy functioning and produce illness when unfulfilled.

Yalom addressed existential meaning from a strictly existentialistic stance. In his view there is no ultimate design or purpose to the universe. Humans essentially choose and create their own circumstances. Meaning does not exist outside of individuals, but they create it themselves. Psychopathology is conceived as the result of defensive and ineffective modes of dealing with the ultimate concerns in life (death, freedom, isolation and meaninglessness). Existential meanings are, in fact, no more than individuals' creative responses to the world's absolute meaninglessness. However, to forget the self-created nature of their existential meanings, individuals need to immerse themselves wholeheartedly in life through active commitment.

The previous summaries illustrate the fundamental differences between theoretical views on existential meaning. Each of these perspectives possesses intellectual merit and has definitively contributed to a deeper insight into the multiple and complex aspects of the existential meaning construct. However, the great variety of contrasting theories causes problems to both clinicians and researchers because they need a framework to evaluate the results of their treatments and research unequivocally. Consider that patients' attempts to achieve a sense of meaning in life hedonistically would be disregarded from a Franklian logotherapeutic perspective given that, for Frankl, only self-transcendent values are believed to lead to fulfillment in life. In contrast, religious patients who believe in a personal, protective God would have a difficult time with a Yalom-like existentialist therapist who holds that the belief in an ultimate rescuer is one of the basic defenses against facing life's meaninglessness and has to be outgrown.

Therefore, the present inquiry avoided an a priori choice for one of the previous conceptions of the nature of existential meaning. The challenge was to find some theoretical perspective that is not biased toward one specific ontology (i.e., theism, atheism, humanism). An article published in *Psychiatry* in 1973, titled "The Development of Meaning in Life," by John Battista and Richard Almond offered such an approach.

Battista and Almond concluded, after studying the various theories on existential meaning, that four basic characteristics of existential meaning could be identified. First, when individuals state that their lives are meaningful this implies that they are positively committed to some concept of the meaning of life. This concept may be taken from a broad, traditional humanistic or religious meaning-giving system or it may be a more idiosyncratic one (e.g., "life is a challenge"). Second, this concept provides individuals with a framework from which life events can be interpreted in some coherent fashion. From this a set of specified life goals or purposes for living are derived. Third, if individuals state that their lives are meaningful, they can see themselves as having fulfilled or as being in the process of fulfilling their framework or life goals. And finally, this process of fulfilling their purposes in life ultimately leads to the experience that their lives and existential existences have significance.

Based on these four commonly held, meta-theoretical notions, Battista and Almond developed their so-called relativistic perspective to existential meaning. Whereas more philosophically oriented models have postulated that existential meaning develops only from the commitment to and fulfillment of some intrinsic meaning of life, such as God (religious models), being (existential models), or man (humanistic models), this relativistic model emphasizes that commitment to any system of beliefs can serve as a life framework for the development of existential meaning. This perspective acknowledges that diverse ways of reaching a sense of meaningfulness coexist, and that these are not reducible to one 'true' or ultimate principle identical for everyone. The process of believing is regarded as more important than the specific content of these beliefs. The crucial factor in deriving a sense of meaningfulness is the degree to which people are committed to their ideals or purposes for living.

Because of the plausibility and intellectual soundness of Battista and Almond's perspective it was adopted as the general theoretical framework for the various clinical and phenomenal studies in the present research program. A further advantage of this perspective is that it has produced a reliable and valid instrument to measure the existential meaning construct, the Life Regard Index (LRI). Battista and Almond designed the LRI as a value-independent self-report questionnaire. The LRI consists of two subscales. The Framework scale assesses the degree to which individuals can envision their lives within some meaningful perspective or have derived a set of life goals or philosophy of life from these. The Fulfillment scale measures the degree to which people see themselves as having fulfilled or as being in the process of fulfilling their framework or life goals. For a review of the psychometric properties of the LRI see Debats (1998).

CLINICAL PERSPECTIVE

Although the previously discussed theorists, Frankl, Maslow, and Yalom, differ regarding the nature of existential meaning, they essentially agree on the centrality of a sense of meaningfulness in developing general and psychological well-being. Frankl (1976) stated that if individuals do not pursue meaning they may experience an existential vacuum or meaninglessness.

> Every age has its own collective neurosis, and every age needs its own psychotherapy to cope with it. The existential vacuum that is the mass neurosis of the present time, can be described as a private and personal form of nihilism; for nihilism can be defined as the contention that being has no meaning (Frankl, 1976, p. 204).

In agreement with this view, Maslow postulated that without the fulfillment of values, individuals in higher stages will become ill.

> The state of being without a system of values is psychopathogenic, we are learning. The human being needs a framework of values, a philosophy of life, a religion or religion surrogate to live by and understand by, in about the same sense that he needs sunlight, calcium or love (1962, p. 206).

And Yalom stated, in accordance with both Frankl and Maslow, that a sense of meaningfulness of life is essential to mental health:

> The human being seems to require meaning. To live without meaning, goals, values or ideals seems to provoke considerable distress. In severe form it may lead to the decision to end one's life. ... We apparently need absolutes, firm ideals to which we can aspire and guidelines by which to steer our lives (Yalom, 1980, p. 422).

So despite their quite different views of life, theistic, humanistic, and existentialistic respectively, Frankl, Maslow, and Yalom emphasized the relevance of the existential meaning concept for psychological theory and practice.

To establish empirical evidence for the above-mentioned claims of clinical relevance for the existential meaning concept we tested several hypotheses that were derived from the literature on existential meaning. First, we demonstrated that people with high meaning are less affected by momentary anxious, depressed, or hostile mood disturbances and are more elated than people with low meaning in life (Debats, 1990). Scoring high on the LRI was strongly associated with happiness and general satisfaction with life. The prediction that psychological distress is significantly related to absence of sense of meaning and purpose in life, as is claimed by the previously discussed theorists was also tested (Debats, van der Lubbe, & Wezeman, 1993). To this end patients' and non-patients' scores on measures for negative well-being (psychological distress), positive well-being (self-esteem and happiness) and existential meaning were compared. As expected, patients were far more psychologically distressed than non-patients. Additionally, the patient sample had a far lower mean LRI score than the non-patient sample.

A further investigation of the clinical significance of existential meaning was conducted in an outpatient mental health institution (Debats, 1996). At the start and at the end of psychotherapeutic treatment, 114 patients were asked to fill out the LRI and questionnaires designed to measure psychological distress, happiness, and self-esteem. Treatment involved eight therapy sessions on average. The focus of this study was on the part played by meaning in life on psychological well-being and on the outcome of the psychotherapeutic treatment. It was hypothesized that patients' degrees of existential meaning play a hidden, yet crucial, role in the process and outcome of psychotherapy. The rationale was that, because psychotherapists generally ignore existential issues during treatment (Yalom, 1980), patients' pretreatment degrees of existential meaning would constitute a critical condition to treatment outcome.

The first analysis addressed the association between patients' pretreatment scores on the LRI subscales Framework and Fulfillment and their scores on measures for psychological distress, happiness, and self-esteem. In accord with our expectations, the linear correlations of Framework and Fulfillment with the three well-being measures appeared moderate to high. Additionally, the separate contribution of Fulfillment and Framework to each of the well-being measures was measured by means of partial correlations. Partial correlations express the linear effects of the one existential measure, for example, Framework, on each of the well-being measures, separately from the linear effects of the second existential measure, for example, Fulfillment, on both Framework and the specific well-being measure. This analysis showed that the partial correlations of Fulfillment with the three well-being measures reached the level of the linear correlations, whereas no such separate contribution to well-being showed up for Framework. In contrast, the partial correlation of Framework with self-esteem was zero, whereas the partial correlation of Framework with happiness even had a negative sign.

These findings are important since they highlight that envisioning oneself as fulfilling one's goals or as having fulfilled goals in life is a more critical factor in deriving a sense of psychological well-being and existential fullness than is the sheer presence of life goals or the belief in a purpose in existence. Persons may find it difficult to perceive life as meaningful if the meaningful beliefs and goals they cherish are not validated by real and fulfilling personal experiences. The findings suggest that having a framework or a purpose for living without a sense of fulfillment may in fact be stressful and may affect psychological well-being negatively.

The evaluation of patients' therapeutic improvement involved two separate analyses. First, improvement during psychotherapy was conceived of as both a decrease of psychological distress and an increase of existential meaning. This analysis showed that at the end of treatment 87% of the patients had improved in terms of symptom relief. This, of course, was expected because short-term treatment in an outpatient clinical environment is normally focused on the alleviation of symptoms only. However, this analysis also revealed that only 34% of the patients had improved in terms of existential meaning. These findings demonstrate that symptoms and meaning in life essentially constitute different criteria for assessing therapeutic outcome and that both need therapeutic attention.

Second, the prediction was tested that patients' pretest degree of existential meaning would constitute a critical condition to the outcome of their treatment. The analyses showed that patients' pretreatment LRI scores do indeed strongly predict the outcome of treatment: the lower a patient's pretreatment LRI score, the poorer the outcome of treatment as measured by degree of self-esteem, happiness, and psychological distress.

The findings of these two analyses clearly indicate that patients with low levels of existential meaning have a significantly lower probability of profiting from psychotherapeutic treatment than subjects with high levels of existential meaning. The findings underline that the existential meaning construct has substantial relevance for clinical practice. The results confirm that, generally, regular psychotherapy fails to be effective with patients having low initial levels of meaning in life. These findings imply that more efficacious treatment should be provided when lack of fulfillment and framework are more pronounced.

PHENOMENAL PERSPECTIVE

The third perspective from which this research investigated the existential meaning concept was a phenomenal one. This approach was influenced by Koehler, who said: "Never, I believe, shall we be able to solve any problems of ultimate principle until we go back to the source of our concepts – in other words, until we use the phenomenological method, the qualitative analysis of experience" (cited in van Kaam, 1959, p. 66). Two separate studies (Debats, Drost, & Hansen, 1995; Debats, in press) were designed from this phenomenal perspective. In the first study, idiographic-essay and nomothetic-inventory techniques were used to investigate the conditions under which individuals experience meaningfulness and meaninglessness. In the second, these were used to examine the sources of meaning of patients and non-patients. By choosing this combined qualitative-quantitative approach an attempt was made to avoid the one-sidedness of traditional positivists, who have been "too concerned with internal validity and conceptual certainty, coming to grief when their data lacked authenticity and meaning, i.e. external reality" (Miles & Huberman, 1984, p. 19).

The first study focused on pinpointing the core elements of the experiences of meaningfulness and meaninglessness. Two guiding assumptions were derived from the literature on existential meaning. First, meaningfulness is associated with relatedness (cf. Buehler, 1968), psychological well-being (cf. Zika & Chamberlain, 1987), and a positive attitude toward life in general (cf. Maslow, 1962). Second, meaninglessness is manifested in alienation and social isolation (cf. Maddi, 1967), disengagement (cf. Frankl, 1973), and is furthermore associated with psychopathology in a roughly linear sense – the less the sense of meaning, the greater the severity of psychopathology (cf. Yalom, 1980). It was hypothesized that the main themes and core elements related to presence and absence of existential meaning as indicated by the content analysis would correspond with these phenomena reported in the literature.

The participants, 122 psychology students, were asked to fill out the LRI and to describe briefly one period or time in which they had deeply experienced a sense of meaningfulness. In addition, they were asked to describe a period or time in which they had profoundly experienced a sense of meaninglessness. Although the concepts of meaningfulness and meaninglessness refer to complex phenomena, they were briefly defined as presence or absence of the feeling that one can make sense, order, or coherence of one's existence.

Analysis showed that presence of existential meaning was associated with social interactions with a variety of people (family members as well as strangers and friends) in which positive interactions (helping, caring) prevailed, with enjoying life fully in leisure, with making new plans, and with well-being and positive appraisals of self, others, and the world. Examples of verbatim answers were: "If I notice that I can mean something to other people (friends) or if I have a nice (deep) contact with certain people (who are important to me)"; and "Life has meaning to me in those moments that I am close to my feelings and I don't cling to expectations and duties anymore." Within the descriptions of meaningfulness a clear pattern of active engagement and commitment, as well as of being received in the mainstream of life, showed up. The results show that meaningfulness is essentially connected with a state of being in contact on three levels: with self (integratedness), with others (relatedness), and with life or the world (being, transcendence).

In contrast, absence of existential meaning showed a general picture of alienation on three levels: from self (blocked potentials, disabilities), from others (separation, isolation) and from life or the world (living marginally, without purpose). Examples of verbatim answers were: "The suicide of a friend. I realized that some people do have an unreasonable lot to bear. I questioned what could be the meaning of life in general, when such injustices exist"; and "When my parents divorced when I was about 15." In the various descriptions of meaninglessness, attitudes and interactions were predominantly negative. Meaninglessness was found to be associated with comparatively little and restricted social intercourse (with family members or partners only) and with a preoccupation with the problematic aspects of life. Furthermore, incidents of being confronted with major traumatic life events, such as divorce of one's parents or the death of a beloved person, are moments of dramatic changes in life regard. Yalom (1980) suggested that confrontations with such boundary experiences may bring people in contact with the ultimate concerns of life (such as own mortality and existential isolation), which may thereby elicit critical shifts – both positive and negative – in the evaluation of the meaningfulness of life.

The second part of this study addressed the relation between existential meaning and coping with trauma and stress. The prediction was tested that participants who show in their descriptions of meaningfulness and meaninglessness clear evidence that they have successfully overcome a personal crisis or effectively coped with highly stressful life events in their past, and who have further derived from these experiences some clear sense of existential meaning, would also show significantly higher current levels of existential meaning, as measured by the LRI, than those who did not give evidence of such transformations. This hypothesis was much inspired by Antonovsky's (1987) "salutogenic" approach in his research on finding answers to the important question of how people manage stress and stay well.

To test this prediction we combined the qualitative and quantitative information and found that high LRI participants did indeed refer more often to having found existential meaning through successfully coping with stressful life events in the past than low LRI subjects. Examples of verbatim answers were: "In my adolescence I sometimes thought about suicide, but then I reflected on the continuation of my life and found that I could help many people and make them happy. And that succeeded"; and "The period I recovered from anorexia nervosa. I experienced meaning because there were people that proved to care about me."

The second study explored the various sources from which young adult patients and non-patients derive a sense of purpose or meaning in life. The 114 patients and 169 non-patients were asked to fill out the LRI and to describe their three most important personal meanings in life. They also had to indicate the degree of their significant commitment to these personal meanings. All the answers were categorized by means of a classification system that was designed by comparing the systems employed by similar studies (e.g., DeVogler & Ebersole, 1980) in which a varying number – from six to nine – main themes or sources of meaning emerged.

It was expected that, because the patients and non-patients were in the same developmental life stage, the same sources of meaning would emerge in both samples (cf. Erikson, 1963). It was also hypothesized that patients, since they are preoccupied with inner conflicts and hence less free to pursue their goals with devotion and consistency (Orbach, Illuz, & Rosenheim, 1987), would exhibit significantly lower levels of existential meaning and commitment to their personal meanings in life than non-patients.

In the exploratory part of this study the content analysis of expressed personal meanings revealed seven main categories. These are given in order of importance: Relationships, commitment to family, partner/lover or friends; Life work, meaning through engagement in one's job, schooling, or main occupation; Personal Well-being, an individualistic orientation with an emphasis on experiencing meaning through appreciation of life, hedonistically striving for pleasure, and maintaining physical and mental health; Self-Actualization, an orientation toward development and achievement of tangible goals and talents or intangible goals and psychological abilities; Service, an altruistic orientation with an emphasis on helping people in general; Beliefs, devotion to or practicing religious/spiritual or social/political beliefs; and Materiality, meaning derived from the pursuit of materialistic objects and gratifications.

Confirming expectations, the results showed that the order of the four most frequent sources of meaning in life is the same for both samples. The category Relationships was found to provide by far most frequent sources of meaning, followed by Life Work, Personal Well-being, and Self-Actualization. However, further analysis revealed that patients as compared to non-patients expressed significantly more personal meanings belonging to Self-Actualization, with an emphasis on developing psychological abilities such as "becoming more confident," and the pursuit of ideals such as "harmony." In contrast, non-patients as compared to patients expressed significantly more personal meanings belonging to Personal Well-being, with an emphasis on enjoying life as it is by "having fun" and being engaged in leisure or sports activities. These findings suggest that patients have a greater motivation to find meanings at a deeper level. We are reminded of Frankl (1973), who stated that, in general, the issue of the meaning of one's personal life has no relevance until some personal or professional crisis occurs.

The second, confirmatory part of the study showed that the participants' LRI scores did relate strongly to their degree of commitment to their personal meanings, both in patients and non-patients, thus confirming Battista and Almond's (1973) theory from which the LRI was derived. Note that this theoretical view holds that it is not so much the specific content of subjects' personal meanings as much as the extent of their commitment to those particular meanings that is the crucial factor in their deriving a sense of existential meaning.

Finally, the combination of the qualitative and quantitative data produced one significant differential effect, namely that patients were significantly less committed to personal relationships than non-patients. This finding suggests that psychological distress, sense of meaninglessness, and decreased commitment to relationships covary significantly. This important issue deserves further attention from both clinicians and researchers.

DISCUSSION

This inquiry was started as a search for adequate answers to two fundamental questions: "What are the components of individuals' experiences of their lives as meaningful?" and, "What are the conditions under which individuals will experience their lives as meaningful?" At the end of this examination, it is time to evaluate the merit of the information that was gathered from the theoretical, clinical, and phenomenal perspectives.

The study of the various theories on existential meaning makes it clear that choosing between these theories, except for a priori reasons, is an impossible task. Each theory possesses intellectual merit and is valid within the range of its corresponding stage of human development and consciousness. There is no scientific evidence that favors the overall position of one theory over the others. Consider the criticisms of Frankl, Maslow, and Yalom on each other's perspective to existential meaning, because the theories of these three influential thinkers were initially weighted as possible theoretical frameworks for the present research. Frankl has been criticized by Maslow (1966) because of his postulate that self-transcendence is the ultimate source of existential meaning that is positive for anyone at any time. Maslow correctly pointed out the 'danger' of premature self-transcendence, for instance in adolescents and young adults, because this may lead to the failure to fulfill deficit needs at the proper time, which may eventually hamper psychological growth. Conversely, Frankl (1966) criticized Maslow's theory because of the rigidity of his postulated hierarchy of human values. Based on his own experiences as a concentration camp prisoner, Frankl correctly pointed out that, in contrast to animals, humans are quite capable of voluntarily surpassing the satisfaction of lower needs and of transcending directly to the fulfillment of higher values, for instance out of concern for their loved ones. Yalom (1980), in his turn, criticized both Frankl and Maslow because of their views on the position of the source of existential meaning: according to Frankl this can only be found outside the person, whereas Maslow stated that meaning is found only within the person. Opposed to Frankl's and Maslow's conceptions of the discovered nature of existential meaning, Yalom pictured meaning as essentially a unique creation, a conscious or unconscious projection from the person onto the world.

The inquiry shows that the dilemma of having to chose between equally appealing and valuable theories can be solved by switching the theoretical focus from the postulated 'true' or ultimate nature of existential meaning to a meta-theoretical position that respects the merit and validity of the various theories. We conclude that Battista and Almond's (1973) approach presents such a perspective. It offers researchers a way out of the insoluble controversies on the content level of existential meaning, and it invites scientists to investigate more fundamental aspects of existential meaning at a structural level. It is fortunate that this approach has produced a reliable and valid instrument, the LRI, because the lack of an adequate measure has long hampered empirical research in this area.

The LRI may help clinicians estimate the extent to which existential meaning is related to clinical symptomatology and detect persons who are especially vulnerable and in need of special care. A person scoring low on the LRI experiences feelings of meaninglessness, which in itself does not necessarily reflect an abnormal state of mind. However, low LRI scores may also point to a profound and pervasive sense of meaninglessness of personal existence, which is associated with severe dysfunctions in the cognitive (nihilism), affective (cynicism), and motor (apathy, vegetativeness) domains (cf. Maddi, 1967). Therefore, in clinical examination one must be cautious about relying solely on LRI scores. Like scores on any other self-report questionnaire, these scores may inherently suffer from the possibility of response bias, such as subject denial. For instance, non-distressed persons may honestly believe that their lives are meaningful and, hence, score high on the LRI out of a defensiveness to really question their existential situation. Conversely, patients may well minimize their LRI scores out of a sudden awareness that their sources of meaning are no longer providing a sense of order or purpose in life.

The findings of the various studies have important clinical implications since they demonstrate that existential meaning is strongly related to psychological and general well-being. The widespread assumption among clinicians is that problems with finding meaning in life deserve no special attention within the psychotherapeutic process because they disappear along with the alleviation of psychiatric and psychological disturbances (cf. Yalom, 1980). This is called into question by the present results, which demonstrate that low meaning patients have a significantly lower probability of profiting from regular psychotherapeutic treatment than high meaning subjects.

The fact that only one third of the psychotherapy patients in this research improved in terms of existential meaning points to the need for a professional perspective on how to handle existential issues adequately in clinical practice. The development of such a perspective starts with the recognition that the ways in which people find or create meaning in life are many, and that these are not reducible to one true and ultimate meaning identical for everyone. Therapists can no more hide their own values than they can fail to communicate. Hence, because therapists cannot avoid influencing the personal meanings and values of their clients, their training should help them raise their awareness of how their own values and purposes for living affect their patients. Therapists should neither circumvent existential issues nor take the pastoral role of actively telling patients what values or meanings in life they should pursue. Problems with finding some purpose or meaning in life are a natural part of human existence and, hence, need be respected and dealt with in therapy, much like problems in other areas of life, such as work or interpersonal relationships.

Given the special relevance of the interpersonal dimension to existential meaning, as was demonstrated on several occasions by the present research, psychotherapists should help patients above all in removing the obstacles that keep them from relating at a deeper level to others. Therapists are good existential models if they really commit themselves to make genuine contact with their low meaning patients in their experiences of (existential) loneliness and powerlessness. This therapeutic strategy may instill in these patients some hope that they themselves will eventually find their way out to some personal fulfillment in life. Our view accords with Frank (1974) who stated that psychotherapy is ultimately about the restoration of morale.

Taken as a whole, the phenomenal findings point to commitment and positive affiliation as the two most relevant factors in developing existential meaning. It remains an important question for further study whether commitment and engagement in personal relationships create the conditions necessary for the experience of meaningfulness or whether the relationship is the other way around, namely that presence of a sense of meaning leads to greater commitment and relatedness. We hypothesize that these variables are interdependent and that they operate interactively in their influence on subjective well-being (Reker, 1985).

While interpreting the present findings one should keep in mind that the participating patients and non-patients were predominantly young adults. The fact that there is a gradual evolution of meanings throughout an individual's life cycle (Erikson, 1963) was the reason that participants in all studies except one (Debats et al., 1993) were selected from the same developmental life stage of young adulthood. Hence, the generalizability of the phenomenological results is limited to subjects of the same age.

To conclude, we believe that this inquiry shows that existential meaning can be fruitfully investigated by means of idiographic and nomothetic research methods. The combined qualitative-quantitative approach meets the growing recognition among researchers that there is need to reestablish the qualitative grounding of empirical research in order to be truly scientific (Campbell, 1979). This research offers substantial evidence that existential meaning is a most relevant issue in modern life. It is astonishing that social scientists have not paid much attention to this subject until recently. One major reason for this relatively late admission of existential meaning to empirical inquiry may be that meaning is of an ontologically different order than the observable data of regular empirical science. Wilber (1983) correctly noted that meaning is in the realm of ideas and not in the realm of things or in the empirical world, and, hence, that it may never be fully grasped or detected by the five human senses or their extensions. However, one only has to look at the world of politics to understand that values and meanings play a crucial role in human actions and decisions, peace-keeping and war-making, and that these in turn lead to consequences that can be investigated very well. Therefore, let us welcome the empirical study of existential meaning as an important and innovative scientific contribution to modern society.

REFERENCES

Antonovsky, A. (1987). *Unravelling the mystery of health.* San Francisco: Jossey-Bass.

Battista, J., & Almond, R. (1973). The development of meaning in life. *Psychiatry, 36,* 409-427.

Buehler, C. (1968). The general structure of the human life cycle. In C. Buehler & F. Massarik (Eds.), *The course of human life* (pp. 12-27). New York: Springer.

Campbell, D. T. (1979). Degrees of freedom and the case study. In T. D. Cook & C. S. Reichardt (Eds.), *Qualitative and quantitative methods in evaluation research.* Beverly Hills, CA: Sage.

Debats, D. L. (1990). The Life Regard Index: Reliability and validity. *Psychological Reports, 67,* 27-34.

Debats, D. L. (1996). Meaning in life: Clinical relevance and predictive power. *British Journal of Clinical Psychology, 35,* 503-516.

Debats, D. L. (1998). Measurement of personal meaning: The psychometric properties of the Life Regard Index. In P. T. P. Wong & P. S. Fry (Eds.), *The human quest for meaning* (pp. 237-259). Mahwah, NJ: Lawrence Erlbaum.

Debats, D. L. (In press). Sources of meaning: An investigation of significant commitments in life. *Journal of Humanistic Psychology*.

Debats, D. L., Drost, J., & Hansen, P. (1995). Experiences of meaning in life: A combined qualitative and quantitative approach. *British Journal of Psychology, 86*, 359-375.

Debats, D. L., van der Lubbe, P. M., & Wezeman, F. R. (1993). On the psychometric properties of the Life Regard Index (LRI): A measure of meaningful life. An evaluation in three independent samples, based on the Dutch version. *Personality and Individual Differences, 14*, 337-345.

DeVogler, K., & Ebersole, P. (1980). Categorization of college students' meaning of life. *Psychological Reports, 46*, 387-390.

Erikson, E. (1963). *Childhood and society* (2nd ed.) New York: Norton.

Frank, J. D. (1974). Psychotherapy: The restoration of morale. *American Journal of Psychiatry, 131*, 271-274.

Frankl, V. (1966). Self-transcendence as a human phenomenon. *Journal of Humanistic Psychology, 6*, 97-106.

Frankl, V. (1976). *Man's search for meaning*. New York: Pocket Books.

Frankl, V. (1973). *The doctor and the soul*. New York: Vintage.

Hepburn, R. W. (1965). Questions about the meaning of life. *Religious Studies, 1*, 125-140.

Janoff-Bulman, R. (1992). *Shattered assumptions: Toward a new psychology of trauma*. New York: Free Press.

Kaam, A. L. van (1959). Phenomenal analysis: Exemplified by a study of the experience of "really feeling understood." *Journal of Individual Psychology, 15*, 66-72.

Maddi, S. (1967). The existential neurosis. *Journal of Abnormal Psychology, 72*, 311-325.

Maslow, A. M. (1962). *Toward a psychology of being*. Princeton, NJ: D. Van Nostrand.

Maslow, A. M. (1966). Comments on Dr. Frankl's paper. *Journal of Humanistic Psychology, 6*, 107-112.

Miles, M. B., & Huberman, A. M. (1984). *Qualitative data analysis*. Beverly Hills, CA: Sage.

Orbach, I., Illuz, A., & Rosenheim, E. (1987). Value systems and commitment to goals as a function of age, integration and personality, and fear of death. *International Journal of Behavioral Development, 10*, 225-239.

Reker, G. T. (1985). Toward a holistic model of health, behavior and aging. In J. E. Birren & J. Livingston (Eds.), *Cognition, stress, and aging* (pp. 47-71). Englewood Cliffs, NJ: Prentice Hall.

Wilber, K. (1983). *Eye to eye: The quest for the new paradigm*. Garden City, NY: Doubleday.

Yalom, Y. D. (1980). *Existential psychotherapy*. New York: Basic Books.

Zika, S., & Chamberlain, K. (1987). Relation of hassles and personality to subjective well-being. *Journal of Personality and Social Psychology, 53*, 155-162.

Zika, S., & Chamberlain, K. (1992). On the relation between meaning in life and psychological well-being. *British Journal of Psychology, 83*, 133-145.

CHAPTER 7

The Personal Meaning System in a Life-Span Perspective

Freya Dittmann-Kohli and Gerben J. Westerhof

THE PERSONAL MEANING SYSTEM

There are two basic meanings of the term *meaning*. One refers to what is signified and represents the ideas associated with something, for example an event or experience. In this sense the term *meaning of life* refers to the interpretation of life events and life in general. A second meaning of the term refers to the goals and motives that one has with respect to life events or one's life. The term meaning of life can thus be understood as the interpretation of what it means to live one's life, on the one hand, and the goals and purposes one has in life, on the other hand.

The meaning of life has been reflected on in ideologies like religious or philosophical systems. Individual persons in modern societies without a dominant religion or philosophy, however, do not regularly develop for themselves a comprehensive, overarching philosophy that explains the meaning of life. What everybody does acquire as a member of a society and culture, however, is a set of cognitive categories and frameworks as well as goals and purposes, which together are mentally used to represent one's life and oneself as an actor in it.

Phrased in this psychological perspective, the study of meaning combines self-concept research (Markus & Wurf, 1987) with research on goals (Austin & Vancouver, 1996) and can be subsumed under the concept "personal meaning system." In this chapter, we will introduce this concept and describe it in a life-span perspective.

The "personal meaning system" (PMS; Dittmann-Kohli, 1990, 1995) integrates both the interpretative and the directional aspects of meaning. The PMS is conceptualized as an affect-laden network of cognitions. The cognitions represent positively or negatively valued aspects of oneself and one's life: the things one likes or loves as well as the things one finds unpleasant or disturbing. The mental representations about motivations, the motivational cognitions (Nuttin, 1984), are also positively or negatively valued: they comprise plans, goals, and purposes in life as well as fears and anxieties.

The cognitions of the PMS comprise various meaning domains that are relevant to a person. First, we can speak of cognitions concerning one's own person and its various stable or unstable characteristics. Within these, we may differentiate between representations of psychological processes, states and traits, and of one's physical state. Second, cognitions may refer to various aspects of the world one is living in: activities (both work and leisure), the persons in our private environment and in society at large, material conditions, as well as life in general. These domains of person and life are represented as being in the past, the present, or the future. Hence, the PMS also includes a temporal perspective on self and life.

The PMS is assumed to serve three main psychological functions. First, the cognitive schemata of the PMS are used to interpret the stream of sensations and experiences. In other words, the PMS gives meaning and coherence to one's experience. Second, based on general psychological assumptions on the individual as a seeker of meaning and fulfillment in life (cf. Baumeister, 1989; Frankl, 1972), the PMS can be thought of as a subjective theory about the various aspects of self and life that may impede or facilitate the quest for meaning and fulfillment. Third, the PMS as a representation of one's most important goals and the ways to reach them is used to guide our daily life and our short- and long-term decisions.

In sum, we assume that the PMS is part of what relates human beings to their world in terms of experience and action. In the following, we will discuss the PMS in a life-span perspective.

ADAPTATION TO CHANGING LIFE CONDITIONS

We see the PMS as a dynamic structure that is continuously developed and adapted in the course of one's life. The process of building a theory about one's place in the world is thought to depend on our interactions with our environment and our experience in it as well as on the general cognitive endowments of the human mind (Epstein, 1973; Neisser, 1988).

In the course of one's life, biological, psychological, social, and material aspects of one's life conditions may change, resulting in new experiences that call for an adaptation of the PMS. Insofar as the world and/or the person change, the individual must respond by correcting his or her perceptions, beliefs, assumptions, goals, and purposes. When incentives or rewards no longer exist, an individual will not be able to maintain fulfillment in life, if he or she keeps them as resources of present or future meaning.

Research on cognitive life-span development from early to late adulthood has focused on processes of adaptation to changing life situations. Different processes have been described in recent years: the processes of assimilation and accommodation (Brandstädter & Greve, 1994); the mechanisms of primary and secondary control (Schulz & Heckhausen, 1996); and the strategies of selection, optimization, and compensation (Baltes & Baltes, 1990). These adaptation processes have been conceptualized without paying much attention to structural changes in meaning content, that is, in structured bodies of knowledge like the PMS. However, such structural changes of meaning over the life span can be expected if there are changes in life situations. Two cognitive processes that may account for such structural changes will be discussed briefly: changes in "chronic availability" and "strong change."

Higgins (1990) coined the concept of chronic availability of personal constructs, which is useful in understanding the reorganization of cognitive structures in the course of aging. Chronic availability is described as a characteristic of cognitions in long-term memory: these cognitions are easily, mostly automatically retrievable from long-term memory. In the case of changes in one's life situation, the chronic availability of a cognition might be changed. For instance, if durable changes in an individual's bodily sensations occur, as is the case in biological aging, the chronic availability of cognitions about health and physical functioning will increase and can develop into an enduring concern about physical integrity. Occupational work is an example for the opposite phenomenon. After retirement, there are no more work-related sensations and experiences, so the work-related cognitions of the PMS might loose their chronic availability.

In her work on intuitive theories of children, Carey (1985) has shown that strong change occurs in these theories during development. Strong change is comparable to a change in scientific paradigms. It is set in contrast to a weak change, where only certain elements of a lower order are exchanged, added, or left out, but the subjective theory as a whole can be retained in its main structure and content. For example, one can substitute means, while keeping one's goal intact. Strong change in the PMS will involve transformations within motivational objectives and major categories of self- and world-knowledge. The loss of close friends, of one's partner, or of health may involve a strong change in the subjective theory of life goals and a rewarding life. Strong change requires deep and time-consuming processes of affective adaptation and reorganization.

CULTURAL AND HISTORICAL DIMENSIONS

We have seen that there are various conceptualizations of mechanisms that can be used to account for adulthood changes in the PMS. Thus far, reorganizations of the PMS were portrayed as being an individual response to changing internal and external living conditions. However, the concepts in this reorganization of meaning are taken from the surrounding environment and culture. The process of meaning reconstruction should therefore also be seen as guided and constrained by the availability of cultural models and concepts. Hence, the result of the reorganization of meaning will not just be a 'copy' of objective reality.

The concepts that individuals use in articulating the meaning of life are transmitted to them from their environment. These concepts may be described as social representations, that is, widely shared social cognitions in a society, a social group, or a cultural region (Moscovici, 1984). In contacts with other persons, like parents or friends, as well as in contacts with societal institutions like the school or the mass media, people learn how to use these social representations in accounting for their own experiences. The construction of meaning is therefore not just an individual but also a sociocultural process.

From this assumption, it follows that in different historical periods, the construction of meaning will differ. We find philosophical reflections about the meaning of life occurring for at least two millennia. In particular, Greek philosophers have generated a body of thought about what the good life should be and how it should be achieved. In Christian times, the ideas and beliefs about oneself as a person and about the nature and purpose of one's life were intricately connected with the very substance of religion. Modern times, with their loss of religious ties, established everyday reality as a point of reference, for instance, by making work and family the basic values and standards of the good life (cf. Taylor, 1989). Modern times also brought individualization: there is no longer a ready made and comprehensive blueprint and orientation for how to select and organize the purposes and the course of one's individual life. In spite of these individualizing tendencies, modern social systems do provide standardized pathways for life courses and define the requirements and entrance conditions to desired routes and opportunities, as well as stages and exits, such as schooling and retirement (Kohli, 1990). To a certain extent, just following those routes gives direction to life to a certain extent, but to achieve the more desirable routes, effort, planning, and careful choices are usually required.

These characteristics of modern times have invaded the everyday life of larger groups of citizens only relatively recently. The rapid dynamic societal changes in the last century resulted in changes in life conditions and social representations even within one life span. As a result, grandparents, parents, and children may have learned different self- and life-conceptions to a certain extent. These generational differences in the PMS will be enlarged by specific historical events, such as war or economic recession, that leave deep imprints on individual lives.

In sum, from a life-span perspective the PMS at a certain age is the result of socially constructed adaptations to changing life conditions. From this perspective, an empirical study on the PMS of young and older adults will be described.

A STUDY OF PERSONAL MEANING SYSTEMS OF YOUNGER AND OLDER ADULTS

In the empirical study, the PMS of younger (17-25 years) and older adults (60-90 years) were compared. A comparative study of the PMS in young and late adulthood will help to understand the specific constellations of meaning systems in different phases of life. Of course, a comparative study cannot be as conclusive about development as longitudinal or even cross-sequential studies. Rather, the study was used to produce clues on how to further develop our theory on the construction of the PMS in social contexts.

SELE-Instrument

In the study, the so-called SELE-Instrument (from the German *SElbst* (self) and *LEben* (life); Dittmann-Kohli & Westerhof, 1997) was used. The instrument consists of a sentence completion procedure and an accompanying coding scheme. According to our conceptualization of the PMS, sentence stems were used to stimulate statements about positively and negatively valued characteristics and observations about the self and one's life; for example, abilities, weaknesses, feelings, and evaluations of self and life. Furthermore, a series of sentence stems asks for aspects that give direction to one's life, like plans, goals, desires, future expectations, fears, and anxieties. Subjects were asked to finish the sentence stems so as to describe what they consider as true and important about themselves.

In order to structure the sentence completions and make comparisons between the age groups possible, a coding system delineating the content and structure of the PMS was developed. The coding system contains a large number of categories that are organized according to meaning content. The categories were initially derived inductively by sorting the statements according to similarity of content. A similar coding system for categorizing motivational cognitions (Nuttin & Lens, 1985) was adopted and modified to fit also the cognitions about the self and life in the present and past. The main categories of the coding scheme were used to structure the presentation of the results in this chapter. They include the various meaning domains as well as the temporal and evaluative dimensions making up the PMS: physical and psychological self; activities; social relations; time and change; self- and life evaluations.

Other work on personal meaning differs in the manner of empirical assessment and conceptualization in that its main emphasis lies in measuring the strength or intensity of experiencing a meaningful, purposeful, or fulfilled life (e.g., Antonovsky, 1993; Debats, 1996; Reker, Peacock, & Wong, 1987). The cognitions activated by the SELE-instrument also describe the person or his/her life as (not) satisfying, (un)fulfilled, or the self as being (un)happy. However, the focus of our research is primarily on the meaning content of these descriptions.

Description of the Younger and Older Samples

Three hundred younger and 300 elderly German adults participated in the age-comparative study on the PMS. The age range of the young group was 17 to 25 years (mean 20), the age range of the elderly adults was 60 to 90 years (mean 74). For the young group, the SELE sentence completion questionnaire was applied in a school setting, whereas the elderly completed it at home. About equal numbers of full-time students and apprentices make up the younger group. The sex distribution was about even in the younger group (55% females). The older group was comparable to the younger group with regard to educational level, although the spread was somewhat wider, ranging from unfinished primary to college education. The older group consisted of more females (68%). Although it was found that higher educated respondents produced more complex and ambivalent answers than lower educated respondents, the latter were perfectly able to complete the sentence stems in meaningful ways.

DIFFERENCES IN THE PERSONAL MEANING SYSTEMS OF YOUNGER AND OLDER ADULTS

In the following section, the findings of the above described study are presented. Here, it is only possible to give summarized findings. The detailed findings on which these summaries are based have been reported in Dittmann-Kohli (1995). Overall, the results show marked differences in the frequency and configuration of categories used in self- and life-descriptions of young and elderly adults.

Physical Self

Among the very consistent and prominent findings of the study are differences relating to the physical self. The subjective significance of one's present physical functioning and of future changes in one's health status is much larger among the elderly than among the young. Young adults direct attention especially to the positive implications of their physical self, mostly in relation to attractiveness to the opposite sex or in relation to enjoyment and sports. The elderly are concerned about loss and maintenance of physical integrity and psychophysical functioning. Many different aspects of physical functioning, such as energy, vitality, and physical and mental fitness become manifest in their self-descriptions. In opposition to what one might expect, no difference was found in frequencies of responses on physical integrity between the "young old" (60-73) and the "old old" (over 73 years).

There are also characteristic qualitative and quantitative age differences in the concerns about death and dying. Young respondents would mention, for instance, that they fear to die at a young age. The elderly adults are concerned with good or bad circumstances of dying, like being left helpless and in pain, having a good death, and being able to die at an appropriate time.

The elderly men and women also expressed an interest in continuing awareness. Statements about the desire to see what might happen in the next century or being sad about not being able to experience how their grandchildren grow up are examples. The young respondents produced only a few self-statements in these categories and if they did, as in the case of health or death, their cognitions were less differentiated and vivid.

In sum, it can be stated that bodily functioning is a more central domain in the PMS of the elderly, signaling a major change in the structure of the self-concept. This change appears to mirror an age-related decline in objective psychophysical functioning. Since the oldest old do not mention health concerns more often, there appears to be no perfect relationship between health concerns and objective health status.

Psychological Self

The psychological self shows fewer age differences than the physical self. Cognitions of one's model of the mind or inner self were found to differ quantitatively, but not qualitatively between age groups. In both age groups, temperament and personality dispositions are important elements in describing the psychological self. However, the younger group more often used cognitions about intrapersonal or self-directed behaviors and attitudes. The young are also concerned about personal growth more often than the elderly. These cognitions are indicative of a search for identity among the young. However, since these aspects of the self are mentioned especially often by students, they may also result from their higher education level.

Besides the meaning domains relating to the physical and psychological self, meaning domains relating the person to his or her environment were identified, namely, activities and social relations.

Activities

With regard to the meaning domain activities, it was found that young people are mainly concerned about their achievements. Education and vocational training are portrayed often as a source of negative meaning: the young worry about having enough abilities for school subjects, being able to speak well in class, or being disciplined enough. We also found many fears about finding a job and worries about its quality. Work stress and competence deficits are also mentioned by the young. In contrast to the statements about the problematic features of school, university, and jobs, the young adults attribute very positive meanings to leisure time and vacation, enjoyable activities, and having fun. Present life fulfillment is often found in free time used for oneself.

While the elderly are free from worries of doing well in school or a job, they are also no longer able to look forward to rewards such as future career and occupational fulfillment or wealth and status. However, work and career can still function as sources of positive meaning: the elderly's pride frequently lies in past achievements. The lack of stress from enforced work load reduces the elderly's need for regeneration. There are some elderly who express concerns abc•t being stressed, or being interested in too many things, but the emphasis on maintenance of functioning in everyday activities is more salient.

Among the elderly, life fulfillment through leisure time is often focused on traveling. Anticipation of late life activities also include more passive activities like reading, going for walks, or home-bound hobbies. These imply that the elderly take notice of decreasing physical functioning in their cognitions about activities. As an illustration, wishes and plans to travel are often mentioned in connection with thoughts about changing physical potential: "I like to travel, if I'm healthy enough."

In sum, cognitions of young and elderly adults relating to activities are very different in content. In general, the observed age differences suggest that there are prototypical ideas about suitable and desired life course patterns that are related to the institutionalized life course of school, work, and retirement.

Social Relations

The social world is an important motivational focus for both young and old adults. The persons of whom fulfillment is expected or over whom concerns are voiced, however, are clearly different. The type of interaction and the social and emotional needs are at variance, too. Subjectively, young and elderly adults seem to live in a rather different social world.

Friendship, belonging to a group, and being accepted are among the central needs of the younger adults. Cognitions about love and erotic attractiveness, about finding a partner and founding a family are also concerns of the young. Parents are mentioned by only some of the youngest of the younger group. The elderly are less often subject to suffering from worries over being rejected, unpopular, left by a friend, and so on. In contrast, the family, the marriage partner, and children and grandchildren are central sources of meaning to the older adults. The elderly derive interpersonal rewards from thinking of their children's well-being. At the same time, they hope to continue their life with their partner.

A part of the answers coded as social relations did not refer to particular persons belonging to family, partners, or friends. Rather, they referred to human beings in general, to politicians, to political and environmental issues in society, or to peace or lack of harmony in mankind. A subsection of these were statements about one's own actions and involvements in trying to do something for the general good. Especially among the older adults, there were many references to helping, often specifying that the help was directed to other older people.

At least partly, the different meaning structures relating to social relations mirror differences in the position on the life course of young and elderly adults. The first are concerned with finding a partner and founding a family, the latter have already done so and are concerned about maintaining good relationships within the family and express hope for good lives for their children and grandchildren.

Time Perspective

Besides the age differences in meaning domains, we also found differences in the time perspectives of the young and the old. Young and elderly adults situate themselves and their lives in clearly divergent structures of personal time. While young adults live in a timeless present and a seemingly endless future, the elderly live partly in the past, in a present where time is passing by too quickly, and a future where meaningful aspects of life are seen as threatened. Nevertheless, the elderly expressed many goals and purposes for their future lives.

There are clear differences in the subjective significance of the past self. A large number of spontaneous references to the past were made by the elderly, but hardly ever by the young. Past life events and achievements are an important aspect of the elderly adults' identity: they are proud of having achieved social status, of their former occupations, of children raised successfully, of having been able to cope successfully with critical life events. In addition, the past was mentioned in terms of its positive or negative quality and in terms of the positive and negative contributions the subject thought he or she had made. Other sentence completions indicated that one would probably make the same mistakes or choices again if one could live one's life again, or that one would now know how to do things differently. Such references to the past were not mentioned by the young adults. The students and apprentices stated only occasionally that their past life was not very long and not full of events, and was not really worth mentioning.

In respect to future orientations, the age differences do not reside primarily in the extension of the future time perspective (i.e., in the number of years) but rather in its qualitative structure. The answers to the sentence stems referring to the coming years, to a time later on as well as to goals, desires, dreams, and perceived possibilities were answered completely differently. Young adults cognize a future where they will become what they are not yet. The future is a temporal domain where aspired roles and activities are located. These contain passing examinations, finding and having a job, and advancing vocationally. A great number of statements also refer to a future partner and family. The topic of hopes and dreams becoming true or not was also addressed directly. For the young adults, the future is the domain where the positive potential of the self can be unfolded and realized – or may fail to be realized – by entering into the future.

In opposition to this, the elderly adults' future is not so much a domain where new and partly unknown potentials can be realized but where present positive conditions should be maintained as long as possible. Hopes are directed toward continuing contentment, maintenance of health, or a life together with one's partner. The word *still* is often used by the elderly, stating that they are "still able to do something" or that something "still" is the case. This use of the word *still* as well as other words like *continue, maintain,* or *for a few more years* suggest that the elderly expect that good functioning, well-being, and enjoyment of life is not going to last. Indeed, some elderly describe their fears and expectations about decreasing opportunities for self- and life-realization.

When younger adults hope that there will be a positive change in the future, they imply that the present is less positive than the future might be. The young persons' concept of development is growth and positive change, that is, reducing a negative Is-Ought discrepancy by attaining the more positive Ought. The elderly, on the other hand, hope that their present life and their present self will remain as they are now. The prototypical elderly's expectations for personal development does not consist of growth but of either preservation or reduction.

Self- and Life-Evaluation

Young and elderly adults apply different frameworks for self- and life-evaluation, not only in terms of positive or negative outcomes of evaluation processes, but also in the kind of standards they use in evaluating themselves and their lives.

With regard to positive or negative evaluations, young subjects were found to be more self-critical. The elderly adults were more positive about their present life and self. For example, older respondents more often reject sentence stems that imply negative valuations, like "I am afraid of ...." Furthermore, it was found that the elderly use multiple cognitive strategies for self-enhancement. For example, although their health status may be worse than that of the younger group, they achieve positive evaluations of their health by comparing themselves with aged peers and seeing that they are better off.

With regard to the different standards used in evaluations, the younger persons think of their character and competencies more often, whereas the elderly think of their former or present life in general. There is also a strong tendency for the older respondents to judge self and life in terms of satisfaction, whereas the young adults prefer to use affective valuations like happiness.

These differences point to changes in the quality and role of well-being from young to late adulthood. In old age, it is no longer as important what type of character and personality one has or whether happiness is experienced, but whether one's life situation is satisfactory and one is content.

CONCEPTUALIZING LIFE-SPAN CHANGE OF THE PERSONAL MEANING SYSTEM

What can we learn about the meaning of life as seen by younger and older adults in this study? In contrast to current life-span theories that focus on adaptational mechanisms without resorting to the level of meaning, we made meaning the primary object of study. The advantage of our approach is that personal meanings and its changes can be studied directly by asking persons for what they see as important and characteristic of self and life. The method provides us with information about how young and elderly adults perceive and interpret themselves and their lives. By qualitative and quantitative comparisons we were able to discover the similarities and differences in their perspectives.

Adaptation of the Personal Meaning System to Changing Life Conditions

The prototypical configurations of meaning in the young and the old suggest that they have generated an understanding of self and life that at least partly reflects their position on the social and biological life line.

The results show that the age-related changes of the human body should be considered as a context influencing the elderly adults' self-conception. Not only does physical integrity acquire direct relevance in the elderly's self-concept and their concerns, but the elderly's preferences and expectations for activities also reflect their reduced physical prowess and orientation to comfort. Full possession of one's physical potential is reflected in the patterns of young people's leisure time preferences – for example in the type of sports they mention.

The cognitions about social relations partly reflect (quasi-)universal patterns of age-related social structures. The biologically determined family cycle is clearly reflected in the answers: students and apprentices talk about their hopes and intentions for their future families, and sometimes about their parents. The elderly talk about their existing family, about children and grandchildren, and about growing old together with their partner. The PMS of the younger and elderly adults also reflect changing socio-emotional needs: friends and acquaintances are mentioned by the young subjects, as well as corresponding social needs and feelings, such as concern for status in the group or for intimate relationships, whereas the old are interested in the life of their children and grandchildren.

Cognitions about education and work reflect the institutional embeddings of the younger group; they are no longer found in the older group. To a certain extent, the psychological self-concept is also influenced by these aspects of the life-situation of early adulthood. The seemingly general dimensions of the self-concept in adolescence are tied to the existence of schools, parents, and the vocational future. Traits, skills, and potentials of all kinds, which are constantly evaluated at school and on the job, are indeed less important in self- and life-evaluations of the elderly.

In sum, the PMS of the young takes into account the life conditions that are typical for early adulthood, like finishing an education, founding a family, or finding one's identity. The elderly's PMS mirrors life conditions of old age, like retirement, biological changes, being nearer to the end of one's life, and having established a family life with children and grandchildren. Hence, we might conceptualize many of the differences in the meaning constellations of the two age groups as a systematic adaptation of the PMS to changing life conditions throughout the adult life span. The findings of our study suggest that 'strong change' and changes in 'chronic availability' are found from early to late adulthood.

In an ongoing research project, the German Aging Survey, the relations between life conditions and the PMS in the second half of life are studied in detail in a large representative sample of East- and West-Germans (Dittmann-Kohli, Kohli, & Künemund, 1995). A first publication on this study shows that concerns about physical integrity are indeed related to one's health status (Westerhof, Kuin, &

Dittmann-Kohli, 1998). They are also related, however, to socially constructed representations of one's own aging as a process of decline in health, which brings us to the role of social representations in the PMS.

The Role of Social Representations in the Personal Meaning System

In the introduction, we theorized that changes in life conditions are rendered meaningful by use of social representations. Therefore, we assumed that the reorganization of meaning will not just be a copy of objective changes in living conditions. The use of social representations becomes evident when we turn our focus not so much to what has been said by our respondents, but to what they did not say.

As an example, we found that most self-descriptive statements explicitly concerned the private life and self. Some statements were also found that referred to more general concerns about society, humanity and other people in general. Compared to the personal themes, these topics of humanitarian concerns and societal issues make up only a relatively small number of the sentence completions. The dominant reference to the private self and life is partly, but not completely, attributable to the SELE-instrument. On the one hand, the instructions and sentence stems probably activate the private self. On the other hand, the few answers about the non-private domain give evidence that it is at least grammatically easy to complete the sentence stems with statements about the world beyond the private self. The dominance of personal themes over more general societal concerns, which is true for young as well as elderly adults, may be related to an individualistic orientation of modern societies where life is seen as part of a private self. One's life is one's own business and is not primarily seen as an element of the larger system.

Another example is the fact that the statements hardly ever mention religious content, which implies that one's person and life are not seen as a matter of a higher being or will. As described in the introduction, everyday reality, including self, work, and family, is the reference point for meaning in life in modern societies. Religious ideologies have lost significance in providing frameworks for finding meaning in life (Taylor, 1989).

Some cross-cultural studies on the PMS, also using the SELE-instrument, have indeed shown that in other countries, such as Zaire and India, societal and religious topics are mentioned more often. These findings lend support to our interpretation that cultural models and concepts are used in the construction of the PMS.

Besides these cultural differences, which apply to both younger and elderly adults, we also found differences in cultural constructions regarding the aging process. In one of our cross-cultural studies (Westerhof & Dittmann-Kohli, 1997), we found that both in the Netherlands and in Zaire health is a more central concern for older than for younger adults. However, the age differences were larger in the Netherlands than in Zaire. Furthermore, the Dutch elderly described health as a general goal, were concerned about their health behavior, and about losing their independence, whereas the Zairean elderly referred to their health mostly as a means in order to reach goals, like professional activities. The Zaireans also described their hopes for support by their children instead of hopes for remaining independent. These findings suggest a rather universal pattern in the concerns about health in different age groups, as well as culturally divergent ways of giving meaning to biological aging and health.

Generational Differences

Although many of the differences between the young and the old might be interpreted as changes in the PMS that are adaptive to changing life situations over the life span, some generational differences might also be reflected in the PMS of the younger and elderly adults. Living conditions and social representations may be subject to historical change. Hence, when they have grown older, the younger subjects may in some aspects have a different PMS than the elderly of today.

Some social changes are already becoming manifest. For instance, a decreasing stability in the domains of work and family can be observed, which is exemplified by more and quicker alternations in one's work life, changing retirement patterns, and higher divorce rates. These changes will have an influence on the lives of the future elderly, which might be reflected in the corresponding meaning domains of their PMS.

On the other hand, in spite of historical changes, the PMS of the future elderly will continue to reflect many of the prototypical biological and social living conditions that are found today in young and old age. As we have argued above, many cultural and individual perceptions of aging reflect existential conditions that are of relevance everywhere, like the patterns of biological development and the family cycle, as well as the passing of time. In addition, we can also safely assume that our language concepts and basic categories for understanding the world do not change so radically that we do not understand what people thought a hundred years ago. Indeed, accounts by Cicero or Montaigne on the aging process are perfectly intelligible today.

One further example may be mentioned here. Despite scientific and public discussion about a lengthening of the human life span up to 120 or 150 years, it seems likely that physical decline in very old age will remain with us. In order to remain a good theory and provide for good predictions and planning, the PMS of individuals must take this aspect of the Conditio Humana into account. On the other hand, it may not be necessary that psychophysical functioning will remain a central concern. Rather, it seems possible that the meaning and motivational texture around biological aging will change in the future and that more stress will be laid on using an individual's potentials that remain in spite of physical aging. Once again, we see an intricate balance between universal aspects of aging and specific cultural ways of giving meaning to these. It seems to be a matter of scientific discovery just which factors should work toward historical continuity or change in regard to composition and structure of the PMS.

Life-Span Theories and the Personal Meaning System

We can thus affirm our earlier position that individual perceptions and experiences, mechanisms of cognitive representation and processing, as well as socio-cultural models are relevant determinants of the PMS. The different processes – the reorganization of the PMS in light of new experiences, the use of social representations in giving meaning, and generational influences – should not be conceived of as contradictory, but as working together in the formation of personal meaning systems.

In line with current theorizing, it seems sensible to conclude that assimilation and accommodation (Brandstädter & Greve, 1994), primary and secondary control strategies (Schulz & Heckhausen, 1996), as well as compensation, optimization, and selection (Baltes & Baltes, 1990), all describe valid processes of the life-long development of personal meaning. Although it is not easy to identify empirically which mechanism is at work, they all involve a restructuring and reorganization of the meaning system. The reorganization of the PMS indeed presupposes that there are adaptive psychological processes. However, these adaptive psychological processes have most often been described and studied without taking into account the substantive meaning involved. The cognitive reorganization of meaning content, as found in our study on the PMS, emphasizes that there must be certain systematic changes in subjective theories, including the development of completely new parts of theory.

Although explanatory mechanisms for life-span developmental changes in meaning systems need much more careful discussion than is possible here, it can be suggested that the age-related changing balance of gains and losses is perceived differently by aging persons themselves than by researchers using an outside gerontological perspective (cf. Dittmann-Kohli, 1989). Although from an outsider's perspective aging may include many losses and declines, aging persons themselves do not always experience their aging process as such. Indeed, the second half of life, perhaps especially the time after (early) retirement, may even be seen as the best stage of life. The widespread life satisfaction and the desire that things stay as they are now point to an interpretation that there is not so much a decline as a stability in deriving positive meaning from life. Although there may be critical life events and phases of detachment involving feelings of loss and a sense of generalized or more specific meaninglessness (van Selm, 1998), most people are able to regain a new sense of meaning that provides the same level of life fulfillment, albeit a qualitatively very different kind of fulfillment. It has often been found that the strength or intensity of meaning in life is unrelated to one's age, but we have shown in our study that the qualitative content of the cognitions that are used in constructing meaning in life differs largely between the young and the old. Our findings indicate that Erikson's developmental task in the last stage of life, "integrity versus despair," seems to be a matter of wisdom in the sense of changing one's personal meaning system.

REFERENCES

Austin, J. T., & Vancouver, J. B. (1996). Goal constructs in psychology: Structure, process, and content. *Psychological Bulletin, 120*, 338-375.

Antonovsky, A. (1993). The structure and properties of the Sense of Coherence Scale. *Social Science and Medicine, 36*, 725-733

Baltes, P. B., & Baltes, M. M. (1990). Psychological perspectives on successful aging: The model of selective optimization with compensation. In P. B. Baltes & M. M. Baltes (Eds.), *Successful aging: Perspectives from the behavioral sciences* (pp. 1-34). New York: Cambridge University Press.

Baumeister, R. (1989). The problem of life's meaning. In D. M. Buss & N. Cantor (Eds.), *Personality psychology* (pp. 138-148). New York: Springer.

Brandstädter, J., & Greve, W. (1994). The aging self: Stabilizing and adaptive processes. *Developmental Review, 14*, 52-80.

Carey, S. (1985). *Conceptual change in childhood*. Cambridge, UK: Cambridge University Press.

Debats, D. L. (1996). *Meaning in life: Psychometric, clinical and phenomenological aspects*. Doctoral dissertation, Rijksuniversiteit Groningen.

Dittmann-Kohli, F. (1989). Erfolgreiches Altern aus subjektiver Sicht. *Zeitschrift für Gerontopsychologie und Psychiatrie, 2*, 301-307.

Dittmann-Kohli, F. (1990). The construction of meaning in old age. *Ageing and Society, 10*, 270-294.

Dittmann-Kohli, F. (1995). *Das persönliche Sinnsystem: Ein Vergleich zwischen frühem und spätem Erwachsenenalter*. Göttingen: Hogrefe.

Dittmann-Kohli, F., Kohli, M., & Künemund, H. (1995). *Lebenszusammenhänge, Selbstkonzepte und Lebensentwürfe: Die Konzeption des Deutschen Alters-Survey*. Internal Report Forschungsgruppe Altern und Lebenslauf. Berlin: Freie Universität Berlin.

Dittmann-Kohli, F., & Westerhof, G. J. (1997). The SELE-Sentence Completion Questionnaire: A new instrument for the assessment of personal meaning in research on aging. *Anuario de Psicologia, 73*, 7-18.

Epstein, S. (1973). Entwurf einer integrativen Persönlichkeitstheorie. In S.-H. Filipp (Eds.), *Selbstkonzept-Forschung* (pp. 15-45). Stuttgart: Klett-Cotta.

Frankl, V. E. (1972). *Der Wille zum Sinn*. Bern: Hans Huber.

Higgins, E. T. (1990). Personality, social psychology, and person-situation relations: Standards and knowledge activation as a common language. In L. A. Pervin (Ed.), *Handbook of personality* (pp. 301-338). New York: Guilford.

Kohli, M. (1990). Lebenslauf und Lebensalter als gesellschaftliche Konstruktionen: Elemente zu einem interkulturellen Vergleich. In G. Elwert, M. Kohli, & H. K. Müller (Eds.), *Im Lauf der Zeit* (pp. 11-32). Saarbrücken: Breitenbach.

Markus, H. R., & Wurf, E. (1987). The dynamic self-concept: A social psychological perspective. *Annual Review of Psychology, 38*, 299-337.

Moscovici, S. (1984). The phenomenon of social representations. In R. Farr & S. Moscovici (Eds.), *Social representations*. Cambridge, UK: Cambridge University Press.

Neisser, U. (1988). Five kinds of self-knowledge. *Philosophical Psychology, 1*, 35-59.

Nuttin, J. (1984). *Motivation, planning, and action: A relational theory of behavior dynamics.* Hillsdale, NJ: Lawrence Erlbaum.

Nuttin, J., & Lens, W. (1985). *Future time perspective and motivation.* Hillsdale, NJ: Lawrence Erlbaum.

Reker, G. T., Peacock, E. J., & Wong, P. T. P. (1987). Meaning and purpose in life and well-being: A life-span perspective. *Journal of Gerontology, 42,* 44-49.

Schulz, R., & Heckhausen, J. (1996). A life-span model of successful aging. *American Psychologist, 51,* 702-714.

Selm, M. van. (1998). *Meaninglessness in the second half of life.* Nijmegen, The Netherlands: University of Nijmegen Press.

Taylor, C. (1989). *Sources of the self: The making of the modern identity.* Cambridge, MA: Harvard University Press.

Westerhof, G. J., & Dittmann-Kohli, F. (1997). Zingeving, levensloop en cultuur: Verschillen en overeenkomsten tussen jong en oud in Nederland en Zaire. *Medische Antropologie, 9,* 115-136.

Westerhof, G. J., Kuin, Y., & Dittmann-Kohli, F. (1998). Gesundheit als Lebensthema. *Zeitschrift für Klinische Psychologie, 27,* 136-142.

CHAPTER 8

The Development of a Culturally Sensitive Measure of Sources of Life Meaning

Edward Prager, Rivka Savaya, and Liora Bar-Tur

The increasingly popular concept of hermeneutics in the humanities and use of life story narratives in qualitative research have brought about a return to meaning as an area of phenomenological exploration and understanding of the aging process. The question of meaning appears to be universal. There is no area that is not touched by this theme (Peseschkian, 1983).

It is through meanings that individuals experience, understand, and manipulate themselves, each other, and their worlds (Ford, 1975). Deriving from the symbolic interaction and phenomenological perspectives is the helpful insight that it is individual interpretations rather than some objectively defined reality that are the bases for behavior and social interaction (Breytspraak, 1984). Personal meaning is an expression of the value people place upon the events and flow of life and the significance they attach to their existence (Reker & Wong, 1988). It is a tool for controlling the world, for self-regulation, and for belongingness. While life involves constant change, meaning is based on stability and permanence (Baumeister, 1991).

Kaufman (1987) contends that "old people ... maintain an ageless sense of self that transcends change by providing continuity ..." (p. 161). Consistent confirmation of such continuity comes from a variety of studies. Ebersole and DePaola (1989), in their investigation of meaning in the active married elderly, found no significant differences in depth of meaning between younger marrieds and older (65+) ones. Baum and Stewart (1990), studying 185 subjects, observed that the amount of purpose in life did not vary with age or sex, and sources of meaning did not alter across time. In their study of mothers and elderly, Zika and Chamberlain (1992) found support for Yalom's (1980) position, namely that while the sources of meaning may change over a life span, the relation between the strength of life meaning and psychological health may remain consistent regardless of where meaning is embedded.

Personal meanings drive and/or are driven by the themes people create and the values they live by. For Kaufman (1987), themes, or cognitive areas of meaning, explain, unify, and give substance to people's perceptions of who they are and how they see themselves participating in social life. Values may be understood to be expressions of widely held ideals of human behavior, clearly locating the individual within a historical cultural cohort. Thus, a sense of personal meaning is derived from, or closely reflects the interaction between the macro level historically and culturally determined value system and its integration and the micro level life themes by which people know themselves and explain who they are to others.

Disparate explorations into the content of meaning have produced what appears to be a general consensus as to the major sources of meaning in life for individuals of all ages. Fiske and Chiriboga (1991) delineate seven goals: achievement and work; good personal relations; philosophical and religious goals; social service; freedom from hardship; seeking enjoyment; and personal growth. Closely paralleling these are the eight meaning categories found by DeVogler and Ebersole (1980): understanding (trying to gain more knowledge); service (a helping, giving orientation); relationship (interpersonal orientation); belief (living according to one's beliefs); expression (through art, athletics, music, writing); obtaining (respect, possessions, responsibility); growth (toward developing personal potentials, obtaining goals); and existential-hedonistic (the importance of the pleasures of daily life). Similarly, in studies by Thurner (1975), Hedlund and Birren (1984), Klinger (1977), Levi (1996), and others there seems to be a consensus around a few major sources of meaning, namely personal relationships, personal growth, success, altruism, hedonism, creativity, religion, and legacy.

During the period from 1993 to 1995, the first author interviewed more than 800 Australians and Israelis, using the Canadian-developed Sources of Meaning Profile (SOMP; Reker, 1988). The SOMP was created to measure the sources and degree of personal, present meaning in one's life. As tempting as it was to look for similarities and/or differences between cultures in sources of meaning, the author encountered a number of instrument-related limitations that the current study attempts to address. First, for some populations the limited number of SOMP sources (16 or 17, depending upon the version) was constraining. A legitimate question goes to the issue of whether more diverse, comprehensive lists of meaning sources would produce similar or very different results. In both Australian and Israeli studies based upon the SOMP instrument (Prager, 1996, 1997), between 25% and 33% of the respondents wrote in additional sources of meaning, including personal and family health, personal honor, peace, and nature, among others.

Second, though translations of an original instrument may be faithfully rendered into the language of the respondents currently being studied, linguistic nuances of the original culture persist. Though care was taken to make necessary adaptations, some items by their phrasing (e.g., "everyday needs," "hedonistic activities") or the inclusion of compound statements (e.g., "personal relationships with family and/or friends") force a response to a question that may be perceived to mean one thing when it actually may mean another. Other items, such as "participation in religious activities" reflect, at the least, a narrowness in definition.

A third source of difficulty, related to the above two, pertains to the issue of cultural and ethnic specificity in research in general, and in instrument development in particular. The author was well aware of the fact that "the SOMP was designed as a culture-specific instrument" (Reker, personal communication, 1997). In recent years there has been increasing recognition of the need to anchor social and psychological research of minority or ethnic populations in the culture of the group under investigation (Hughes, Seidman, & Williams, 1993; Hui & Triandis, 1989; Sasao & Sue, 1993; Seidman, 1993). Noting that culture affects every stage of the research process, researchers have called for the development of culturally sensitive research methods that take into account the values, belief systems, and behaviors of the population under study, as well as its place in, and its relationship with the dominant culture in whose midst it lives (Hines, 1993; Maton, 1993; Tran, 1992). It is therefore our view that, in studying personal meaning, while it may be important to compare young or old respondents *across* cultures on an item-by-item basis, it may be even more worthwhile an endeavor to study what sources of meaning are generated by specific cultures (culture-specific instrument conceptualization) and how those sources of meaning identify and differentiate between different groups *within* those cultures. In order to properly document how cultural norms, values, and experiences influence the relevance of a set of constructs to respondents, qualitative contextual comparisons of personal meaning may be much more valid than quantitative comparative measurements of magnitude of specific meaning sources.

The study undertaken by the authors, and still in progress at this writing, relates to the above issue of cultural specificity, as reflected in the construction of an instrument that we are tentatively calling the Sources of Life Meaning (SLM). The SLM examines the sources of meaning in life for younger and older Arab and Jewish Israelis. In this study, which focuses on the formulation and definition of meaning constructs, we attempted to represent our participants' reality as faithfully as possible. Qualitative research methods provided us with a broad-based description and deeper understanding of meaning phenomena from the participants' viewpoints and perspectives. At the same time, in our attempt to create a viable, parsimonious instrument validly measuring meaning-in-life sources, quantitative measures were used in order to obtain reliability estimates and assessments of other psychometric properties, including the factorial structure and distribution of the subscales.

CONSTRUCTION OF THE SOURCES OF LIFE MEANING SCALE

To develop the culturally sensitive SLM measure referred to in this study, a mixed-methods approach was adopted, in several stages. First, a concept mapping procedure (Trochim, 1989) was first employed in order to learn about the culturally specific sources of meaning in life from our young and elderly volunteer respondents. In the second stage, based on the information obtained from the first stage, a survey questionnaire was developed to learn about the properties of the instrument. In a third stage, SLM differences between younger and older Arabs and Jews were analyzed, with emphasis on cultural background, age, and gender.

Stage 1: Concept Mapping

The concept mapping procedure, selected in this study for identifying the sources of meaning in life, enables an individual or group to present their ideas pictorially or graphically and can be used to help articulate a theory, to provide the basis for measurement, or as a framework for analyzing research results (Trochim, 1989). Concept mapping involves several steps:

(1) Determining the focus for the mapping, which in this study was the observation of variables relevant to the meaning-of-life concept.

(2) Generating statements relevant to the focus. The first task addressed was the selection of methods and participants for generating variables relevant to the focus. Two methods were employed: focus groups and questionnaires. In this study, four focus groups were employed: one each for elderly Arab men and women ($N = 14$) and one each for elderly Jewish men and women ($N = 30$), all of whom were recruited from two community centers for the aged in Tel-Aviv. Participants' ages were similar for Jews and Arabs, ranging from 62 to 78 years. An open discussion was conducted on the questions: "What are the most important things in life?", "What are the things that you consider most meaningful and necessary in life?", and "What gives you a taste for life?" Two moderators, an experienced psychologist and social worker, and a recorder, all of whom were ethnically matched to the respective groups, were present in each of the four groups. Duration of each of the focus group meetings was approximately 90 minutes. These groups generated a sum of 72 different meaning items.

Due to problems of logistics, we were unable to conduct similar focus groups to generate statements from younger people. It was thus decided to employ a different method. One hundred and ten Israeli Arab and Jewish male and female students between the ages of 21 and 36 were recruited from the Tel Aviv University student body and were asked to respond to the open-ended question: "What are the things you consider most meaningful and necessary in life?" An additional 21 meaning items were obtained from the students and then added to the items obtained from the older group, rendering a total of 93 meaning items obtained from 154 individuals. Though SOMP data were also collected from the students, an analysis of those findings, including validation data for the SLM, is beyond the scope of this chapter.

(3) Sorting of statements into groups. The researchers wrote all the meaning sources down on cards, one statement per card. We approached seven social workers, giving each one a complete set of cards with the instruction that they were to arrange them in piles, in whatever way made most sense to them, being sure that there was more than one pile.

(4) Analyzing the sorting, resulting in a visual mapping of concepts. To analyze the combined data obtained from the sorters, we used the Concept System software, developed by Trochim (1993), that performs two main analyses: multi-dimensional scaling and cluster analysis. The multi-dimensional scaling prepares a series of [N x N] matrices, yielding a two-dimensional dot map of the statements, with each dot on the map representing one statement. Statements that were frequently sorted together into the same group are located close to each other on the map and those that were not sorted together are far apart. The second analysis is a hierarchical cluster analysis (Andeberg, 1973; Everitt, 1980), grouping individual statements (dots) on the map into clusters of statements that presumably reflect similar concepts. The end products are two visual maps of the statements: a dot map and a cluster map (for more details on concept mapping, see Trochim, 1989).

(5) Interpreting the cluster or concept map. The cluster map may be interpreted on two levels. First, one examines the items comprising each cluster and attempts to discover their common denominator in order to identify and label the underlying concept. Second, the spread of the clusters in the two-dimensional space (north-south and east-west) is examined in an effort to understand the underlying meaning of the clusters' locations relative to each other.

The Dot and Cluster Maps. As mentioned above, in dot maps each of the statements is graphically represented by a dot on a map. Dots that are close together on the map represent items that were often sorted into the same category by the sorters, for example: "to find a suitable partner" and "to live with a partner." Dots that are farther apart were sorted into separate groups and represent dissimilar items, for example: "to gain social status" and "the satisfaction derived from helping others." Statements that all sorters placed in the same cluster appear as dots one on top of the other.

Cluster maps present the results of the cluster analysis. Statements within a cluster are those that were more often sorted into the same pile than the statements in the other clusters. Furthermore, clusters that are closer to each other will in general be more similar in content than clusters that are farther apart on the map. The program allows the researcher to determine how sensitive the analysis should be, and it is possible to generate solutions based on any number of clusters. The ultimate decision regarding the number of clusters to be retained for interpretation is made by the researcher based on conceptual and practical considerations. This process resulted in the identification of eight major clusters of sources of life meaning, as determined in the qualitative phase of this study. The following is a list of the clusters with two examples of entries for each cluster.

1. *Being respected by others*: to be respected by family; to be respected by community.

2. *Closeness to family*: to feel enjoyment and satisfaction with family; to maintain good relationships with all close kin.

3. *Belonging to a social group*: to be with people; to enjoy good social relationships.

4. *Living according to values*: to preserve the honor of the family; to maintain values and traditions.

5. *Spiritual and mental/intellectual pursuits*: to participate in religious and spiritual activities; to participate in educational and cultural activities.

6. *Physical and mental health*: to function independently, without help; not to be a burden or dependent on anyone.

7. *Personal status and success*: to be successful financially/materialistically; to succeed in all aspects of life.

8. *Self-fulfillment*: to derive personal satisfaction from accomplishments; to feel self-fulfilled.

Interpretation of Dimensionality. Examination of the location of clusters in the quadrants created by the north/south and east/west axes revealed four principal underlying dimensions very similar to those reported by Reker (1998): a self-preoccupation dimension (physical and mental health, personal status and success); a self-actualization dimension (self-fulfillment, being respected by others); a collectiveness and connectedness dimension (closeness to family, belonging to a social group); and a self-transcendence dimension (living according to values, spiritual and mental activities). The positioning of the clusters on the axes appeared to lend additional support to the conceptualization of the four basic dimensions: self-preoccupation and collectiveness were at opposite poles on the north-south axis, while the self-actualization and self-transcendence dimensions were at opposite poles on what was roughly an east-west axis.

Stage 2: Construction of the Questionnaire

The eight clusters that emerged from the concept mapping procedure provided us with a contextual structure for the SLM. From the pool of 93 statements we chose, after eliminating clearly redundant items, those 41 statements that best captured the essence of the eight meaning clusters. We then rewrote the items in a 5-point Likert-type questionnaire format (1 = not important at all as a source of meaning; 5 = very important as a source of meaning). The final interview schedule, in both the Hebrew and Arabic versions, consists of a section on demographics and background information, the 41 Likert-type meaning items, and a third section containing three summary questions dealing with the respondent's global assessment of meaning in his or her life.

To test the psychometric properties of the SLM, the responses of a convenience sample of 405 men and women were surveyed. Ages ranged from 20 to 97 years; the mean age was 50 years. Of the total, 57% were Jewish and 43% were Arab. The younger Jews and Arabs again were recruited from the rosters of the Tel Aviv University. The older respondents were interviewed in their senior citizens' organizations, in community centers, or in the northern Arab villages in which they lived.

As expected there were significant differences between the two cultures in areas of religious observance, country of birth, and education. On the whole, Arab respondents reported poorer health than Jewish subjects. These differences closely reflect the population parameters for these variables.

Exploratory Factor Analysis. Table 8.1 presents the results of factor analytic procedures and the alpha coefficients for each of the 11 factorially derived scales. The principal components factor analysis method with varimax rotation was used in this study. The reader's attention is called to the fact that the items listed for each factor are only examples and do not represent the total of all items in the factor.

Two factor analyses were conducted. In the first, we found a considerable amount of missing data in three items. Two of the items ("to live with a suitable partner" and "having good relationships with a partner") may not have been relevant for part of the sample and were therefore left blank. A third item ("to attain social status") was not understood, especially by the Arab subjects, due in large part to a poor translation of the Hebrew into Arabic, and also left blank by many. This might also have been due to culture-bound nuances relative to "social status." In the second factor analysis, the third item was removed completely. However, in keeping with the exploratory nature of the study at this early stage, and owing to the importance we intuitively assigned to the first two items, an additional factor, Factor 11, was created, and given the label "reflecting relationships with partner."

For 8 of the 11 factors, the number of valid responses ranged from 359 to 372. The missing data in these factors are more likely due to random non-completions rather than to group or culture-related misinterpretations. As such, given the number of useable questionnaires, we saw no statistically significant problems in using these eight factors even with their varying number of valid responses. Factor 2, with its 303 valid responses, presents a potential factor analytic problem. There are too many missing responses to be random; more likely they are due to either issues of relevancy, age and/or cultural interpretations, or both. Nonetheless, at this stage of the research it was decided to treat Factor 2 as we did the others, albeit with some caution in interpreting results. A similar decision was taken with regard to Factors 10 and 11, each with 345 valid responses, in which the missing data might have been random non-completions or problems of relevancy rather than of cultural-based (mis)interpretation.

TABLE 8.1 Summary of Factor-Analytically Derived Subscales

Factor Example Items	N Items	Explained Variance	Alpha
1. **Reflecting Family and Communal Values** "to preserve the honor of the family" "to be respected by the community"	7	23.4	0.75
2. **Reflecting Materialistic Concerns/Values** "to be successful financially/materialistically" "to be gainfully employed"	5	8.3	0.79
3. **Reflecting Life Satisfaction/Autonomy** "to determine how I wish to lead my life" "to enjoy life" "to function independently, without help"	6	6.9	0.65
4. **Reflecting a "Sense of Connectedness"** "to feel loved" "to be with people" "to enjoy good social relationships"	6	4.7	0.78
5. **Reflecting Communal Consciousness/ Awareness** "to feel proud of my country's accomplishments"	3	4	0.7
6. **Reflecting Attainment of Tranquillity/Peace** "to live a quiet life" "to be at emotional peace with one's self"	3	3.8	0.67
7. **Reflecting Leisure Pursuits; Self-Development** "to pursue hobbies (reading, music, writing, art)" "to broaden knowledge; to continue learning"	3	3.5	0.66
8. **Reflecting Family Relationships** "to maintain good relationships with all close kin" "to feel enjoyment and satisfaction with family"	3	3.1	0.67
9. **Reflecting Leisure Activities Away From Home** "to go on trips, go to movies, vacation activities"	2	2.8	0.45
10. **Reflecting Enjoyment from Animals** "to be with pets"	1	2.6	–
11. **Reflecting Relationship with Partner** "to share my life with a suitable partner"	2	1	0.84

NOTE: Cumulative alpha for all 41 items = 0.87; Total variance explained by all factors = 64.1%

A number of factor structure anomalies were encountered and have not yet been dealt with. For example, originally the six items in Factor 4 were grouped under the label *interpersonal relationships.* However, among those six items is the item "to feel satisfied with the accomplishments of the country." Its loading on the factor is .40 and conceptually it would appear to be out of place. If removed, however, the alpha for the subscale would decrease from .78 to .75. A reconsideration of the factor name, to sense of connectedness, provides the items with increased conceptual connectedness, and all but the name was left unchanged. A similar situation was found in Factor 8, *family relationships*, with the item: "to feel physically and emotionally healthy" having the lowest of the three loading weights (.51) and being conceptually misplaced. If removed, the alpha would increase from .67 to .70. As above, we left it in place at this stage of the research.

One- and two-item factors will require a reconsideration of their utility. In future stages of this research these scales will either be augmented by additional items or, in the interest of economy, will be removed since their structure is at best questionable and their contribution to explained variance is marginal. Focal items that were either misunderstood or not understood at all, as, for example, in Factor 3, *life satisfaction/autonomy:* "to accept life as it is," and in Factor 7, *leisure pursuits; self-development:* "to have an inner feeling of self-fulfillment" will be reworded. Items that were interpreted as having political undertones, such as "to attain a state of peace and security in the country" (loaded on Factor 6, *attainment of tranquillity/peace*), and showed as missing values on many questionnaires, will also be reworded. Lastly, though Factor 11 (*relationship with partner*) is shown here more for heuristic than empirical purposes, it is too weak to be considered a workable subscale. Its item loadings were less than .40 and explained variance was less than 1%. The items will be augmented by additional ones from the 93 items generated and submitted to further testing.

Test-Retest Reliability. In order to obtain test-retest reliability estimates, 79 individuals unfamiliar with the instrument or its development, and ranging in age from 27 to 88 years, were administered the 41-item SLM. For most, administrations were carried out over a 2-week period; for some the interval was 3 to 4 weeks. Of the 79 interviewed, complete and valid responses were obtained from 64 persons (81%). The reliability coefficient obtained was .77. A more rigorous test-retest reliability estimate might have been obtained had the psychometrics for each factor-scale been tested individually. Owing to the fact that the scales are still in the process of being developed, and in the interest of space here, individual scale reliabilities are not reported.

Stage 3: Observing SLM Differences Between Younger and Older Arabs and Jews: The Quantitative Phase of the Study

Four groups were the focus of our attention: two young groups of males and females (ages 20-40) of 101 Jews and 81 Arabs, and two older groups of males and females (ages 60-97) of 83 Jews and 100 Arabs. The differences between ethnic groups were not constant and tended to vary according to the age group in question. That is, the differences between Jews and Arabs were usually apparent only in one age group, or were greater in one age group than in the other, in most of the areas examined. The following is a brief comparison, by factorialized meaning scales, of the significance of the sources of life meaning for younger and older Arabs and Jews.

- Factor 1. *Family and Communal Values:* This factor was found to be significantly more important for Arabs than for Jews (main effect for ethnicity), and the difference between the two ethnic groups was most pronounced among the young (much more important for younger Arabs than for younger Jews).

- Factor 2. *Materialistic Concerns/Values:* This source of life meaning was generally given a low ranking. However, it was substantially more important for the young groups than for the old. In addition, it showed a significant three-way interaction manifested in the differences of gender in the older groups. This source of meaning was of least importance to older Jewish men, but of most importance to older Arab men. Arab and Jewish elderly women positioned themselves between these two extremes.

- Factors 3 & 4. *Life Satisfaction/Autonomy* and *Connectedness/Belonging:* Both of these factors were important sources of meaning overall (M = 4.53 and M = 4.41, respectively). In addition, both sources were found to be more important for Jews than for Arabs among the older groups, whereas no differences were found among the younger subjects.

- Factor 5. *Communal Consciousness/Awareness:* This factor, though relatively low in overall importance, was found to be significantly more important for Arabs than for Jews, especially among younger subjects. Gender was more significant than ethnicity in this dimension.

- Factor 6. *Attainment of Tranquillity/Peace:* This meaning dimension was rated highly by all groups (M = 4.68) and especially by older Jewish subjects (M = 4.88).

- Factor 7. *Leisure Pursuits/Self-Development:* This dimension was also rated highly by all groups (M = 4.09) but it drops somewhat in significance among the older groups, and especially among the Arab aged (M = 3.56 for Arab aged; M = 4.35 among younger Arabs).

- Factor 8. *Family Relationships:* This was the most highly rated source of life meaning overall (M = 4.71). It was of similar importance to both Jews and Arabs, but it seems to be slightly less important to older Arabs than to younger ones. There are no observable differences between younger and older Jews in this dimension.

- Factor 9. *Leisure Activities Away From Home:* This source of meaning was relatively low in significance (M = 3.66). It is also one of the few areas where differences were found between the sexes. It generally appears to be of less importance to Arab women than to Arab men or Jews of either sex. Among the younger groups it is more important to men than women (in both culture groups). Furthermore, its significance seems to decrease with age for Arab men and women and for Jewish men. For Jewish women, there is a reverse trend in that its importance as a source of life meaning is more important for older Jewish women than for younger Jewish female subjects.

- Factor 10. *Enjoyment From Animals:* This was the lowest rated source of life meaning overall (M = 2.55). This was the dimension with the most widespread differences between the sexes: it was rated more highly by men than women in both age groups, and in both culture groups. In addition, there was a strong interaction between ethnicity and age: its importance increases with age among Arabs of both sexes, whereas it decreases with age for Jews.

- Factor 11. *Relationship With a Partner:* This was one of the most important sources of meaning overall (M = 4.65). It was more important for Jews than for Arabs among both sexes and both age groups. In addition, while it retains its importance with age for men (both Arabs and Jews), it becomes less important with age for women. This may be due to the fact that so many elderly women are without mates compared to elderly men.

Summarizing, results showed substantial main effects for age as well as for ethnicity, and a two-way interaction effect for ethnicity by age. Though significant statistically, total meaning differences were quite small; the groups were all very similar in *overall amount of meaning in life* that they reported. The data revealed, as expected, that the differences in *total amount* of meaning reported for the age and ethnic groups is almost inconsequential as compared with the main differences reported by the groups in *sources* of meaning. This finding supports earlier studies by Reker (1988) and Prager (1996, 1997) with Canadian and Australian samples, respectively. The SLM appears to be an age and ethnically sensitive instrument for measuring sources of life meaning.

CONCLUSIONS FROM THE EXPLORATORY PHASE OF THE STUDY

This chapter describes the development of a culturally sensitive instrument, the SLM, to measure sources of life meaning. A mixed methods qualitative and quantitative approach to instrument construction was utilized with younger and older Arab and Jewish subjects whose ages ranged from 20 to 97 years. Focus group techniques were used, followed by the identification of the major domains of meaning and their referent items, employing the processes of dot and concept mapping. The resultant 41 meaning items, representing four major dimensions of Sources of Life Meaning (11 factorially derived scales) were administered to 405 Arab and Jewish Israelis. Through quantitative procedures, including factor analytic methods, the psychometric properties of the instrument were determined. Most of the factorially derived scales attained creditable Cronbach alpha levels, and test-retest reliability was similarly respectable. As expected, while there were no significant differences between the two culture and gender groups in total magnitude of meaning-in-life, substantial differences were found between them with respect to which sources of meaning were most significant for each group.

The study of what sources of meaning are generated by specific cultures (culture-specific instrument conceptualization) and how those sources of meaning identify and differentiate between different samples within those cultures may be a more empirically valid and useful undertaking than comparing respondents across cultures, using instruments created in foreign cultures, requiring considerable linguistic and semantic adaptation. The combination of qualitative and quantitative methodologies, though time-consuming and draining on precious resources was, from our perspective, the most appropriate way of exploring sources of meaning in life within a bi-cultural Arab-Israeli study sample. In choosing Arabs and Jews to participate in our study we consciously selected two cultures markedly different from each other on traditional/spiritual dimensions, but similar to each other in historic roots. In choosing both young and old to participate in our study we hoped to ensure that the items generated would be contextually appropriate for all respondents, and that the resulting instrument could be used validly and reliably in studying similarities and differences between age heterogeneous populations.

The qualitative phase of the research, in acknowledging the fact that our aged have considerable native ability to know and share things about their own lives and their respective worlds, was the suitable methodology for ferreting out information in such a culturally grounded area as personal meaning. We felt that through our utilization of focus groups and the analysis of the content generated we were able to gain some additional clarity, understanding, and relevancy in the exploration of personal meaning in the lives of Arabs and Jews, both young and old. One example of this would be the emphasis we observed on personal honor and respect from others as a source of meaning in life, especially emphasized by the Arab respondents. The qualitative methodology served as a means to acquire an in-depth culturally empathic insight into a phenomenon not previously explored in Israel, in any age group.

The clustered content of the 93 statements generated by the focus groups supported the thesis of Rokeach (1973) and the later work of Reker (1988) in revealing four basic dimensions or levels of meaning: areas of meaning reflecting preoccupation with material comforts and the outward manifestations of material and other achievements; sources of meaning concerned with realization of personal potential; areas of meaning lying beyond the realm of self-interest; and sources of meaning that transcend the self and others, encompassing "cosmic" meaning and ultimate purpose.

At the time of this writing the quantitative part of the study is only in its rudimentary stage. As mentioned above, much needs to be done before we can consider the SLM to be a completely valid and reliable instrument. Items that are unclear or were not answered for other reasons need to be reconsidered and either made clearer or dropped. Items with factor loadings below .40 also need to be reconsidered; either additional items will be added to strengthen these otherwise weak factors, or such items (and factors, as the case may be) will be dropped. Randomly chosen Arabs and Jews in much larger numbers than recorded in this study will provide us with data enabling us to finalize the factorial structure of the SLM, more clearly analyze the variance in sources of personal meaning within and between groups of younger and older Arabs and Jews, and develop baseline data for meaning magnitude and diversity within the different subsamples. If feasible, computer simulations of a longitudinal analysis will help establish the extent of meaning continuity during the adult years. Lastly, as our final questionnaire will include biographic variables that are both general and socioculturally specific, we may be able to make some determinations as to the effects, if any, of certain personal and communal life events on current perceptions of sources of meaning and their relative importance to the individual.

In closing we would like to take this opportunity to invite our readers, who no doubt represent cultures quite different from the one described here, to join us in developing similar research ideologies and methodologies so that, together, we may be able to observe how different younger and older ethnic groups, living in disparate socio-environmental settings, differentially determine those sources of meaning that are most significant in their lives.

REFERENCES

Andeberg, M. R. (1973). *Cluster analysis for applications.* New York: Wiley.

Baum, S. K., & Stewart, R. B. (1990). Sources of meaning through the life span. *Psychological Reports, 67,* 3-14.

Baumeister, R. F. (1991). *Meanings of life.* New York: Guilford.

Breytspraak, L. (1984). *The development of self in later life.* Boston: Little, Brown.

DeVogler, K. L., & Ebersole, P. (1980). Categorization of college students' meaning of life. *Psychological Reports, 46,* 387-390.

Ebersole, P., & DePaola, S. (1989). Meaning in life depth in the active married elderly. *Journal of Psychology, 107,* 171-178.

Everitt, B. (1980). *Cluster analysis* (2nd ed). New York: Wiley.

Fiske, M., & Chiriboga, D. A. (1991). *Change and continuity in adult life.* San Francisco: Jossey-Bass.

Ford, J. (1975). *Paradigms and fairy tales: An introduction to the science of meanings.* Vol. 1. London: Routledge & Kegan Paul.

Hedlund, B., & Birren, J. E. (1984, November). *Distribution of types of meaning in life across women.* Paper presented at the Gerontological Society of America, San Antonio, TX.

Hines, A. M. (1993). Linking qualitative and quantitative methods in cross-cultural survey research: Techniques from cognitive science. *American Journal of Community Psychology, 21,* 729-746.

Hughes, D., Seidman, E., & Williams, N. (1993). Cultural phenomena and the research enterprise: Toward a culturally anchored methodology. *American Journal of Community Psychology, 21,* 687-703.

Hui, C. H., & Triandis, H. C. (1989). Effects of culture and response format on extreme response style. *Journal of Cross-Cultural Psychology, 20,* 296-309.

Kaufman, S. R. (1987). *The ageless self: Sources of meaning in late life.* Madison: University of Wisconsin Press.

Klinger, E. (1977). *Meaning and void*. Minneapolis: University of Minnesota Press.

Levi, D. (1996). *Determining sources of meaning in life using focus groups of Israeli aged*. Unpublished master's thesis (Hebrew). Bob Shapell School of Social Work, Tel Aviv University, Tel Aviv, Israel.

Maton, K. I. (1993). A bridge between cultures: Linked ethnographic-empirical methodology for culture anchored research. *American Journal of Community Psychology, 21*, 747-773.

Peseschkian, N. (1983). *In search of meaning: A psychotherapy of small steps*. Heidelberg: Springer-Verlag.

Prager, E. (1996). Exploring personal meaning in an age-differentiated Australian sample: Another look at the Sources of Meaning Profile (SOMP). *Journal of Aging Studies, 10*, 117-136.

Prager, E. (1997). Sources of personal meaning for older and younger Australian and Israeli women: Profiles and comparisons. *Ageing and Society, 17*, 167-189.

Reker, G. T. (1988, November). *Sources of personal meaning among middle-aged and older adults: A replication*. Paper presented at the Annual Meeting of the Gerontological Society of America, San Francisco, CA.

Reker, G. T., & Wong, P. T. P. (1988). Aging as an individual process: Toward a theory of personal meaning. In J. E. Birren & V. L. Bengtson (Eds.), *Emergent theories of aging* (pp. 214-246). New York: Springer.

Rokeach, M. (1973). *The nature of human values*. New York: Free Press.

Sasao, T., & Sue, S. (1993). Toward a culturally-anchored ecological framework of research in ethnic-cultural communities. *American Journal of Community Psychology, 21*, 705-727.

Seidman, E. (1993). Culturally anchored methodology: An introduction to the special issue. *American Journal of Community Psychology, 21*, 83-685.

Thurner, M. (1975). Continuities and discontinuities in value orientation. In M. F. Lowenthal, M. Thurner, D. Chiriboga, & Associates (Eds.), *Four stages of life: A comparative study of women and men facing transitions*. San Francisco: Jossey-Bass.

Tran, T. V. (1992). Subjective health and subjective well-being among minority elderly: Measurement issues. *Journal of Social Service Research, 16*, 133-146.

Trochim, W. M. (1989). An introduction to concept mapping for planning and evaluation. *Evaluation and Program Planning, 12*, 1-16.

Trochim, W. M. (1993). *The concept system*. Ithaca, NY: Concept Systems.

Yalom, I. (1980). *Existential psychotherapy*. New York: Basic Books.

Zika, S. & Chamberlain, K. (1992). On the relation between meaning in life and psychological well-being. *British Journal of Psychology, 83*, 133-145.

PART III

APPLICATIONS AND
INTERVENTIONS

CHAPTER 9

Finding Meaning in Caregivers of Persons with Alzheimer's Disease:
African American and White Caregivers' Perspectives

Carol J. Farran, Karen Lowe Graham, and Dimitra Loukissa

In recent years, researchers have given increasingly more attention to understanding the positive aspects of caring for persons with Alzheimer's disease (AD) (Kramer, 1997). Recent attempts have also been made to examine whether these positive aspects vary by culture and ethnicity, particularly between African American and White family caregivers (Farran, Miller, Kaufman, & Davis, 1997; Lawton, Rajagopal, Brody, & Kleban, 1992). This chapter reports the results of a secondary analysis to determine whether previously identified themes of the positive construct, finding meaning, were reflected by African American and White family caregivers. Researchers collected original data to better understand how outreach to African American family caregivers might be improved. The original study examined African American and White caregivers' perceptions of AD, the caregiving process, information most needed, and how to best package that information.

Framework for Understanding Meaning in Family Caregivers

Four earlier studies that focused on the construct finding meaning through

139

caregiving were conducted. In the first qualitative study ($N = 94$), which included primarily White family caregivers (White 81% and African American 17%), six major themes were identified, Acknowledging Present Loss, Acknowledging Powerlessness Over the Situation, Making Personal Choices About Life and Caregiving, Valuing Positive Aspects of the Caregiving Experience, Searching for Provisional Meaning, and Searching for Ultimate Meaning (Farran, Keane-Hagerty, Salloway, Kupferer, & Wilken, 1991). Data from this qualitative study were used to develop the measure, Finding Meaning Through Caregiving (FMTCG). Two subsequent measurement studies involving caregivers ($N = 46$, $N = 215$) determined psychometric properties of this measure and collapsed the six original themes into three subscales: Loss/Powerlessness, Provisional Meaning, and Ultimate Meaning (Farran et al., 1998). Loss/Powerlessness refers to those feelings of loss, grief, and powerlessness that occur during difficult life experiences. Provisional Meaning refers to the day-to-day or transitory experiences that give meaning to life, while Ultimate Meaning refers to those deeper meanings in life often associated with one's spiritual nature (Farran, 1997; Farran et al., 1991).

Data in the fourth study ($N = 215$) suggested that, while there were mean FMTCG differences between African American and White caregivers, there were no differences by race in terms of how FMTCG subscales predicted caregiver depression and role strain. Namely, caregivers who expressed higher levels of Provisional Meaning, reported lower levels of depression and role strain (Farran et al., 1997).

Theoretical support for the construct, finding meaning through caregiving, is derived primarily from Viktor Frankl's (1978) work, which suggests that loss and powerlessness are fundamental aspects of human suffering; and that when persons suffer they are afflicted physically, mentally, spiritually, and socially (Soelle, 1975). Frankl (1978) suggests four assumptions about finding meaning: (1) Persons create meaning by making choices, (2) Values provide basis for meaning, (3) Each person has responsibility for right action and conduct, and (4) Provisional and ultimate meaning exist. When applied to caregiving, these assumptions suggest that caregivers can make choices about whether and how to care for their family member; that creative, experiential, and attitudinal or life belief values assist persons in the process of caregiving; and that as humans we have certain moral responsibility for right action and conduct.

THE PRESENT STUDY

Five focus groups were conducted throughout the Chicago metropolitan area in churches, community service agencies, and several health maintenance organization sites. Intentional efforts were made to oversample for African American caregivers, as prior studies have included primarily White family caregivers. Persons unable to attend one of the scheduled focus groups participated in an individual telephone interview (Smith, Scammon, & Beck, 1995).

A total of 27 persons participated in focus groups and another 7 persons participated in individual telephone interviews (*N* = 34). The majority of participants were African Americans (68%), followed by Whites (29%) and Hispanics (3%). The majority of participants were female (74%), including daughters and wives (44%), followed by other family/friend caregivers (38%), husbands (12%), sons (3%), and paid caregivers (3%). Caregivers' age most frequently ranged from 40 to 59 and 60 to 79 years (40% each), followed by those over 80 years old (12%), and by those 20 to 39 years old (8%).

A structured questionnaire was designed by the investigators at the outset, and modified during initial phases to facilitate information gathering. Three investigators, representing diverse ethnic and cultural groups, participated in each focus group. One person assumed leadership responsibility for conducting the focus group, with two recorders assuming responsibility for summarizing caregiver comments. Following each focus group, recorders combined their verbatim comments into one summary for each session. Individual interviews were conducted by one person who then summarized comments for all interviews.

Data for all focus groups and individual interviews were combined into one large data set by interview question. The investigators used the following process to analyze the original qualitative data: (1) identification and clarification of themes by interview question; (2) observation of patterns and clustering of themes across questions; and (3) establishment of a logical chain of evidence from these data (Miles & Huberman, 1984). Secondary analysis of these data was conducted to determine to what extent caregivers addressed the three themes commonly associated with finding meaning, Loss/Powerlessness, Provisional Meaning, and Ultimate Meaning.

THEME 1: LOSS/POWERLESSNESS

The theme, Loss/Powerlessness, is thought to be particularly relevant to African American caregivers because African American characteristics have been viewed as being shaped by involuntary immigration, slavery, racism, and oppression (Proctor, 1995). An unanswered question is how this broader sociocultural context has shaped a difficult experience such as caring for a person with AD.

In this study, caregivers expressed feelings of loss for themselves, and feelings of powerlessness concerning relationships with other family members and the health care system. Furthermore, potential effects of powerlessness appeared to involve emotional, physical, financial, and sociocultural aspects, as well as affecting caregivers' ability to care for themselves.

Loss Concerning Oneself

Caregivers described a range of feelings such as loss, uncertainty and fatigue, depression, and unsuccessful coping strategies, not unlike responses reported earlier (Farran et al., 1991). Caregivers expressed feelings of sadness and frustration over the loss of their relationship with their relative, and confusion and uneasiness about the impact of the reversed roles. "He will never be the same person you married ...." "You feel that you loose them over and over again."

Feelings of Powerlessness Concerning Family Relationships

Differences were noted when data were compared to an earlier qualitative study where caregivers were quite positive about family members (Farran et al., 1991). In this study, considerable discussion focused on feelings of powerlessness and anger directed toward family members. These feelings are not unlike those reported in an earlier study where African American caregivers expressed more anger than White caregivers when their friends/family did not provide them with adequate support (Fink & Picot, 1995), in spite of cultural expectations of the family to provide support (Chatters & Taylor, 1993). Caregivers chided family members who did not help, explained why some family members could not assist them, and expressed frustration when there were disagreements concerning how to provide care. Caregivers expressed their feelings, identified behaviors, and made resolves in response to these feelings of powerlessness.

Chiding Family Members Who Don't Help. Caregivers had negative feelings about family members who did not help and these comments did not appear to vary by ethnicity. There were what family members considered *empty offers* – "Call me if you need me." Caregivers also talked about family being *so close and yet so far* – "My husband has a brother who lives six blocks from my house. He's been here once since May."

Explaining Lack of Assistance. Family members explained this lack of assistance in a number of ways. One general category could best be described as *the don'ts.* Caregivers shared that family members *don't think about it* – "Nobody will say that I need to help Aunt Grace for a day, a week, a weekend." Caregivers also noted that some family members *don't want to deal with it* or deny that there is a problem – "His brother doesn't want to face what's happened to him."

Other caregivers found that some family members *don't know* about the disease and in some cases *don't want to understand.* During early stages of the disease, many caregivers felt they were not supported by their families. Other family members did not accept the diagnosis and sometimes became over-protective. "The diagnosis was very definitive. Her side of the family refused to believe that she was sick."

In some families, these attitudes continued throughout the process of caregiving. "They think that when they visit they will be the ones to help her – to connect with her. When that doesn't happen, they get frustrated and don't know what to do." And finally, caregivers noted that some family members *don't want to be involved.* One caregiver summed up all of these issues by saying, "Some people don't deny, they just don't think about it. It isn't that they don't care, they don't want to deal with the illness. They don't want to understand because they don't want to be involved."

Another way of explaining lack of assistance from some family members could be referred to as *the can'ts.* Caregivers said some people *can't deal with it* – "Her sister can't deal with it except for a short time." Caregivers explained that family members' feelings of fear and an inability to deal with their own emotions made it difficult for some persons to help – "Some of them are afraid of a nursing home. They are the type of people who fear it. They are squeamish."

Disagreements in How to Provide Care. A number of caregivers talked about disagreements they had or criticisms they received from other family members about how to provide care – "I would take my mother to the hairdresser twice a week but my sister thinks she doesn't need it." One family member concluded, "Sometimes its harder to deal with the family than it is the AD patient."

Caregivers' Feelings, Behaviors and Resolves. Caregivers expressed anger toward other family members for not helping, "My mother-in-law would always help a lot of people. This is what makes me so mad now that his family doesn't help." Because of this lack of help, caregivers also made certain statements of resolve – "I don't ask for help from family and friends because of their negative responses." Said another caregiver, "You have to know how to say no to relatives who expect everything from you."

Feelings of Powerlessness Concerning the Health Care System

Caregivers' feelings of powerlessness were also directed toward "the system." They expressed frustration in getting a diagnosis, lack of information to help them with providing care, and concerns about financial aspects of care. Caregivers expressed uncertainty about the diagnosis, unpredictability, lack of resources, and lack of direction from health care professionals. They expressed doubt, suspicion, confusion, and frustration with the health care delivery system. Caregivers also expressed frustration about health care providers, especially at the initial stage of the illness, for not providing them with adequate information about the illness and referrals for support and community resources (Loukissa, Farran, & Graham, 1998).

African American caregivers, particularly, expressed that they had less knowledge about and access to services, which might be interpreted as a type of institutional racism (Jackson, Taylor, & Chatters, 1993). "As Black people we don't know where resources or services are. We are not educated about the resources. If you don't speak up as a Black person you will not get proper medical treatment." Disappointment was also expressed about State regulations and "fine print." In addition, caregivers expressed needing more information about financial resources than was available to them.

Potential Effects of Powerlessness on Caregivers

Feelings of powerlessness appeared to be closely related to the stress of caregiving and appeared to have emotional, physical, financial, and sociocultural effects on caregivers, as well as influencing how caregivers perceived their own self care.

Emotional Effects. General expressions of emotional stress included that of an African American daughter who said, "When I get home from work I'm tired and really don't want to hear what's going on during the day for anyone else." Feelings of depression were expressed by both African American and White caregivers. Said one African American caregiver, "I was crying. Mentally I was in a crying spell all the time."

Physical Effects. Several caregivers reported difficulties with their blood pressure, "My blood pressure was very high" and "I now have to take blood pressure medication." An African American daughter described her health as faltering and said she now experienced a number of different physical ailments: "I kept coming to the doctor and he said nothing was wrong. They kept saying I was under stress, when in fact I was allergic to animals and then I had a ruptured appendix." She continued by describing the combined mental, physical, and financial effects of this stress, "By this time I am no longer insurable. I became self-employed and can't afford to go the doctor because I have too many medical bills. I drink a quart of beer and that doesn't help."

Financial Effects. Financial strain was also noted for impaired family members who became sick while in the work force. "He lost his job because of the doctor's note ... we went for 6 months without a job. Now we live on his sick pay. Later he will be on disability. He is 59. His supervisor gave him a job at a lesser pay ($15,000 less)."

Sociocultural Effects. Sociocultural issues appeared to both effect the caregiving process as well as influence potential outcomes. Cultural characteristics and socioeconomic status have been identified as two factors relevant to caregiving in African Americans (Dilworth-Anderson & Anderson, 1994). In this study, both African American and White caregivers reflected that class, financial, and educational differences exist. An African American wife caregiver shared, "Its more of a class issue. There are certain groups that would be more 'ghetto' that are not used to dealing with different groups. We are more middle class and people in our support group are used to dealing with a variety of people." Another African American caregiver said that education plays a big role, "The caretaker we had was

Hispanic. There was a big difference because she was educated. Her conversations were more family oriented. She interacted with my mother."

Difficulties with Self Care. In spite of attention to self care, caregivers often talked about some of the difficulties and tension associated with caring for themselves. Some of their comments were prefaced by *I need to, I tend to, I try to,* and *I have to* – "I have to exercise more. I need to go to the doctor. I try to buy a few nice things."

Self-care was difficult because of the responsibilities and changes brought about by caregiving, and family demands, particularly for daughter caregivers – "You are sort of living in a vacuum. You forget what day it is. You get up and do what you usually do. Come back and eat. Its not much of a life." Some caregivers also found that self-care was a process – "For the first three years my dad didn't go anywhere. Now he's adjusted. He's a lot happier, but it took him a couple of years."

Analysis of Loss/Powerlessness

Caregivers' feelings of Loss/Powerlessness in four areas are of note: negative feelings about family members, negative perceptions concerning the health care delivery system, negative mental and physical health effects, and negative financial/sociocultural effects of caregiving.

Caregivers' negative feelings concerning family members were somewhat surprising given the often-expressed importance of the extended family and the strong sense of "we-ness" often noted as an African American characteristic (Dilworth-Anderson & Anderson, 1994). One potential interpretation of these data is the concern that has been expressed about whether caregivers of aged African Americans will be able to meet competing demands of different needy generations in the family, because of changing demographics in the African American community. These demographic changes include trends that suggest African American families are becoming poorer, that fewer males are obtaining a college education, and that caregivers may often be single mothers with dependent children who are poor and in need of assistance themselves (National Urban League, 1989). Future studies must address these sociocultural issues and examine their impact on family caregivers.

Caregivers' negative perceptions and feelings of powerlessness concerning the health care delivery system were similar to previously reported concerns (Jackson et al., 1993). African Americans' lack of knowledge of the availability of services has also been noted in unpublished raw data (Picot, personal communication, May 28, 1997). Caregivers' perceptions of the availability of services to African Americans, by both African Americans and Whites, provides further support for feelings of institutional racism so often expressed. These perceptions have been associated with distrust in the health care delivery system, and may promote a passive problem-solving style on one hand, or an increased personal efficacy in the face of potential discrimination on the other hand (Dilworth-Anderson & Anderson, 1994). The issues of institutional racism confront clinicians and researchers alike, and require careful attention by both practitioners and researchers.

The negative mental and physical health effects associated with feelings of Loss/Powerlessness reported by study participants deserve further comment. Quantitative data in recent studies that compare family caregivers note that African Americans report lower levels of emotional distress and/or depressive symptoms (Lawton et al., 1992; Miller, Campbell, Farran, Kaufman, & Davis, 1995). Qualitative data from the present study, while limited, suggest that although both African American and White caregivers experience emotional distress, there may be different underlying causes or expressions of this distress (Dilworth-Anderson, 1998). Further research in this area is certainly warranted. Of note though, concerning physical health effects of caregiving, is that in such a small study, the issue of high blood pressure was reported by several caregivers. Existing research documents a higher incidence and earlier occurrence of hypertension in African Americans when compared to Whites (Anderson, 1989), and suggests a major area of concern for future caregiver studies.

Feelings of powerlessness associated with the financial and sociocultural effects of caregiving are not surprising. While there is considerable economic diversity in African Americans, it is well documented that African Americans suffer disproportionate economic hardship as reflected by higher rates of poverty, lower median incomes, and higher unemployment rates between African American men and teenagers, when compared to Whites (Bureau of Labor Statistics, 1995; Wilson, 1996). Future research must address these sociocultural issues, as existing research suggests that some of the reported differences between African American and Whites may incorporate social system and life span issues, in addition to ethnic/cultural issues (Chatters, 1988).

THEME 2: PROVISIONAL MEANING

Provisional meaning refers to short-term and transitory experiences that give meaning to life (Frankl, 1978). In an earlier study, caregivers noted that they found provisional meaning through the choices they made about life and caregiving, and by valuing the positive aspects of the caregiving experience. In many cases caregivers found that while they would not have consciously chosen to have become a caregiver, or for their relative to have dementia, they could say that they had grown and become a better person as a result of this experience (Farran et al., 1991). Existing literature suggests that the concept of provisional meaning might be particularly relevant to African Americans because of their values (Lawton et al., 1992), and the influence of religious faith, family kinship ties, and community support or their methods of appraisal and coping (Peters & Massey, 1983).

Provisional, or day-to-day, meaning was expressed by caregivers through the values they expressed concerning their relationships, in personal choices they made about caregiving, and by their approaches to creating a positive environment for their impaired family member.

Valuing Relationships

Caregivers' values were expressed concerning relationships with impaired family members, as well as other family members and friends.

Impaired Family Member Relationships. While caregivers talked about changes in the relationship with their family member, they often interrupted this train of thought by affirming their present relationship with a *but* – "our relationship is still close and based on trust and love, we still have a good time when we go out, she still knows me." Often times caregivers made positive comments about their relatives and stressed positive areas of their personality or level of functioning. "His past memory is excellent – better than mine." And despite care receivers' dependency and relationship changes, caregivers often said, "I am grateful that I am still able to take care of everything."

Relationships with Other Family Members and Friends. Although caregivers talked about their negative experiences in relationships, at the same time relationships appeared to play a big part in how caregivers dealt positively with the process of caregiving. An African American caregiver said, "There is a lot of love in my family. It came from my family and I am passing it down. We are people that love. When you know God, it really makes a difference." A White husband caregiver wrote a monthly family newspaper that went out to 13 states and 125 people.

Making Personal Choices

Caregivers reported making personal choices in the attitudes they developed toward caregiving, as well as in their behaviors and activities. Concerning their own attitudes, caregivers had a list of imperatives that they were ready to share with other caregivers.

Caregiver Imperatives. Concerning his own self-care, a White husband caregiver said, "Don't feel sorry for yourself. You have to look out for yourself. If you don't, you can't take care of you." An African American wife caregiver said, "I try to stay positive. The only people who don't have problems are in cemeteries. Sometimes you have to be thankful." And an African American daughter said, "You have to find humor where you can, but also have to create space for yourself. Its part of your role or you get overwhelmed."

Caregivers also talked about setting limits for themselves, on others, and on their impaired relative. An African American wife caregiver said, "There is a time when I say, 'I'm going to read the paper.' I tell others, 'you handle it.' When I need it, I will cry out for help. When I feel overwhelmed, I just take time out." Concerning priorities for her relative, a White wife caregiver said, "I let some things go for him." Other suggestions for dealing with their impaired family member included, "You have to handle an Alzheimer's patient like you handle a child." "Be patient and don't give up on them."

Caregiver Self-Care Activities. Caregiver self-care could be described as focusing around four major categories: being involved in activities, participating in relationships, using outside assistance, and maintaining rituals and routines. Activities that caregivers engaged in as a part of their self-care ranged from the routine home-based activities such as doing chores and housework, baking, crafts, mowing the lawn and tending the flowers, and watching television, to participating in activities outside the home such as working, volunteering, going out for shopping or movies, doing exercise or participating in sports, traveling, and attending conferences.

Caregivers described that rituals and routines provided a structure for themselves and for their impaired family members – "You get into a routine. I have my breakfast while preparing hers." "I get up at 4 am and exercise, talk to the Good Master at 5 am, and read the Bible until 7 am."

Creating a Positive Environment for Impaired Family Members

When caregivers were asked to tell their most successful stories, they described how much attention they gave to creating a positive environment for their impaired family members.

Doing the Little Things. Caregivers talked about feeling good about the little things, including both the physical and emotional care that they provided to their relative, "Fixing breakfast for her. It's the one meal I'm sure she eats." "Making a meal together. Cooking as a family, allowing her to help. She always asks if she can help." "Talking with her. Not cursing. Not pulling at her. My dad said you never kick a dog when they're down." "One Saturday I gave him a shower and he said, 'I forgive you.' This was his way of asking for forgiveness. He knew that he was going to die." "My mother likes to go out, she talks to everybody and enjoys the interaction. I feel so good when I fix her up."

Being Flexible, Finding Creative Solutions, Working Around the Dementia. Caregivers also reported that their ability to be flexible, find creative solutions, or ways to work around the dementia was a success story for them. They shared, "I ask him if he wants to take a shower. If he says yes, I waste no time and give him a shower. If he says no, I give him a sponge bath. The easiest thing is to ask him." An African American son caregiver said, "I asked family members to set up a kitty to give to the primary caregiver. That allowed for respite care to be paid for when needed." And finally, an African American daughter caregiver said, "Mom used to order lots of things over the phone. I kept returning them. I asked mother to have the things she ordered sent to my house. When they arrived I would refuse them. My mother caught on and now she has things delivered to her own house again. It doesn't have a good ending yet, but it will."

Maintaining Functioning, Preventing Complications. Caregivers prided themselves in being able to maintain their care receivers' functioning as well as preventing complications. A White wife caregiver said, "He was able to work an extra year and drive. It made him happy." Another caregiver said, "Putting him on medication turned things around. He's able to concentrate better and is not disruptive at the day care center." An African American wife caregiver said, "I took care of my husband for 17 years. He never had a sore on his body. He was well cared for."

Doing Things the Care-Receiver Enjoys, Going Beyond. Caregivers reported seeing the impaired person's response when they planned special occasions and went beyond the routine. An African American caregiver said, "She likes music, old time records. I ordered $124 worth of CDs. I got her some Benny Goodman. She comes to life when the music is playing."

An African American daughter caregiver described, "I gave my parents a 50th wedding anniversary party. I picked out three dresses for her and brought them home. She picked out one and the next morning she picked out the same dress. I got her hair done. She was in a white and gold gown and he was in a white and gold tuxedo. Near the end of the party I told her that her limousine was here. She said that she could not leave the party before her guests left. It was like a Cinderella story. They had a good time." Another African American wife caregiver shared, "I had a birthday party for my husband in December with a clown, then he died in March."

An African American minister talked about helping a family in her congregation, "I help the family to go and dress him and bring him to church every Sunday. I try to pick up the kids (7, 11, 13 years old) and after church we will have dinner and I take him out and have the boys make sure his plate is full. The kids love pets so I took everyone to a pet store and he fell in love with that parakeet. He will let the bird sit on his arm for hours ... it brought him alive. It has done a lot for his morale because he was just sitting staring at the wall, drooling."

Maintaining the Care Receiver's Dignity. Many caregivers' success stories centered around maintaining the care receivers' dignity: "I was able to keep laughter in my house over the duration of my mother's illness. When she passed away, she had a smile on her face." An African American wife caregiver said, "You have to decide whether you will give or withhold from a person who becomes like a child. You either abandon them or embrace them and help them have the best day possible. I try to treat people the way you want to be treated. We all know how we're going to come into this world but don't know how we will leave."

Analysis of Provisional Meaning

The general themes reflected by caregivers in this study were quite similar to those noted in an earlier qualitative study (Farran et al., 1991). Namely, caregivers talked about the positive feelings and values they held concerning their impaired family members and other family members and friends. Caregivers were adamant about making personal choices about life and caregiving, and readily generated a list of imperatives, "Things you have to do in order to cope with caregiving" and "What you have to do for yourself." Asking caregivers to share their most successful stories elicited a multitude of approaches for maintaining a sense of normalcy in their impaired members' lives, as well as "going beyond the call of duty" in providing daily care and celebrating special occasions.

Three areas deserve further attention concerning African American caregiver perspectives, however. First, these data support the importance of examining the interpersonal context of caregiving, which commonly include family, friends, and the church for elderly African Americans (Dilworth-Anderson & Anderson, 1994). Second, while these data do not allow for in-depth examination of differences between African American and White family caregivers, they document the need to further examine caregivers' appraisal style. Prior work has suggested that African Americans in general tend to express more positive attitudes toward the elderly (Mutran, 1985); and that they may express personal feelings of efficacy and a behavioral disposition to succeed in life no matter what the obstacles (Dilworth-Anderson & Anderson, 1994). African American caregivers, more specifically, have expressed higher positive levels of traditional ideology, greater satisfaction, and lower levels of caregiving intrusiveness and burden (Lawton et al., 1992) and higher levels of rewards than White caregivers (Picot, Debanne, Namazi, & Wykle, 1997).

And finally, these data support the notion that caregivers in this study assumed an active coping style in response to stress and squarely faced their problems (Neighbors, Jackson, Bowman, & Gurin, 1983), although few studies have examined differences in coping styles between African American and White family caregivers (Picot, 1995). Greater attention in future research is needed to address how it is that African Americans get past oppressive life events and experience the power of transcendence, as expressed by Proctor (1995) in his description of values taught by his family, "It is a habit of the heart that constrained us to focus on the stars rather than the canopy of darkness" (p. xxii).

THEME 3: ULTIMATE MEANING

Ultimate meaning has been linked to the process of exploring deeper meanings in life, and meaning associated with, or based upon one's spiritual perspective (Frankl, 1978). Caregivers in an earlier qualitative study talked about their spiritual beliefs providing them one means by which to "make sense of" past and present experiences. Likewise, religious practices such as attending church, praying, and reading the Bible provided a structure by which they could regularly feel "refueled" or "grounded" in something greater than themselves and their daily experiences (Farran et al., 1991).

A deliberate decision was made not to initiate questions concerning religious/spiritual or ultimate meaning issues to decrease the chance of bias and the possibility of caregivers giving socially acceptable answers. However, if the topic was spontaneously raised by family caregivers, group leaders asked a series of structured questions concerning this topic.

The topic of religion came up in all African American groups, and in groups with both African Americans and White caregivers. In the one focus group with all White caregivers, the topic of religion did not spontaneously emerge. Of all the spiritually oriented comments, 80% were made by African American caregivers. Earlier studies have also noted that levels of spontaneously acknowledged religiosity are higher among African Americans than Whites (Koenig, Moberg, & Kvale, 1988; Wykle & Segall, 1991).

Potential reasons for this freedom of expression about one's spiritual beliefs and perspectives might be based in what has been referred to as the Black sacred cosmos. This Black sacred cosmos is described as being related to an African heritage where the whole universe is viewed as being sacred; African American's conversion to Christianity during slavery and its aftermath; and African American's creation of a unique and distinctive forum of culture or worldview that paralleled the United States' culture in which they were unwelcomed guests (Lincoln & Mamiya, 1990). Caregiver responses to these questions were organized around five themes.

Caregiving as a Calling

Both African American and White caregivers appraised caregiving as a means of fulfilling a spiritual calling. One African American caregiver said, "I ask the Lord to use me. I like taking care of the sick." Another African American daughter said, "I find passages in the Bible on how to respect your parents and to love them. Since I am single, I can take the time to care for them." These comments may be further supported by references to the Black sacred cosmos, which suggests that if God calls you to discipleship, or in this case caregiving, God may also call you to freedom, a major theme in African American's culture and religious experiences. Furthermore, God wants you free because persons are made in God's image (Lincoln & Mamiya, 1990). Freedom, in this sense, may focus on freedom to choose one's responses and attitudes toward a situation such as caregiving.

Religion as a Means of Explaining and Interpreting Life's Experiences

One African American wife caregiver was particularly poignant in her description and interpretation of life experiences. Her comments may be reflecting another aspect of the Black sacred cosmos that suggests that African-based religion may include deities and spiritual forces that play a prominent role in the rituals and worship of the people (Lincoln & Mamiya, 1990). She said, "I have explored the philosophy of reincarnation. If you don't do your best in this life you will have to pay and make up for it at another time ... you're going to go through something worse. I had a few psychic experiences when I was 13 so there is more to what we see ... there is an energy that we don't know about ... I am deeply Christian but know there's more to this life than just being born and dying. I have found answers. I'm not conventional and this is taking me through life, helping me through. I know I had to find answers or I would be ill. Answers for me, this has helped me get through."

She continued to appraise her situation by saying, "God put me here for a purpose. We are traveling on a highway. You can't just stay on the highway, you have to stop and rest. Sometimes you get disoriented and lost. But don't fear, someone will send you back. You may ask the policeman and you will get back on the highway. You get lost if you don't pay attention. It's a quiet voice you have to listen to ... it's not a big thunder. If you hear this whisper you can get through."

She continued with an affirmation of God's presence and empowerment, "God promised me, 'I will be with you ....' So I'm confident the good result is there waiting for me on the expressway. I can't change the script, so I play it well ... I'm not a star, I'm one of the billions." Another African American wife caregiver concluded, "It's not so much religion. It's faith that things are not going to be so bad all the time."

Religion as a Source of Strength and Blessing

Praying, being optimistic, having hope and faith, and keeping on trying were some of the coping strategies used by caregivers to manage their relatives' symptoms, needs, and personality changes. Both African American and White caregivers frequently referred to their feelings of being blessed. A White wife caregiver shared, "My strength comes from Christ and the knowledge that there is a place for me and my husband. I go to this nice little church. Its steeped in the Bible and I even got myself baptized in water. If I didn't have this peace and joy that I won't be let down I wouldn't be able to handle it. I am very blessed. I have people who help me."

An African American wife caregiver commented, "God has blessed me. I feel blessed that God helped me give the best care possible. I got sick and had to go to the hospital but couldn't stay long. I said I had to go home and take care of my husband."

Other caregivers said, "That's what I say, you pray for patience." "Patience is what you need. You need understanding ... I pray every day. I ask the Lord to give me strength. You have to have strength."

Appeal to God for Help and Use of Rituals

Both African American and White caregivers identified that they called upon God for help in difficult situations and that religious rituals were helpful: "I pray every day. I ask the Lord to give me strength. You have to have strength." Commenting further on rituals, several African American caregivers shared: "I pray at 5 am. Read the Bible until 7am." and "I pray, and find passages in the Bible which reflect strength and weaknesses."

The Paradox of Pain and Growth

An African American minister talked about how she helped people deal with difficult life situations, "There are crises in people's life that they haven't dealt with and as they grow older they are confronted with reality. There's this whole denial thing. You need to help people resolve their guilt, pain, lost love, bereavement .... One's mental health is important as you grow older – it can destroy them. I try to teach the Bible in a different way so people can resolve the pain. You have to do it in a psychological and theological way. You let them cry it out within the body of Christ .... A lot of choices in life have not to do with that we age but how we age." Another African American wife caregiver concluded her comments with, "Together with roses come the thorns." These experiences with the paradox of pain and growth are deeply rooted in the broader African American cultural and religious experiences of slavery and discrimination (Lincoln & Mamiya, 1990; Proctor, 1995).

Analysis of Ultimate Meaning

Data in this study supported the notion that what is referred to as ultimate meaning is similar to what other researchers refer to as spirituality or religiosity. These findings verified the multidimensional nature of this construct and also support that ultimate meaning/spirituality/religiosity may serve a variety of functions for African Americans. Namely, a religious/spiritual structure may assist persons with: causal attributions; transcending what is unbearable; appraisal and reappraisal; empowerment due to interaction with a Supreme Being; social support through formal participation in church activities; and specific coping strategies such as prayer and reading the Bible (Dilworth-Anderson & Anderson, 1994; Picot et al., 1997).

   Numerous questions remain to be answered in the future. The spontaneous initiation of discussions concerning spiritual/religious perspectives by African Americans raises questions such as whether this means that African American caregivers are more spiritual than White caregivers, more comfortable expressing their views without intentional questions pertaining to this area, or assume that others in their company will share similar views. The close identification of African Americans with the church and spirituality also raises questions concerning clinical and research programming. Is it enough to use churches as places of contact and information dissemination, or do spiritual perspectives need to be more closely intertwined with programmatic and service delivery?

SUMMARY AND CONCLUSIONS

The purpose of this study was to conduct a secondary analysis of focus group data collected primarily for the purpose of examining outreach strategies with African American and White caregivers, to determine to what extent caregivers reflected three themes commonly associated with finding meaning: Loss/Powerlessness, Provisional Meaning, and Ultimate Meaning. The striking observation from these data was that, even though the primary intent of the interviews was focused on general caregiver issues and outreach strategies, caregivers' underlying philosophical and moral perspectives emerged and could be reflected in the larger themes often associated with finding meaning. One possible interpretation of this finding is that these data reflect the close relationship between the Black sacred cosmos and Black culture, that Lincoln and Mamiya (1990) say is often missed by social analysts.

While the scope of this study was not to determine if differences existed between African American and White family caregivers, the observations noted in this study were interpreted within the context of the African American community because this perspective is often overlooked and fewer African Americans are generally included in other caregiver studies. Due to the small sample size, the sampling methods used, and the nature of focus group data, however, transferability of these qualitative data is limited to other similar caregiver groups using similar methods of data collection.

In summary, this study supports the increasing number of caregiver studies that point to the importance of examining the broader ethnic and sociocultural issues that underlie the positive aspects of caring for elderly persons with Alzheimer's disease. As these questions are answered, clinicians and researchers, respectively, will be able to provide more culturally sensitive services and interpretations of data.

ACKNOWLEDGMENTS

This study was funded by the National Institute on Aging, Alzheimer's Disease Center Core Grant (P30 AG 10161, Denis A. Evans, MD, Principal Investigator). The helpful comments of Dr. Peggye Dilworth-Anderson and Dr. Sandra Picot, and the assistance from the following community agency sites are gratefully acknowledged: Greater Chicagoland Chapter Alzheimer's Association Southeast Side Support Group; Phoebes' Place Support

Group; South Suburban Senior Services Center; and Rush Anchor Health Maintenance
Organization.

REFERENCES

Anderson, N. B. (1989). Racial differences in stress-induced cardiovascular reactivity and
hypertension: Current status and substantive issues. *Psychological Bulletin, 105*, 89-105.
Bureau of Labor Statistics. (1995). *Employment and wages, annual average.* Washington,
DC: U.S. Department of Labor.
Chatters, L. M. (1988). Subjective well-being among older Black adults: Past trends and
current perspectives. In J. S. Jackson, P. Newton, A. Ostfield, D. Savage, & E. L.
Schneider (Eds.), *The Black American elderly: Research on physical and psychosocial
health* (pp. 237-258). New York: Springer.
Chatters, L. M., & Taylor, R. J. (1993). Intergenerational support: The provision of
assistance to parents by adult children. In J. S. Jackson, L. M. Chatters, & R. J. Taylor
(Eds.), *Aging in Black America* (pp. 69-83). Newbury Park, CA: Sage.
Dilworth-Anderson, P. (1998). Emotional well-being in adult and later life among African
Americans: A cultural and sociocultural perspective. In K. W. Schaie & M. P. Lawton
(Eds.), *Annual Review of Gerontology and Geriatrics, 17,* 282-303.
Dilworth-Anderson, P., & Anderson, N. B. (1994). Dementia caregiving in Blacks: A
contextual approach to research. In E. Light, G. Niederehe, & B. D. Lebowitz (Eds.),
Stress effects on family caregivers of Alzheimer's patients (pp. 385-409). New York:
Springer.
Dilworth-Anderson, P., Burton, L. M., & Johnson, L. B. (1993). Reframing theories for
understanding race, ethnicity, and families. In P. G. Boss, W. J. Doherty, R. LaRossa,
W. R. Schumm, & S. K. Steinmetz (Eds.), *Sourcebook of family theories and methods:
A contextual approach* (pp. 627-646). New York: Plenum.
Farran, C. J. (1997). Theoretical perspectives concerning positive aspects of caring for
elderly persons with dementia: Stress/adaptation and existentialism. *The Gerontologist,
37,* 250-256.
Farran, C. J., Keane-Hagerty, E., Salloway, S., Kupferer, S., & Wilken, C. S. (1991).
Finding meaning: An alternate paradigm for Alzheimer's disease caregivers. *The
Gerontologist, 31,* 483-489.
Farran, C. J., Miller, B. H., Kaufman, J. E., & Davis, L. (1997). Race, finding meaning and
caregiver distress. *Journal of Aging and Health, 9,* 316-333.
Farran, C. J., Miller, B., Kaufman, J., Davis, L., Donner, E., & Fogg, L. (1998). *Finding
meaning through caregiving: Development and testing of a measure.* Manuscript
submitted for publication.
Fink, S. V., & Picot, S. F. (1995). Nursing home placement decisions and post-placement
experiences of African-American and European-American caregivers. *Journal of
Gerontological Nursing, 21,* 35-42.
Frankl, V. E. (1978). *The unheard cry for meaning.* New York: Washington Square Press.
Jackson, J. S., Taylor, R. J., & Chatters, L. M. (1993). Roles and resources of the Black
elderly. In J. S. Jackson, L. M. Chatters, & R. J. Taylor (Eds.), *Aging in Black America*
(pp. 1-18). Newbury Park, CA: Sage.
Koenig, H. G., Moberg, D. O., & Kvale, J. N. (1988). Religious activities and attitudes of
adults in a geriatric assessment clinic. *Journal of the American Geriatric Society, 36,*

362-374.

Kramer, B. J. (1997). Gain in the caregiving experience: Where are we? What next? *The Gerontologist, 37*, 218-232.

Lawton, M. P., Rajagopal, D., Brody, E., & Kleban, M. H. (1992). The dynamics of caregiving for a demented elder among Black and White families. *Journal of Gerontology: Social Sciences, 47(4)*, S156-S164.

Lincoln, C. E., & Mamiya, L. H. (1990). *The Black church in the African American experience.* Durham, NC: Duke University Press.

Loukissa, D., Farran, C. J., & Graham, K. L. (1998). *Caring for a relative with Alzheimer's disease: The experience of African-American and White family caregivers.* Manuscript submitted for publication.

Miles, M. B., & Huberman, A. M. (1984). *Qualitative data analysis.* Beverly Hills, CA: Sage.

Miller, B., Campbell, R. J., Farran, C. J., Kaufman, J. E., & Davis, L. (1995). Race, control, mastery and caregiver distress. *The Journal of Gerontology: Social Sciences, 50B(6)*, S374-S382.

Mutran, E. (1985). Intergenerational family support among Blacks and Whites: Response to culture or to socioeconomic differences. *Journal of Gerontology, 34*, 48-54.

National Urban League. (1989). *The state of Black America: 1989.* New York: National Urban League.

Neighbors, H., Jackson, J., Bowman, P., & Gurin, G. (1983). Stress, coping, and Black mental health: Preliminary findings from a national study. *Prevention in Human Services, 2*, 1-25.

Peters, M., & Massey, G. (1983). Mundane extreme environmental stress: The case of Black families in White America. In H. McCubbin, M. Sussman, & M. Patterson (Eds.), *Social stress and the family* (pp. 193-215). New York: Haworth.

Picot, S. J. (1995). Rewards, costs, and coping in African American caregivers. *Nursing Research, 44(3)*, 147-152.

Picot, S. J., Debanne, S. M., Namazi, K. H., & Wykle, M. L. (1997). Religiosity and perceived rewards of Black and White caregivers. *The Gerontologist, 37*, 89-101.

Proctor, S. D. (1995). *The substance of things hoped for: A memoir of African American faith.* New York: G. P. Putnam.

Soelle, D. (1975). *Suffering* (E. R. Kalin, Trans.). Philadelphia: Fortress Press. (Original work published 1973)

Smith, J. A., Scammon, D. L., & Beck, S. L. (1995). Using patient focus groups for new patient services. *Journal on Quality Improvement, 21*, 22-31.

Wilson, W. J. (1996). *When work disappears: The world of the new urban poor.* New York: Knopf.

Wykle, M., & Segall, M. (1991). A comparison of Black and White family caregivers' experience with dementia. *Journal of Black Nurses Association, 5*, 29-41.

CHAPTER 10

Making Meaning Within the Experience of Life-Threatening Illness

Doris D. Coward

Some persons with serious illness perceive their life situation as being devoid of personal meaning. Such persons also may believe they lack control over any part of their lives and may make comparisons only to persons they view as more fortunate than themselves. Other persons (even in advanced illness) perceive meaning in their lives, maintain control over some aspects of their care, and continue to initiate efforts to maintain self-esteem. This chapter describes a program of research with persons with AIDS and women with breast cancer, exploring the manner through which people discover and/or create meaning within the context of life-threatening illness. The intervention phase of the research program is based on theoretical literature and empirical findings suggesting that the human capacity for self-transcendence (defined as the expansion of self-boundaries) is a resource for making meaning and for healing at the end of life. The ultimate goal is to learn how best to facilitate self-transcendence perspectives and behaviors in those persons who are having difficulty making meaning within a living-while-dying trajectory.

I first will discuss life-threatening illness as crisis, followed by a discussion of crisis as an opportunity for constructing meaning. Theoretical and empirical connections between self-transcendence and meaning-making and healing will be presented, followed by descriptions of human responses to crisis that are growth promoting and meaning making within three potential crisis turning points of a cancer trajectory. I will end with a description of my current work in facilitating self-transcendence views and behaviors in women who are participating in breast cancer support groups.

LIFE-THREATENING ILLNESS AS CRISIS

The primary definition of *crisis* is that of a time of great trouble or danger. Crisis is a turning point, a decisive or critical time, the outcome of which may have bad consequences. A pivotal life event, such as the diagnosis of a life-threatening illness, may be considered a crisis or turning point because choices made within the context of that life event may have far-reaching consequences. The time period between diagnosis and recovery or death is filled with many decision-making opportunities that may or may not alter the final consequence of the illness, but that can influence the manner by which a person's life is lived and the perceived quality of that life.

There are at least three potential crisis points within a serious illness trajectory. Diagnosis of a life-threatening illness is accompanied by shock and disbelief for the person afflicted as well as for that person's loved ones. Diagnosis may precipitate feelings of disequilibrium, fear, and uncertainty. For many persons, there is at first a period of intense aloneness and isolation that is followed by an urgency to reach out to others for information and support. During the diagnosis period, many people feel they have lost control and have an urgent need to educate themselves about their disease and treatment options. Regaining control may be enhanced by assigning an attribution for why this bad thing has happened to them. Assigning an attribution may help people believe they are able to do something to prevent disease progression in themselves or to help prevent the disease from happening in others. The fear of dying is present to some degree in most persons at the time of diagnosis, but the hectic time of treatment choice, and treatment itself, may necessitate placing that concern on a "back burner" while energy is focused on control and cure. Informed decisions during the period following diagnosis are made through obtaining information related to the disease and choices of treatment, and garnering instrumental and emotional support.

A second potential crisis point is at the time when active treatment for the illness is completed. During this period, people return to their home environment and begin to manage their own care with occasional assistance from an agency and/or other support systems. The person and family may feel unprepared to manage the many, and sometimes complex, intricacies of dealing with a serious illness within the current health care system. The high-tech drama is over and the person is now faced with learning how to live with and manage a condition that has an uncertain end. The decisions made during this period involve how to live with uncertainty while doing all that is possible to promote one's health in order to live fully and to prevent progression of the illness.

A third crisis period occurs at the time of recurrence of disease, or the finding of disease progression, that indicates a 'cure' was not obtained. This may signal probable death in the near future or, at the very least, signal that palliation may be the only medical option available. This situation may rekindle the sense of doom that occurred at the time of diagnosis of disease, or this may be the first occurrence of the death fear. In either case, the person and the others who care about him/her can no longer ignore the possibility of death. This realization leads to a return of feeling alone and, in an ideal situation, stimulates motivation to think carefully about how to plan one's remaining life.

Jean's story provides an example of the first crisis point within a trajectory of living and dying from AIDS. Jean, a nurse, discovered she was HIV positive in 1989 when she was tested after being informed by the police department that a man who raped her several months earlier had AIDS. She described going through a long period of an overwhelming sense of aloneness. Her aloneness was accentuated by her belief that she was abandoned by God, who let this happen to her. Her feelings of isolation increased when she moved from her own small town to a large city that had more comprehensive AIDS services. In describing her decision to talk to groups of nurses and other health professionals about the plight of women with AIDS, she said, "When I first reached out to others, I did it out of a conscious need to save myself from becoming totally isolated" (Coward, 1995, p. 315).

The second crisis point was explored in a recent study of the experience of nine women living with uncertainty after treatment for breast cancer (Nelson, 1996). Women's experience of uncertainty, even 2 to 6 years after treatment, was related to the unpredictable nature of breast cancer and to their fear of recurrence. Their uncertainty forced them to consider new ways of living within the context of an uncertain or limited life. Helen's experience is an example of a woman who is struggling to find a way to live after treatment. Helen, aged 62, has just completed 6 months of chemotherapy following radiation therapy and mastectomy surgery for an aggressive form of breast cancer. She will not return to her oncologist for follow-up for 4 months. She is mentally and physically exhausted from the intensive treatment of her cancer. She and her family are concerned that her treatment has left lasting effects. They know that the high dose doxorubicin that was part of her chemotherapy has already resulted in signs of heart damage that may not permit her to be as physically active as she was before her therapy. They also know that, despite her aggressive therapy, her type of cancer is likely to metastasize to her bones.

Mary is an example of a person at the third potential crisis point within the trajectory of life-threatening illness. Mary, now aged 56, was treated initially for breast cancer in 1975 when she was 35 years old. In 1987, she was treated for metastasis to her left lung and to her esophagus. In 1995, cancer was diagnosed in her right lung. Now, in 1997, she is receiving palliative radiation therapy for brain metastases and knows that she also has cancer in her liver. With each recurrence of cancer, Mary and her family felt less hopeful for her recovery and now are faced with the reality of her probable death in the next several months.

CRISIS AS OPPORTUNITY FOR MAKING MEANING

Pivotal life events, such as the diagnosis, treatment, and progression of life-threatening disease, may lead to cognitive restructuring processes within the individual. The meanings that women like Jean, Helen, and Mary (and their loved ones) discover or intentionally create during these crisis periods are influenced by the choices they make within the context of their illness crisis points. There is a large body of literature concerning psychosocial adaptation or adjustment to life-threatening illnesses such as cancer and AIDS. Much of that literature focuses on maladaptive behavior and adjustment. However, there is additional literature that suggests that human beings have a resiliency that helps them transcend personal misfortune (Antonovsky, 1987, 1992; Frankl, 1963, 1969; Rosenbaum, 1990; Taylor, 1983; Thompson & Janigian, 1988; Yalom, 1982). Taylor's work with women with breast cancer and other individuals facing life-threatening events indicated that people may maintain or even improve in their sense of the quality of their lives after the event (Taylor, 1983). Yalom (1982) wrote of the importance of meaning systems in helping his patients who were dying with cancer live more fully and to face death with less despair than persons whose lives seemed devoid of meaning. His discussion revolved around the term *terrestrial meaning* which he defined as the meaning *of* one's life, the purposes or goals to be obtained.

Frankl, from the beginning of his career as a psychotherapist, studied the role of meaning in helping people find and maintain both coherence and purpose in their lives. His most widely read book, *Man's Search for Meaning*, is the chronicle of his life as a prisoner in Nazi concentration camps during World War II. His experiences in the camps supported his previously developed theory that a sense of meaningfulness is the essential motivation for living and that a sense of the meaningfulness in one's life can be maintained even in the face of the most degrading of circumstances (Frankl, 1963).

MAKING MEANING, SELF-TRANSCENDENCE, AND HEALING

The concept of meaning, in the context of the search for meaning described by Frankl (1963) and Taylor (1983), refers to making sense or coherence of something. Personal attempts to understand how life events fit into a larger context are examples of this type of search for meaning. Discovery and creation of meaning are processes that are facilitated by having a reason for existence and purposes to fulfill. The terms *purpose* and *meaning* often are used together, but have different connotations. Yalom (1982) discussed purpose in reference to intention, aim, or function. He proposed that people's understanding of how life events fit into a larger context (i.e., coherence) was associated with the belief that they had a purpose or function to fulfill. Having a purpose or function to pursue is connected to having a reason for existence. Both are resources for making meaning from life events.

Frankl (1969) described several ways through which persons make meaning:

by creating a work or doing a deed; by experiencing goodness, truth, and beauty; by experiencing nature and culture; and through encountering another unique being through loving them. Frankl reserved the highest (i.e., most valued) source of meaning for people who have been deprived of the opportunity to find meaning through work, deeds, or loving another. Such persons have the opportunity to find meaning through the attitude with which they face that predicament. The stand a person takes to a situation that cannot be changed, the manner in which he or she faces inescapable suffering, may be the only way to make meaning from circumstances such as pain, guilt, and death.

Frankl's four ways to make meaning (creating, experiencing, loving another, and taking a courageous stance) are congruent with nurse scholar Pamela Reed's (1991) definition of self-transcendence as the expansion of self-boundaries inwardly (through increased self-awareness and introspection), outwardly (in terms of investing oneself in relationships with others and the surrounding environment), and temporally (by integrating perceptions of one's past and future so as to enhance present life). Self-transcendence literally means reaching beyond a present conceptualization of self through an extension of one's self-boundaries. Self-boundaries are extended through reaching inside oneself for increased self-understanding, through reaching outside one's own concerns to interact with others, and through using memories from the past and hopes for the future to enhance present reality. Frankl (1966, 1969) also defined self-transcendence as reaching beyond oneself. He described the capacity for self-transcendence as an inherent characteristic of being human, and stated further that human existence was not authentic or meaningful unless lived in terms of self-transcendence.

Making meaning within the context of an adverse situation can be healing for all persons involved. Healing is a process of bringing together all dimensions of self at deep levels of inner knowing to regain a sense of integration and balance (Dossey, Keegan, Guzzetta, & Kolkmeier, 1995). Being healed is not the same as being cured. Descriptions of curing emphasize the application of an external agent (such as a drug or treatment) to eliminate or alleviate a harmful situation. Healing comes from within a person rather than from an external source acting upon the person. This distinction between healing and curing is important in situations such as life-threatening illness where healing can, and does, occur in the absence of a biomedical cure.

Self-transcendence views and behaviors are posited to facilitate the process of making meaning and to function as resources for healing in persons facing end-of-life issues (Coward, 1996b; Coward & Reed, 1996). Descriptions of how persons with life-threatening illness made meaning and found healing through self-transcendence were reported in three phenomenological studies (Coward, 1990b, 1995; Coward & Lewis, 1993). In Coward's first study (1990b), five women verbalized or wrote of experiences since their diagnoses of advanced breast cancer, from which they derived an increased sense of self-worth, purpose, and interconnectedness with others. Women reported experiences of physical and emotional pain associated with their disease that forced them to look beyond their usual self-boundaries for new purposes to fulfill that would make their remaining life more meaningful for them. The effort involved in learning to accept help *from* others and in doing *for* others led to changes in their perspectives about their illness and a sense of healing that lessened the pain, fear, and regrets associated with dying. One woman described how several negative encounters with her health care providers prompted her to form a group for women with breast cancer and to teach them how to be more assertive with their physicians. She believed that she, a nurse educator, had fared better than most during her negative experiences because she knew what questions to ask and had little difficulty being assertive. She revealed that, early in her treatment, she kept asking why this bad thing (cancer) was happening to her. Two years after her initial treatment she said, "I now believe the Lord can heal, and I have strong positive feelings I am being healed and guided by the Lord to serve him in a very special way" (Coward, 1990b, p. 166).

In two later studies, 20 persons with AIDS, although they had feelings of fear, isolation, and depression associated with their illness, described experiences of enhanced self-understanding and increased connectedness to self, others, and God that helped them to make meaning within the context of their illness (Coward, 1994). Men with AIDS gave to their community by helping others with AIDS individually, through support groups and volunteer activities in the AIDS community, and through participation in research. Women with AIDS focused on caring for their children, helping other women with AIDS, and working in AIDS education and prevention activities. Both men and women experienced accepting help from others and an increased appreciation of how things within their environment helped them to feel better. The broadened views and behaviors that resulted from choices made related to having AIDS led to new purposes to pursue and to creation of meaning from adversity.

The following statement of a 50-year-old Black woman is an example of creating meaning through both a reason for existence and a purpose to fulfill: "I really believe that helping to educate people about AIDS is my reason for still being here" (Coward, 1995, p. 317). Jean (the nurse with AIDS discussed earlier), although she had first reached out to tell others about her experience only to save herself from feelings of profound isolation, unexpectedly found that her experience was invaluable in increasing the understanding of health professionals about the plight of women with AIDS. The realization that what she had to say was useful to others was a source of self-worth, purpose, and meaning that felt healing to her. The following quote illustrates healing that occurred in a young man through joining an AIDS support group for which he eventually became a leader. "Paradoxically, having AIDS has given me a sense of membership I had never before experienced. I had never felt close to my family, never felt inclusion in any group, never really felt I belonged anywhere. Always on the outside. That has changed" (Coward & Lewis, 1993, p. 85).

GROWTH-PROMOTING RESPONSES TO LIFE-THREATENING ILLNESS

Growth-promoting responses are those that involve the expansion of self-boundaries. The expansion of self-boundaries (or self-transcendence) serves to assist persons to discover and create meaning and to facilitate healing during the potential crisis periods in the course of a life-threatening illness. The ill person and family, after the initial shock of diagnosis, focus on obtaining information about treatment options and on arranging for instrumental and emotional support during treatment. Information on prognosis and treatment options may be obtained directly from health professionals, but choosing also to reach out to others who have experienced a similar diagnosis is helpful in several ways. The sharing of experience with similar others alleviates the sense of aloneness. Learning how others have coped with similar problems may provide ideas for managing the current situation. Most important, such connections also become resources if previous sources of purpose and meaning are disrupted by disease or treatment.

For example, an elderly gentleman with advanced prostate cancer and newly diagnosed bone metastases expressed sadness and decreased self-worth at no longer being able to toss a ball or carry on other physical activities with his 4-year-old grandson. Members of his cancer support group helped him come to understand that, while physical activity was one way to interact with his grandson, reading a story or watching TV together also would provide a meaningful and memorable activity for the man and his grandson. In another example, breast cancer support group members helped a woman resolve her feelings of failure from not being able to fulfill her role of family caretaker during her chemotherapy. The woman was able to redefine her purpose from that of caregiver to that of encouraging family members to be more responsible for themselves and for asking her family to provide help to her when she needed it.

Helen was discussed earlier as being within a second potential crisis period in her life-threatening illness trajectory. Now that the intensive treatment phase of her cancer is complete, Helen and her family are concerned with making choices related to restoring her mental and physical strength, promoting her health in ways that will help to prevent recurrence, and living with the threat of recurrence. Helen has chosen to continue as an active participant in an on-line breast cancer discussion group through which she keeps in contact with other women with breast cancer. These women are resources for emotional support and information. That network also gives Helen an opportunity to share what she has learned with others who are just starting the treatment process. Both she and her husband recently retired from high school teaching and had long planned visits to remote parts of the world after their retirement. Because they are aware of her uncertain future, they have chosen to start traveling as soon as she feels strong enough. They are starting with a short trip from their home in Texas to rural Mexico. They also have planned visits to their out-of-state children's homes to keep in contact with family and to build up energy for longer trips.

A third crisis, or turning point, occurs at the time of disease progression. With her third metastasis from breast cancer, Mary and her two children (25 and 27 years old) now are faced with the probability of her death in the next few months. The decisions she and her family make related to her remaining time affect the meaning made and the degree of healing obtained from the experience. All three persons need to articulate their hopes for the future and to assess the impact of Mary's current and potential treatment on those hopes.

Calman (1984), in discussing quality of life in persons with cancer, stated that quality of life can only be described in individual terms, and depends on present life experience (including the impact of illness and treatment), past experience, and hopes for the future. Quality of life for an individual is the difference, at a particular moment in time, between his/her hopes and aspirations and the present reality. The gap between one's hopes and the present reality can be decreased by either reducing one's expectations or changing the current reality.

An example of reducing expectations was found in the earlier story of the elderly gentleman with bone metastasis. Because of his physical limitations, he chose to redirect the focus of his interactions with his grandson from playing ball to less physically demanding activities. Changing the current reality, for a woman with inoperable advanced stage lung cancer, might be to choose an aggressive course of chemotherapy that (although it could have unpleasant physical side effects) would allow her to live a few months longer to experience her youngest child's graduation from college.

Mary and her family, after discussing their hopes for her remaining life, were able to make choices that would create meaning for all of them. Mary worked hard after her other recurrences to control the cancer but she now recognizes that, with metastasis to her brain and liver, the odds this time are against her recovery. She is thankful that she was able to help both of her children grow to become adults. Her hope now is to be as comfortable as possible, to see a brother from whom she has been alienated for several years, and to die at home. Her children want to be with her as much as possible during this time. They are trying to arrange a visit from her brother, and have contacted a local hospice to provide palliative care. The hospice program not only will provide expert pain management care for Mary, but will help other family members shape the dying experience to be as meaningful as possible for them all.

FACILITATING SELF-TRANSCENDENCE VIEWS AND BEHAVIORS IN PERSONS WITH CANCER

After the initial shock of diagnosis of a life-threatening illness, most persons reach out for informational, instrumental, and emotional support. Although many persons and their families manage purpose- and meaning-related concerns through using their own internal resources and with support from extended family, friends, and spiritual advisors, health professionals also can help to facilitate the process of maintaining or restoring a sense of purpose and meaning within the context of the illness. My current program of research is based on the assumption that self-transcendence views and behaviors assist in the creation of meaning and healing and that such views and behaviors can be consciously facilitated within a support group setting.

The traditional role of cancer support groups is to provide basic information about cancer and cancer treatment, to offer emotional support, and to teach coping mechanisms. Findings from recent studies of cancer support groups report improved psychosocial adjustment in participants (Braden, Mishel, & Longman, 1998; Cunningham et al., 1991; Fawzy, Cousins et al., 1990; Spiegel, Bloom, & Yalom, 1981; Telch & Telch, 1986). Further, there is beginning evidence that these support groups may foster positive changes in immune function (Fawzy, Kemeny et al., 1990) and longer survival (Fawzy et al., 1993; Spiegel, Bloom, Kraemer, & Gottheil, 1989). The mechanism(s) responsible for the changes documented in persons participating in cancer support groups has not been studied. The "healing" factor may be the expansion of previous self-boundaries that occurs through sharing of a sense of common experience and identity, through giving of support and help to others, and through existential factors associated with having a sense of common purpose (Cella & Yellen, 1993; Coward & Reed, 1996).

The goal of the current program of research is to expand the traditional role of cancer support groups by promoting self-transcendence views and behaviors, and to document, over time, improvements in physical and emotional well-being in support group participants. My first intervention pilot study focused on the mechanics of implementing two 8-week support groups for women newly diagnosed with breast cancer, resolving issues of recruitment and retention of support group participants, and developing specific activities to be implemented within support group sessions (Coward, 1998). Support group participants also completed questionnaires assessing self-transcendence and well-being before the start of the support group sessions and within 2 weeks of the end of the eight sessions.

The two pilot support groups met one evening a week for 90 minutes at the newly established Breast Cancer Resource Center (BCRC) in Austin, Texas. During the day, long-term survivor volunteers at the center maintained a print and media library and a telephone helpline for informational and emotional support for women with breast cancer and their families. Volunteers at the center also assisted women to access computer databases to obtain current information on cancer treatment options and clinical trials. Support groups were facilitated by a breast cancer survivor, a psychotherapist, and myself (an oncology clinical nurse specialist). The groups, consisting of seven and nine women each, ran consecutively for 8 weeks.

Specific activities implemented in group sessions to facilitate the self-transcendence process included values clarification (Anderson, Nowacek, & Richards, 1988; Spiegel & Spira, 1991), problem solving (Braden et al., 1998; Telch & Telch, 1986), assertive communication skill training, feelings management

(Braden et al., 1990; Spiegel & Spira, 1991; Telch & Telch, 1986), pleasant activity planning (Grassman, 1993; Telch & Telch, 1986), constructive thinking (Fawzy & Fawzy, 1994; Telch & Telch, 1986), and relaxation training (Fawzy & Fawzy, 1994; Samarel & Fawcett, 1993).

Activities for individual sessions were selected by facilitators as opportunities arose from topics initiated by group participants. The focus was on encouraging women to share their individual experiences and to problem-solve together through sharing of insights. This sharing of personal experience, when encouraged in a group of women with similar concerns, was expected to be a strong trigger for developing self-transcendence views and behaviors that would lead to finding new purposes to pursue and making meaning within the context of breast cancer. Connections among group members also were promoted by: encouraging personal contact between group sessions and after completion of the intervention; planning meals together that included the suggestion to invite other support persons; and maintaining drop-in availability at the BCRC and access to center resources.

Analyses of questionnaire data indicated an increase in self-transcendence views and behaviors and in emotional well-being at the end of the 8 weeks. However, change on self-transcendence and well-being measures after support group participation was interpreted cautiously because of the small sample size and the lack of a control group. The finding of an association of self-transcendence with emotional well-being at both data collection timepoints was similar to the findings of phenomenological and cross-sectional correlational studies (Coward, 1990a, 1990b, 1995, 1996a; Coward & Lewis, 1993) and supports Reed's theory of self-transcendence (Reed, 1991). Evidence of the development of strong connections among the women who participated in the study was evidenced by the fact that some members from both groups continue to meet bimonthly on their own.

A second support group intervention pilot study is being conducted with 22 women with newly diagnosed breast cancer who participated in a breast cancer support group and a control group of 17 non-participants. Data has been analyzed from two of three data collection timepoints. There were no statistical differences between the intervention and control groups on background variables such as age, education, cancer treatment, or months since initial diagnosis of breast cancer. No effort was made to limit study participants' participation in other support groups; seven women in the experimental group and seven control group women attended other local support groups or were active in on-line breast cancer discussion groups. As found in the first study, higher scores on measures of self-transcendence views and behaviors were associated with higher scores on measures of emotional well-being in all study participants. Scores of women in the breast cancer support groups on self-transcendence and emotional well-being also were higher than those of control women, indicating that the support group sessions had a positive effect.

Narrative data, obtained from 10 women at the same time as the questionnaire data, is providing context for the findings of the statistical analyses. One woman, who drove 30 miles in rush hour traffic to attend her support group, said:

I guess I really knew I had gotten something [from the group] when I realized how eager I was to come that first time some of us met after the group had ended. I just felt like I needed to be there; there wasn't particularly anything going on that I needed to discuss. I just cared about the people and I wanted to be there .... Right after our last meeting, a friend of mine at work was diagnosed with breast cancer (it just plunged me right back into that whole time of confusion) and she was trying to make so many decisions so quickly and understand so much that she had never even thought about. I was trying to help her and one of the ways that I was able to help her was to reach out to members of my support group who had the surgical procedure she was going to have. I was struck with how genuinely helpful and willing to help they were. Just knowing that there are people out there willing to help ... you develop a sense of community and being able to share. Some of us may not have shared in this way before.

Another woman said the group helped her to feel better because it gave her "someone to talk to that understands. That makes me feel like I'm not the only one having some of the feelings that I've had." She also was a member of an on-line discussion group about which she said, "I feel like I can answer some questions and that makes me feel more useful." A third woman, experiencing her third recurrence of cancer, said:

I think a lot of things have helped me in the last couple of months. That would include both of my support groups, also my relationship with my family and my other friends. And my struggling relationship with God. I think relationship is the key. I want to be more connected with myself, with other people, and with God. I think they are actually interrelated – no one of them is really separate from the others.

This woman also talked of how differently she views the women in her support group than she did after the first session.

The first time we got together I was listening to all the stories but I didn't know the women personally. I left with a lot of anxiety because it reminded me of what I had been through and I wasn't sure if I wanted to be reminded. Sometimes I just want to forget that I have breast cancer. I joined the group because I thought it would help me feel better, and my initial response was that I didn't feel better, I felt worse .... I now feel we are bound together by a common thread of friendship.

Each of these three women voiced a sense of expanded self-boundaries through caring about others faced with a situation similar to her own. Each of them has found ways to share her experience in a manner that helps others and is meaningful to herself.

MAKING MEANING THROUGH SELF-TRANSCENDENCE VIEWS AND BEHAVIORS

Although my research currently focuses on the manner through which support groups assist people to reach out to establish relationships that meet their needs to make meaning and find healing, the story of how the BCRC was established is in itself an example of how self-transcendence behavior leads to making meaning and promoting healing. Four years ago a small group of breast cancer survivors in Austin, although they trusted their health care providers and valued them as professionals, experienced a lack of emotional support and information about quality-of-life aspects of their cancer treatment options. They wanted other newly diagnosed women to have the resources they themselves had lacked. They set about eliciting support from community oncology physicians, oncology nurses, mental health consultants, and other survivors of breast cancer for the development of a survivor established and run breast cancer resource center.

Within 2 years they obtained a donated space for the center and had trained themselves and other survivors to serve on the 24-hour telephone helpline. The support groups were begun as an additional means of providing information and emotional support to women. The survivors who assisted as support group facilitators for my study groups were among the original group of women who had the dream of starting the resource center. The BCRC is a direct result of several survivors of breast cancer reaching beyond their own concerns to create a setting from which they find personal meaning as they assist other women and families shape the course of their breast cancer treatment and recovery. The work of the organization continues to flourish as women who have been helped through center sponsored support groups or through individual contact with center volunteers join the ranks of survivors who contribute time and energy toward helping others make meaning of life-threatening illness.

In summary, my research findings contain many accounts of self-transcendence perspectives and behaviors influencing the construction of meaning within the context of life-threatening illness. Some of those narratives also describe healing that occurred as a result of changes in beliefs that lead to reprioritizing goals and changing behaviors. The findings from questionnaire data consistently demonstrate the association of self-transcendence views and behaviors with emotional well-being. My current research is focused on how to facilitate self-transcendence views and behaviors within a breast cancer support group. Specific activities have been implemented within group sessions to encourage expression of feelings and group problem solving that will help women with recently diagnosed breast cancer expand their previous self-boundaries. The narrative and statistical findings thus far from the women who have participated in the groups provide limited support for promoting self-transcendence as a means to find new sources of purpose and meaning when former life schemes are disrupted by the physical changes and the uncertainty attendant in life-threatening illness. Health care providers cannot create self-transcendence experiences and construct meaning for their clients with life-threatening illness, but they may be able to support and guide clients to make choices to expand self-boundaries in ways that lead to healing.

REFERENCES

Anderson, R., Nowacek, G., & Richards, F. (1988). Influencing the personal meaning of diabetes: Research and practice. *The Diabetes Educator, 14*, 297-302.

Antonovsky, A. (1987). *Unravelling the mystery of health*. San Francisco: Jossey-Bass.

Antonovsky, A. (1992). Can attitudes contribute to health? *Advances, 8*(4), 33-49.

Braden, C., Mishel, M., & Longman, A. (1998). Self-Help Intervention Project: Women receiving breast cancer treatment. *Cancer Practice, 6*, 87-98.

Calman, K. (1984). Quality of life in cancer patients – An hypothesis. *Journal of Medical Ethics, 10*, 124-127.

Cella, D., & Yellen, S. (1993). Cancer support groups: The state of the art. *Cancer Practice, 1*, 56-61.

Coward, D. (1990a). Correlates of self-transcendence in women with advanced breast cancer. (Doctoral dissertation, University of Arizona, 1990). *Dissertation Abstracts International, 524(1)*, 158.

Coward, D. (1990b). The lived experience of self-transcendence in women with advanced breast cancer. *Nursing Science Quarterly, 3*, 162-169.

Coward, D. (1994). Meaning and purpose in the lives of persons with AIDS. *Public Health Nursing, 11*, 331-336.

Coward, D. (1995). Lived experience of self-transcendence in women with AIDS. *Journal of Obstetrics, Gynecological and Neonatal Nursing, 24*, 314-318.

Coward, D. (1996a). Self-transcendence and correlates in a healthy population. *Nursing Research, 45*, 116-121.

Coward, D. (1996b). Self-transcendence: Making meaning from the cancer experience. *Quality of Life: A Nursing Challenge, 4(2)*, 53-58.

Coward, D. (1998). Facilitation of self-transcendence in a breast cancer support group. *Oncology Nursing Forum, 25*, 75-84.

Coward, D., & Lewis, F. (1993). The lived experience of self-transcendence in gay men with AIDS. *Oncology Nursing Forum, 20*, 1363-1369.

Coward, D., & Reed, P. (1996). Self-transcendence: A resource for healing at the end of life. *Issues in Mental Health Nursing, 17*, 275-288.

Cunningham, A., Edmonds, C., Hampson, A., Hanson, H., Hovanec, M., Jenkins, G., & Tocco, E. (1991). A group psychoeducational program to help cancer patients cope with and combat their disease. *Advances, 7(3)*, 41-56.

Dossey, B., Keegan, L., Guzzetta, C., & Kolkmeier, L. (1995). *Holistic nursing: A handbook for practice* (2nd ed.). Gaithersburg, MD: Aspen.

Fawzy, F., Cousins, N., Fawzy, N., Kemeny, M., Elashoff, R., & Morton, D. (1990). A structured psychiatric intervention for cancer patients: I. Changes over time in methods of coping and affective disturbance. *Archives of General Psychiatry, 47*, 720-725.

Fawzy, F., & Fawzy, N. (1994). *A structured psychoeducational intervention for cancer patients*. New York: Elsevier.

Fawzy, F., Fawzy, N., Hyun, C., Elashoff, R., Guthrie, D., Fahey, J., & Morton, D. (1993). Malignant melanoma: Effects of an early structured psychiatric intervention, coping, and affective states on recurrence and survival 6 years later. *Archives of General Psychiatry, 50*, 681-689.

Fawzy, F., Kemeny, M., Fawzy, N., Elashoff, R., Morton, D., Cousins, N., & Fahey, J. (1990). A structured psychiatric intervention for cancer patients: II. Changes over time in immunological measures. *Archives of General Psychiatry, 47*, 729-735.

Frankl, V. (1963). *Man's search for meaning: An introduction to logotherapy*. New York:

Pocket Books.

Frankl, V. (1966). Self-transcendence as a human phenomenon. *Journal of Humanistic Psychology, 6*, 97-106.

Frankl, V. (1969). *The will to meaning.* New York: New American Library.

Grassman, D. (1993). Development of inpatient educational and support groups. *Oncology Nursing Forum, 20*, 669-676.

Nelson, J. (1996). Struggling to gain meaning: Living with the uncertainty of breast cancer. *Advances in Nursing Science, 18(3),* 59-76.

Reed, P. (1991). Toward a theory of self-transcendence: Deductive reformulation using developmental theories. *Advances in Nursing Science, 13(4)*, 64-77.

Rosenbaum, M. (1990). The role of learned resourcefulness in the self-control of health behavior. In M. Rosenbaum (Ed.), *Learned resourcefulness: On coping skills, self-control, and adaptive behavior* (pp. 3-30). New York: Springer.

Samarel, N., & Fawcett, J. (1993). The effects of coaching in breast cancer support groups: A pilot study. *Oncology Nursing Forum, 20*, 795-798.

Spiegel, D., Bloom, J., Kraemer, H., & Gottheil, E. (1989, October 14). The beneficial effect of psychosocial treatment on survival of metastatic breast cancer patients: A randomized prospective outcome study. *The Lancet*, pp. 888-891.

Spiegel, D., Bloom, J., & Yalom, I. (1981). Group support for metastatic cancer patients: A randomized prospective outcome study. *Archives of General Psychiatry, 38*, 527-533.

Spiegel, D. & Spira, J. (1991). *Supportive-expressive group therapy: A treatment manual of psychosocial intervention for women with recurrent breast cancer.* Stanford, CA: Stanford University School of Medicine, Psychosocial Treatment Laboratory.

Taylor, S. (1983). Adjustment to life-threatening events: A theory of cognitive adaptation. *American Psychologist, 38*, 1161-1173.

Telch, C., & Telch, M. (1986). Group coping skills and support group therapy for cancer patients: A comparison of strategies. *Journal of Counseling and Clinical Psychology, 54*, 802-808.

Thompson, S., & Janigian, A. (1988). Life schemes: A framework for understanding the search for meaning. *Journal of Social and Clinical Psychology, 7 (2/3)*, 260-280.

Yalom, I. (1982). The "terrestrial" meanings of life. *International Forum for Logotherapy, 5*, 92-102.

CHAPTER 11

Religion and Meaning in Late Life

Susan H. McFadden

In a time when biomedical and consumerist ideals about long life occupy the attention of researchers, practitioners, and aging persons themselves, questions about late life meaning often become as marginalized as the old people whose lives contradict those ideals. The "meaning questions" may only surface in times of illness or loss and when they do, old people and those who love and care for them may be ill-equipped to formulate these questions, much less find answers to them. Moreover, it is not only the old and their caregivers who confront the existential dilemmas wrought by long life; they arise among the great mass of middle-aged "baby boomers" forced to examine these daunting questions because of unexpected illness, the needs of aging parents, or just a glance in the mirror.

The values of science and a materialistic culture fail to provide reliable signposts pointing toward meaning that can be sustained in light of despair, dissolution, and death. Religions, on the other hand, have through human history provided directions for humans to follow in seeking meaning, as well as definitions of what constitutes ultimate meaning (Pargament, 1997).

Grounded in the work of Victor Frankl and his image of religion as "the search for ultimate meaning" (Frankl, 1948/1975, p. 13), this chapter examines the problems of meaning in late life and the solutions offered by religion. It begins by acknowledging the loss of cultural meanings for old age and the implications of this loss for aging persons. The chapter next moves to a consideration of religion, spirituality, and aging, asking whether it is important to differentiate religion from spirituality. Taking a broad view of religion, which includes much of what people mean when they talk about spirituality, the chapter then utilizes Reker and Wong's (1988) model of the structure and dimensions of existential meaning to examine how religion functions in older people's lives. Although recent research has noted high levels of religiousness in this population (McFadden, 1996), most studies ask only a few simple questions (e.g., "How religious do you consider yourself to be?"). Reker and Wong's approach provides a holistic way of addressing the experience of religion in later life that has implications for research and for ministry.

MEANING AND AGING

Gerontologists have argued for years about what constitutes successful aging and how its components might be objectively measured. A recent paper asserts that successful aging consists of three components: "Low probability of disease and disease-related disability, high cognitive and functional capacity, and active engagement with life" (Rowe & Kahn, 1997, p. 433). In reading such a description, one wonders whether those aged persons whose lives are bounded by illness and frailty, cognitive decline, dependency, and disengagement must then be automatically labeled as "unsuccessful" in their aging.

Thomas Cole asserts that the split between "good" and "bad" aging can be traced to the rise of liberalism in modern culture when "many of the spiritual resources needed to redeem human finitude" (1992, p. 231) were abandoned. Modern culture cannot hold the paradoxes of human life in creative tension and thus casts upon old age a dualistic model of "success" and "failure." Lacking cultural support for late life meaning, and failing to find supportive communities in which to engage the existential dilemmas of the aging process, persons in our time resort to the scientific knowledge provided by gerontology as the "path to salvation" (1992, p. 232). Earlier convictions about "divine grace" and "piety" as providing the route to redemption have lost their hold on the religious and non-religious alike. Moreover, although some persons might locate meaning on an individual level (e.g., my private life has meaning), collective and cosmic meaning seems for many to be unobtainable (Moody, 1985). Unable to find meaning in their own aging, many persons – both young and old – in our time see little or no meaning in the aging of persons who do not meet the gerontological criteria of success. The frail become "other," psychologically and sometimes physically cast out of community.

To counter this, Cole calls for a return to courageous engagement with the paradoxes of old age. He writes:

> Aging is a moral and spiritual frontier because its unknowns, terrors, and mysteries cannot be successfully crossed without humility and self-knowledge, without love and compassion, without acceptance of physical decline and mortality, and a sense of the sacred. (1992, p. 243)

Cole's description of aging depicts a wholeness that is often absent from contemporary writings. Melvin Kimble, a long-time student of Victor Frankl, has argued that limited, biomedical conceptions of aging must be replaced by Frankl's idea of a "dimensional ontology that recognizes the rich and varied multidimensionality of human persons while still preserving their anthropological unity" (Kimble, 1995, p. 134). Kimble's hermeneutic phenomenology recovers the moral and spiritual dimensions of old age that are missing from positivistic accounts by forthrightly addressing the inevitable encounters with suffering and dying experienced by aging persons. Like his teacher, Frankl, Kimble believes that meaning can be located in suffering and that religion offers both the affirmation of meaning in suffering as well as promises of transcendence of the contingencies of human life.

In a success-driven culture that can neither tolerate nor attribute meaning to experiences of frailty, suffering, and dying, religion provides an alternative vision for individuals and their collectivities. Religion utilizes symbols and rituals to bring to consciousness and integrate the paradoxes of human life. Religion promises the presence of the holy in times of suffering; moreover, religious narratives provide both existential and cosmic structures of meaning by conveying the assurance that one is not alone in suffering, and that others have experienced dread and pain, doubt and horrific loss, but have located a pathway to self-transcendence in religious faith. The question arises, however, whether in a skeptical age, religion possesses the credibility and the power to provide meaning for aging persons forced to overcome narcissistic illusions about a successful old age with no threats of suffering, loss, or despair.

AGING, SPIRITUALITY, AND RELIGION IN CONTEMPORARY CULTURE

The aging of the baby boom cohort, whose suspicion of authority was forged in young adulthood, has coincided with the splitting of spirituality from religion (Bellah, Madsen, Sullivan, Swidler, & Tipton, 1985; Roof, 1993). Increasing numbers of persons claim to be spiritual but have abandoned what they consider the superstitions and authoritarian structures of organized religion. However, if one searches beneath the surface of discussions in which people claim to be spiritual but not religious, one finds numerous and varied definitions of terms.

One of the greatest points of disagreement concerns whether spirituality includes a transcendent object outside the self (Wulff, 1997), and if it does, whether that automatically puts it in the camp of religion and its associated institutional structures, dogmas, and history of internecine warfare. Noting the great diversity of definitions of religion and spirituality among scholars and the public in general, Zinnbauer et al. (1997) undertook a study to determine how individuals in various demographic categories define religiousness and spirituality. Interestingly, they found no difference in association of the sacred with religiousness and spirituality. Descriptions of spirituality most often included some reference to a higher power of some kind. Where the definitions diverged, however, was over the connection of religion with religious tradition and institutionalized structures, beliefs, and practices compared to descriptions of spirituality in terms of individual experience. In other words, spirituality for many people has retained an element of the divine. However, in casting off connections to religion, images of the divine risk becoming merely a mirror image of the self. In fact, that is exactly what Bellah and his colleagues discovered in the 1980s; many persons who had abandoned what they considered the narrow confines of organized religion had privatized it, resulting in a radical individualism that "tends to elevate the self to a cosmic principle" (Bellah et al., 1985, p. 236).

In the opinion of Zinnbauer and his colleagues, this splitting of religion from spirituality, in which the former is "bad" and the latter "good," has a number of implications, most notably that it results in an extremely limited view of religion. They urge scholars and researchers to study religion from a "broadband" perspective (Zinnbauer et al., 1997, p. 563) that includes the phenomenon of spirituality as essential elements of religion.

Frankl's (1946/1984) depiction of spirituality as the human drive for meaning and purpose provides a psychological framework for understanding the intersecting dynamics of religion and spirituality uncovered by the work of Zinnbauer et al. (1997). Frankl represents spirituality as a motivational phenomenon and indeed in ordinary language, this is often implied when people talk about being "moved" by the spirit (often referring to their own spirit, and not in a Christian sense to the Holy Spirit). More broadly, spirituality can be considered a motivational-emotional phenomenon wherein people respond to the drive for meaning by seeking that meaning within the self, in relationships with other persons, in contact with the natural and human-created world, and in a sense of connectedness with the sacred. Psychologically, emotion signals the presence of a drive and offers an evaluation of its fulfillment; thus we find people talking about spiritual experiences of connectedness as fundamentally emotional (McFadden, 1996).

Although spirituality inspires humans to seek the experience of meaningful connectedness, it provides no language or belief-structures for thinking about that experience nor does it offer any guidance for its attainment. Moreover, spiritual experience, as comforting or overwhelming or subtle or magnificent as it might be, offers no way for people to come to terms with suffering as an intrinsic part of human life nor does it articulate moral values that would underlie efforts to alleviate suffering whenever possible. Finally, spirituality, particularly in its present privatized form, does not bring together communities of memory and hope. Religion, on the other hand, provides language, symbols, narratives, rituals, beliefs, and a community to nourish human spirituality. Granted, religion sometimes creates stultifying structures that suffocate the spiritual drive for meaning; nevertheless, religion has traditionally offered human beings pathways to existential meaning as well as a resting place of ultimate meaning. When energies wane and active engagement with life becomes impossible, interpersonal relations are broken, and socially valued productivity ceases, religion – unlike secular culture – affirms the continuing value of the human being.

The remainder of this chapter focuses upon Jewish and Christian responses to the yearning for meaning among aging persons, but it should be noted that the world's major religions, whether Eastern or Western, all offer hope of fulfillment despite brokenness and contingency. For the Christian, fulfillment is found in incarnation when God became human, shared the sufferings of humanity, and promised life eternal through faith in Jesus Christ. Jewish fulfillment lies in the ancient covenant given to the people that God would not forsake them even in their darkest trials. Islam declares that submission and obedience to Allah fulfills the human longing for meaning. The sacred texts of Hinduism point toward fulfillment in the unity of all life and the promise of release from the recurring trials of worldly life. Buddhists attain fulfillment in release from desire and the demands of the ego (Courtney, 1981; Payne & McFadden, 1994; Thursby, 1992). By offering pathways to fulfillment and ultimate meaning – however variously defined – religion orders the world through values that transcend the human experience of suffering and death. In religion, persons of faith find resources for actively constructing a sense of existential meaning.

RELIGION AND EXISTENTIAL MEANING

Structural Components

According to Reker and Wong (1988), meaning is experienced in three interrelated ways: in beliefs, feelings, and the values that define goals and ways of attaining them. Unfortunately, by attaching words like *cognition, emotion,* and *motivation* to human experience, we often reify these constructs and assume they represent separate and distinct phenomena. This tendency, of course, has a long history in the Western intellectual tradition, although today it is being questioned not only in psychological theory but also in psychological research, particularly research on the brain, which has revealed dynamic interconnections among all three processes (e.g., Damasio, 1994).

These interconnections appear when one observes that religious beliefs not only can be *about* emotions and values, but they can also *produce* emotions and values. Moreover, beliefs are held with varying degrees of conviction – conviction being a convenient way of describing the intensity of the emotional attachment to the belief (Abelson, 1988). Although there is a long tradition in theology and philosophy of treating religious beliefs – about sin and salvation, about relationships with God and with other persons, about creation and the end of history, and about suffering and death – as purely intellectual entities, a phenomenological view that accounts for the lived experience of persons holding religious beliefs reveals their emotional substrates and their role in prompting and guiding actions.

Beliefs. Religious beliefs have substance, so to speak of "beliefs" in the abstract offers us little insight into how they contribute to existential meaning. Other chapters in this volume present evidence that different levels of existential meaning are associated with various psychological outcomes. Research is needed to test whether types of religious beliefs contribute differentially to existential meaning and thus produce varying effects. This is a subject that has attracted little empirical attention, due in part to the lack of theological knowledge among social scientists (Donahue, 1989). However, emerging work on religious fundamentalism (Hunsberger, 1995) promises to take the psychology of religion in new directions of studying specific beliefs, although clearly this approach could be expanded. Many important questions remain to be examined. For example, how do beliefs about God, sin and salvation, or an afterlife influence aging individuals' sense of meaning and purpose in life?

One study that did attempt to study the effects of types of beliefs utilized a model of religious maturity that evaluated the way Christian beliefs are applied to everyday life (Atkinson & Malony, 1994). The authors found that among older women, religious maturity was a significant predictor of lower levels of life distress. Here, again, we encounter the difficulty of separating beliefs, feelings, and values. For example, one theological dimension reported in this research was the acceptance of God's grace and steadfast love. This implies a certain belief about God and grace, an emotional response, and presumably some action in response to the values generated (e.g., if God can love me, then I should love others).

Feelings. Beliefs about God are interwoven with feelings about God. A recent theoretical development in the psychology of religion has begun to influence research on the various types of emotional attachment people experience toward the deity. The work of Lee Kirkpatrick (1992, 1995) has pointed out that people's religious attachments bear configurational similarity to the biobehavioral dynamics of attachment that begin in infancy. Indeed, Erikson wrote that the human being's first adumbration of the numinous occurs when the infant gazes into the mother's eyes (Erikson, 1977).

The effects of older adults' feelings of religious attachment upon their efforts to secure a sense of meaningfulness in aging remain to be established, although by triangulating research findings about religion, emotions, and health, one begins to get a picture of the significance of religious attachment for late life well-being. The sense of security and safety derived from positive attachment relations has been identified in the social support received from religious organizations, worship participation, and private times of prayer – all of which have been shown to function as stress buffers in elderly people (McFadden & Levin, 1996). More research is needed to determine whether there are connections between insecure attachments formed in children in relation to parents and later experiences of God as inconsistent and unavailable in times of need. If, as Kirkpatrick believes, these affective connections between the parent-image and the God-image influence religious life, then the outcomes of insecure religious attachment can be assessed.

Among the cognitively impaired elderly, the affective component of religion truly becomes salient in the discernment of existential meaning. With the loss of the ability to process the ideas that form beliefs, as well as the very language to express these beliefs, existential meaning for the cognitively impaired individual may derive solely from affect. Although our current "hypercognitive" culture has difficulty finding any meaning or value in the life of a demented elder, nevertheless that elder's continuing ability to experience emotion and to relate to others represents a starting place for addressing the question of existential meaning for a person so severely impaired (Kitwood, 1997; Post, 1995). Ministry with persons with dementia can affirm their core spirituality and the rituals, symbols, language, and music long associated with religion can provide a meaning-filled space in time (Friedman, 1995; Richards & Seicol, 1991). The person with Alzheimer's disease may no longer recognize individuals, recall names, nor have any sense of a self, and yet that person can still be in relationship with others and receive their loving care. Moreover, the religious community itself can function as the keeper of memory for the demented elder, affirming that it will neither devalue nor forget the forgetful (Sapp, 1998) because it rejects the secular culture's embrace of intellect, productivity, and social engagement as sole definers of human value.

Values. The values that motivate participants in faith communities to care for others may be a function of religious beliefs as well as a reflection of their response to what they have glimpsed of ultimate meaning. The effects of religiousness on helping has generated considerable research among psychologists of religion interested to know how religious orientation – whether a person's religion is extrinsic and self-oriented or intrinsic and self-transcendent – influences people's willingness to help others. In general, the literature reports higher rates of helping by those with an intrinsic orientation (Batson et al., 1989; Hunsberger & Platonow, 1986). This research finding would come as no surprise to Victor Frankl, who remarked in a speech to gerontologists in 1989, "the eye can only see when it is blind to itself but dedicated to the world."

Research on the variety of ways older adults offer help to others finds that service is an important source of personal meaning. Despite various obstacles to helping – including health problems, lack of financial resources, and poorly organized community supports for older adult voluntarism – older people are not only generous in informal and formal helping, but they also view this as a highly valued aspect of their lives (Midlarsky & Kahana, 1994). Although Midlarsky and Kahana did not include an analysis of their research participants' religiosity, a recent study of caregiving by older adults found that receiving comfort from religion and having an active prayer life contributed to a greater sense of reward from caregiving, especially among African Americans (Picot, Debanne, Namazi, & Wykle, 1997). Pargament's (1997) theoretical and empirical work on religious coping suggests that because religion influenced how these elderly caregivers appraised their caregiving challenges and their resources for meeting those challenges, these individuals could attach a greater sense of meaning and value to their daily acts of care.

If value and life-meaning are found in service to others, then what can we say of the frail elders who meet none of the criteria for successful aging? Is this component of existential meaning denied to them? Sadly, many institutionalized older people feel their lives have lost meaning because they can no longer "be any good to anybody." Creative religious responses to these questions have demonstrated how even frail elders can respond to God's presence in their lives by reaching out to others. Religious organizations sometimes organize "ministries of prayer and presence" for frail elders. They convert the burden of time into a gift of time through disciplined, frequent prayer for relatives, friends, and strangers. Sometimes these frail persons are even "ordained" to this ministry through rituals in their religious communities.

As another example, Rabbi Dayle Friedman tells of how she organized a group of Jewish nursing home residents to support a young man in Israel. The residents exchanged letters with the young man and sent him small gifts, and in so doing, experienced a sense of meaningful connection not only with him, but with the wider community. Friedman has also written of the sense of obligation in Judaism that requires Jewish elders to join "with community to worship God, to mark the Sabbath or the holiday, and to continue the chain of tradition" (Friedman, 1995, p. 367). Although services for these elders may need to be abridged, nevertheless even the most frail person is valued as a part of the worshipping community. In fulfilling the obligations of the *mitzvot* – obedience to the commandments in response to the Jewish people's covenant with God – frail elders' lives are meaningfully affirmed by the community and indeed, even take on cosmic meaning, "for the redemption of the world is seen to depend upon the Jewish people's fulfillment of the *mitzvot*" (Friedman, 1995, p. 367). Here, again, is evidence of the interrelationship among the components of existential meaning as beliefs, feelings, and values combine in a religious context of commitment, affirmation of an individual's worth within community, and actualization of values sustained since ancient times.

Sources of Meaning in Religion

Reker's empirical work (see Chapter 3, this volume) reveals that religious activities are commonly cited as one source of meaning, although other sources he lists can also have religious significance (e.g., altruism, leaving a legacy, enduring values or ideas, traditions and culture). The nature of the sources of meaning an older adult experiences from religious beliefs, feelings, and practices depends upon the religious denomination, the local religious congregation, and the individual. Gender, race and ethnicity, and denominational differences all shape forms of religious participation and the meanings derived from it. Important religious differences exist in beliefs about and experiences of public worship, attitudes toward private devotion, and support for "works" as expressions of religious values. These external sources of variability, as well as intraindividual variability (Kim, Nesselroade, & Featherman, 1996), reinforce the notion of breadth in the possible sources of meaning in the older person's religious life.

Frankl's (1946/1984) discussion of three meaning systems offers an organizational framework for understanding the various sources of meaning within religion. Creative values are evident not only in the activities of religious persons, but, more importantly, in the interior growth that occurs in those persons who undertake deliberate efforts to promote spiritual development in later life. Experiential values undergird both public and private worship activities as well as service given to others in response to religious commitments. Attitudinal values are richly displayed in the choices older people make to persist in believing that life has meaning beyond the self's experience of suffering, social ostracism, mental incapacity, and the certainty of death. For example, a very elderly woman related to Jane Thibault that although she no longer had the energy to *think* about God, she had decided that what is important is to *be with* God, to look out her window and love God's creation. "Somehow," she said, "I feel that my looking and loving is enough for God – that that's all God ever really wanted from me in the first place" (Thibault, 1993, pp. 93-94). Despite the limitations of her life, this woman had made a choice to continue in relationship with God.

The significance of these choices forms a subtext in the empirical work of Idler and Kasl (1997a, 1997b), who have found that even very disabled older people often make the effort to attend public worship. Their studies offer evidence that communal worship experiences contain many possible sources of meaning for older persons that have heretofore been ignored in research on religion and aging when measures of religiousness included just a few simple questions about frequency of attendance. Much of the earlier research concluded that attendance is a proxy for functional and psychological well-being, but Idler and Kasl's work shows that public worship may have special attributes that contribute to physical and psychological well-being (their measures) and a sense of meaning in life. Other recently published research on older adults' public religious observances is forcing a change in thinking among gerontologists about what happens when people choose to participate in an experience that binds them together with a religious tradition, a community, and with God. For example, Koenig et al. (1997) studied 4,000 persons age 65 and older and found that those who attended religious services frequently were about half as likely to be depressed as infrequent attenders. In a longitudinal study spanning 28 years, Strawbridge, Cohen, Shema, and Kaplan (1997) found significantly lower mortality rates for frequent religious attenders.

In worship, the breadth of religious sources of meaning connects with their depth when religious persons affirm their own contingency in a context that assures them of ultimate and eternal meaning. As Idler and Kasl (1997a) note, worship enables people to experience transcendence through the beauty of music, liturgy, and architecture. Both privately and corporately, worshipers often confess their sins and shortcomings, and receive the affirmation of forgiveness. Rituals link the sacred and the profane, overcoming the separations and paradoxes of human life. The reading of scriptures not only offers narratives of identity for the community, but also of identification for the person who experiences joys and tribulations similar to those depicted in the ancient stories. Worshippers pray for one another, often by name; concerns about individual lives are expressed and support may be offered. Through frequent worship attendance, older people order time. The severely disabled elder may engage in few activities outside the home but regular worship can anchor the week and give meaning to time. Similar observations have been made about worship in institutional settings (Friedman, 1995).

Just as researchers are beginning to recognize that worship is a multifaceted phenomenon, so too are they acknowledging the multifaceted nature of prayer. One person can pray in different ways (e.g., ritual prayer, conversational prayer, petitionary prayer, meditative prayer) and different religious groups can emphasize different forms and theologies of prayer (Levin & Taylor, 1997).

These recently published papers on worship and prayer represent a watershed in research on religion and aging, for they will undoubtedly inspire future quantitative and qualitative work on the breadth and depth of sources of meaning in religious life. Research that relies on measures of the frequency of public and private religious activities and subjective religiosity will benefit from a more finely textured approach to these phenomena by inquiring about the meanings older people derive from them.

CONCLUSIONS

We are entering a new age of aging. Possibilities for life extension through genetic manipulation and organ transplant coexist with debate about assisted suicide. The baby boom cohort may be the last generation to live out what has traditionally been considered the normative human life span. These rapidly proliferating developments in biotechnology are occurring within a sociocultural context that finds people struggling to locate existential meaning in late life, especially when that life is afflicted with suffering.

This chapter has identified the structural components and sources of meaning found in religion that can offer hope to the aging by transcending and transforming the paradoxes of old age. It is important to remember, however, that although older adults report high levels of religiosity, their heterogeneity produces considerable variability in their religious beliefs, the ways they practice religion, and the meanings they derive from religiousness. For some older persons, religion remains encapsulated in the form it was acquired in childhood. While they might, therefore, claim to be religious, in actuality, their religion offers few spiritual resources for facing the burdens of old age (McFadden, 1999). In addition, as Kim et al. (1996)

have demonstrated, individuals can experience variability in their own religious beliefs and practices, sometimes finding worship and prayer to be meaningful and at other times experiencing these practices as empty and dry.

The present cohort of older adults entered adulthood at a time when there was widespread social support for religious participation. However, this was also a period shaped by modernism when sacred language and the mysteries of religious symbols and rituals were denigrated by many religious groups intent upon making religion accountable to science. Therefore, some older people feel extremely uncomfortable when asked to reflect upon their spirituality. Moreover, for various reasons, some older adults have rejected religion altogether, and others were never religious at any point in their lives (although some may claim to be spiritual). The many faces of religiousness and spirituality in aging persons present enormous challenges to researchers and to those called to minister with them.

Kimble (1995) suggests that Frankl's logotherapy offers a model for ministry with aging individuals because it reminds people of their spiritual core and assures them that human life has value that transcends the biological, psychological, and social aspects of experience. Logotherapy, however, is not a substitute for religion. Those aging persons who choose to take religion seriously will find no facile answers to the paradoxes of human life. They may, however, discover a welcoming community of other seekers of existential meaning and glimpses of ultimate meaning – a community that tolerates and even embraces the uncertainties and ambiguities of long life.

REFERENCES

Abelson, R. P. (1988). Conviction. *American Psychologist, 43*, 267-275.

Atkinson, B. E., & Malony, H. N. (1994). Religious maturity and psychological distress among older Christian women. *The International Journal for the Psychology of Religion, 4*, 165-179.

Batson, C. D., Oleson, K. C., Weeks, J. L., Healy, S. P., Reeves, P. J., Jennings, P., & Brown, T. (1989). Religious prosocial motivation: Is it altruistic or egoistic? *Journal of Personality and Social Psychology, 57*, 873-884.

Bellah, R. N., Madsen, R., Sullivan, W. M., Swidler, A., & Tipton, S. M. (1985). *Habits of the heart: Individualism and commitment in American life.* Berkeley, CA: University of California Press.

Cole, T. R. (1992). *The journey of life: A cultural history of aging in America.* New York: Cambridge University Press.

Courtney, C. (1981). Restructuring "The structure of religion." *Logos, 2*, 73-82.

Damasio, A. R. (1994). *Descartes' error: Emotion, reason, and the human brain.* New York: G. P. Putnam.

Donahue, M. J. (1989). Disregarding theology in the psychology of religion: Some examples. *Journal of Psychology and Theology, 17*, 329-335.

Erikson, E. H. (1977). *Toys and reasons: Stages in the ritualization of experience.* New York: Norton.

Frankl, V. E. (1975). *The unconscious God: Psychotherapy and theology.* New York: Simon and Schuster. (Original work published 1948)

Frankl, V. E. (1984). *Man's search for meaning* (Rev. ed.). New York: Washington Square Press. (Original work published 1946)

Friedman, D. (1995). A life of celebration, meaning, and connection: Facilitating religious life in long-term institutions. In M. A. Kimble, S. H. McFadden, J. W. Ellor, & J. J. Seeber (Eds.), *Aging, spirituality, and religion: A handbook* (pp. 362-373). Minneapolis, MN: Fortress Press.

Hunsberger, B. (1995). Religion and prejudice: The role of religious fundamentalism, quest, and right-wing authoritarianism. *Journal of Social Issues, 51(2),* 113-129.

Hunsberger, B., & Platonow, E. (1986). Religion and helping charitable causes. *Journal of Psychology, 120,* 517-528.

Idler, E. L., & Kasl, S. V. (1997a). Religion among disabled and nondisabled persons I: Cross-sectional patterns in health practices, social activities, and well-being. *Journals of Gerontology: Social Sciences, 52B,* S294-S305.

Idler, E. L., & Kasl, S. V. (1997b). Religion among disabled and nondisabled persons II: Attendance at religious services as a predictor of the course of disability. *Journals of Gerontology: Social Sciences, 52B,* S306-S316.

Kim, J. E., Nesselroade, J. R., & Featherman, D. L. (1996). The state component in self-reported worldviews and religious beliefs of older adults: The MacArthur Successful Aging Studies. *Psychology and Aging, 11,* 396-407.

Kimble, M. A. (1995). Pastoral care. In M. A. Kimble, S. H. McFadden, J. W. Ellor, & J. J. Seeber (Eds.), *Aging, spirituality, and religion: A handbook* (pp. 131-147). Minneapolis, MN: Fortress Press.

Kirkpatrick, L. A. (1992). An attachment-theory approach to the psychology of religion. *International Journal for the Psychology of Religion, 2,* 3-28.

Kirkpatrick, L. A. (1995). Attachment theory and religious experience. In R. W. Hood (Ed.), *Handbook of religious experience* (pp. 446-475). Birmingham, AL: Religious Education Press.

Kitwood, T. (1997). *Dementia reconsidered: The person comes first.* Philadelphia: Open University Press.

Koenig, H. G., Hays, J. C., George, L. K., Blazer, D. G., Larson, D. B., & Landerman, L. R. (1997). Modeling the cross-sectional relationships between religion, physical health, social support, and depressive symptoms. *American Journal of Geriatric Psychiatry, 5,* 131-143.

Levin, J. S., & Taylor, R. J. (1997). Age differences in patterns and correlates of the frequency of prayer. *The Gerontologist, 37,* 75-88.

McFadden, S. H. (1999). Surprised by joy and burdened by age: The journal and letters of John Casteel. In L. E. Thomas & S. A. Eisenhandler (Eds.), *Religion, belief and spirituality in late life* (pp. 137-149). New York: Springer.

McFadden, S. H. (1996). Religion, spirituality, and aging. In J. E. Birren & K. W. Schaie (Eds.), *Handbook of the psychology of aging* (4th ed., pp. 162-177). San Diego, CA: Academic Press.

McFadden, S. H., & Levin, J. S. (1996). Religion, emotions, and health. In C. Magai & S. H. McFadden (Eds.), *Handbook of emotion, adult development, and aging* (pp. 349-365). San Diego, CA: Academic Press.

Midlarsky, E., & Kahana, E. (1994). *Altruism in later life.* Thousand Oaks, CA: Sage.

Moody, H. R. (1985). The meaning of life and the meaning of old age. In T. R. Cole & S. Gadow (Eds.), *What does it mean to grow old? Reflections from the humanities* (pp. 9-40). Durham, NC: Duke University Press.

Pargament, K. I. (1997). *The psychology of religion and coping: Theory, research, practice.*

New York: Guilford.

Payne, B. P., & McFadden, S. H. (1994). From loneliness to solitude: Religious and spiritual journeys in iate life. In L. E. Thomas & S. A. Eisenhandler (Eds.), *Aging and the religious dimension* (pp. 13-27). Westport, CT: Auburn House.

Picot, S. J., Debanne, S. M., Namazi, K. H., & Wykle, M. L. (1997). Religiosity and perceived rewards of Black and White caregivers. *The Gerontologist, 37*, 89-101.

Post, S. G. (1995). *The moral challenge of Alzheimer disease*. Baltimore, MD: Johns Hopkins University Press.

Reker, G. T., & Wong, P. T. P. (1988). Aging as an individual process: Toward a theory of personal meaning. In J. E. Birren & V. L. Bengtson (Eds.), *Emergent theories of aging* (pp. 214-246). New York: Springer.

Richards, M., & Seicol, S. (1991). The challenge of maintaining spiritual connectedness for persons institutionalized with dementia. *Journal of Religious Gerontology, 7*, 27-40.

Roof, W. C. (1993). *A generation of seekers: The spiritual journeys of the baby boom generation*. San Francisco: Harper.

Rowe, J. W., & Kahn, R. L. (1997). Successful aging. *The Gerontologist, 37*, 433-440.

Sapp, S. (1998). Living with Alzheimer's: Body, soul and the remembering community. *Christian Century, 115*, 54-60.

Strawbridge, W. J., Cohen, R. D., Shema, S. J., & Kaplan, G. A. (1997). Frequent attendance at religious services and mortality over 28 years. *American Journal of Public Health, 87*, 957-961.

Thibault, J. M. (1993). *A deepening love affair: The gift of God in later life*. Nashville, TN: Upper Room Books.

Thursby, G. R. (1992). Islamic, Hindu, and Buddhist conceptions of aging. In T. R. Cole, D. D. Van Tassel, & R. Kastenbaum (Eds.), *Handbook of the humanities and aging* (pp. 175-196). New York: Springer.

Wulff, D. M. (1997). *Psychology of religion: Classic and contemporary*. New York: John Wiley.

Zinnbauer, G. J., Pargament, K. I., Cole, B., Rye, M. S., Butter, E. M., Belavich, T. G., Hipp, K. M., Scott, A. G., & Kadar, J. L. (1997). Religion and spirituality: Unfuzzying the fuzzy. *Journal for the Scientific Study of Religion, 36*, 549-564.

CHAPTER 12

Logotherapeutic and "Depth Psychology" Approaches to Meaning and Psychotherapy

David Guttmann

This chapter presents the "picture of the human being" and the concept of meaning of two outstanding psychologists: Szondi and Frankl. They are among the many great personalities who have enriched our knowledge of the human psyche and made highly significant contributions to understanding the motivating forces behind human behavior in the twentieth century. Szondi is known throughout the world as one of the major "depth psychologists" and Frankl is the undisputed "height psychologist."

There are many commonalities and parallels in the personal and professional histories of these two personalities. Both are products of the former Austro-Hungarian Empire: Szondi was born in Hungary, and lived and worked in Budapest and in Switzerland; Frankl lived and worked in Vienna. Both were incarcerated in the Nazi death camps: Szondi in Bergen-Belsen and Frankl in Auschwitz and in several other camps. After their liberation, both continued their scientific works with renewed vigor. Both have written a tremendous amount of work: Szondi left behind nine books and well over a hundred articles and monographs, while Frankl has written 31 books, hundreds of articles and chapters in books, and saw several of his books translated into 26 languages. Both have developed their own version of psychotherapy, based on their philosophy about human life in general and on their theory of motivation in particular. Szondi has developed his anancology, or "fate analysis," and Frankl is "the father of logotherapy." Both were physicians, psychologists, and psychiatrists. Both worked with patients suffering from various mental problems, Szondi as teacher of psychopathology in his laboratory, and Frankl as director of the neurologic department of the Rothschild hospital in Vienna. Szondi established his own institute near Zurich, which has become the worldwide center for training in his philosophy and method of psychoanalysis/psychotherapy. Frankl developed the meaning-centered theory and method of logotherapy, and although he did not establish an institute of his own, his followers developed logotherapy centers on all five continents.

SZONDI'S FATE ANALYSIS

Szondi's Scientific Work

The scientific work of Szondi encompassed two main periods. In the first one, lasting from 1936 to 1944 in Budapest, Szondi concentrated his efforts on developing the theory and method of "fate analysis." In the second period, which started in 1945 and lasted until 1954, the question of whether or not it is possible to direct fate was posed as the leading one. Szondi was interested to see how fate analysis could be used for therapeutic purposes. This second period in Szondi's scientific activities laid the basis for the new anancology, or the theory of fate analysis, which was further developed during Szondi's lifetime into a theory of psychotherapy (Szondi, 1963).

Prior to the first period, Szondi undertook his own fate analysis (between 1934 and 1936). This self-analysis played a central role in the development of fate analysis. During that time he originated the concept of the "family unconscious." The family unconscious in Szondi's theory is seen as consisting of the following components.

In our unconscious, as important factors for our existence, there are models of ancestor figures that direct the fate of the offspring by force. Szondi has called this factor "forced fate." It comprises the "family unconscious" of the offspring many generations later. The "family unconscious" contains the aspirations of the ancestors. The opponent of the ancestors is the ego of the offspring, which can take a stand. The ego is capable of choice, despite the interests of the ancestors. This choice forms the basis for the concepts of "free, egotropic choice" and the "freely chosen fate." Szondi called this ability of the human being to choose his fate "directed fatalism." He also made this ability the cornerstone in his "fate-analysis therapy" (Szondi, 1963).

In the ancient Greek language fate is *ananke*. There are two meanings to this concept. The first is a limit on freedom due to some outside force. In this sense, fate means suffering, or worry. The second meaning of *ananke* is "blood relations" such as the family. Thus fate includes both force and family. Until the end of

World War II, fate as a subject of Szondi's scientific investigation developed in two periods.

In the first, it was viewed as an ancient concept, meaning that fate is a compelling force inside our psyche that expresses itself in the choices we make in life. Szondi, in *Fate Analysis* (1944), reported on a case that led to the establishment of fate analysis. This case involved a man, whose mother had fears about poisoning others, who selected for his wife a woman who a few years later in the marriage developed similar fears to those of her husband's mother. Szondi asked himself the most crucial question in fate analysis: "Why that man fell in love with that particular woman, and not with somebody else?" Szondi was not content to accept the common sense answer of "coincidence." This question was the basis for his major work *Analysis of Marriages* (1937). Additional choice-related questions were derived later when fate analysis was reinforced by the thousands upon thousands of cases in which evidence was found for his approach.

In the second stage, examining the "family unconscious," Szondi investigated the opposing interests of the ancestors and found that choice is of outmost importance for the offspring, for the family unconscious speaks in the language of choice. Szondi maintained that despite the genetic inheritance we all carry, people can freely choose part of their fates. And the greater that part, the easier it is to carry one's own fate. Those who succumb to their genetic inheritance (their forced fate) are totally dependent on their family unconscious. Szondi found that there are three tools for discovering the hidden intentions contained in the "family unconscious" of the patient: experiencing of pathological intentions during fate analysis; confrontation of the patient with those intentions on the basis of the patient's genetic inheritance; and confrontation with the latent family instincts via experiential fate diagnosis. The procedure used by Szondi for this was similar to traditional psychoanalysis. The patient would lie on a couch, and his dreams would be analyzed with the technique of free associations. The diversion from the basically passive Freudian psychoanalysis was based on the observation in patient behavior during analysis. Szondi found that the chain of associations was interrupted by something deeper than the regular opposition, and this opposition was usually expressed by sudden, traumatic behaviors and attacks. These required an active response from the therapist, and his help to let the patient express all those fears and anxieties that are connected to his "family unconscious" and to take a stand against them (Szondi, 1996b).

Components of the Concept of Fate

Szondi maintained that fate analysis requires a solid understanding of all the factors that shape fate, both causative and formative ones. In his use of the term, fate has seven main meanings: forced, selected, character, mental, social, instinctual, and spiritual fate. Each of these seven factors are components of the concept of fate. And each factor or component contains pairs of opposing traits. For example, in "selected fate" we must take into account that there are many things contained in that concept, such as masculinity-femininity; spirit-nature; conscious-unconscious; objective-subjective, and so on. Fate, in Szondi's analysis, is always the result of the behavior exhibited by the subject in relation to the opposing forces. And the human quest is always to attain wholeness. In Szondi's work, the ego, as in Freud's theory, is the mediator between opposing forces, but, unlike in Freud's theory, this mediation gives birth to the individual's fate.

Of the seven factors, spiritual fate is the closest to Frankl's concept of the spiritual dimension that occupies a central position in human life. According to fate analysis, the ego and the spiritual fate together form a hand that directs to a large degree the activities of the instinctual forces of man. These two factors in combination are capable of turning the instinctual forces against their original goals. This turning of the destructive forces in people (which Szondi calls "the nature of Cain") by virtue of the spiritual fate and the ego corresponds to a degree with Frankl's concept of the human being as capable of "self-transcendence," of which more will be said later. The concept of "spiritual fate" is seen by Szondi as the highest instance among the seven components of fate (Szondi, 1987).

The importance of "spiritual fate" becomes evident in the theory of Szondi when he speaks about those who succumb to their fate, those who suffer from fate that is forced on them. These are the people who are incapable of solving the opposing forces in their instinctual fate and the environmental influences acting on them. There are many people who suffer throughout all their lives from the fate they have inherited from their ancestors. They lack ego and spiritual strengths to overcome the compelling forces in their inheritance, and they are incapable of choosing from among the many possibilities open before them a "piece" of individual and private life. They are sick because the functions of their faith are paralyzed.

As Frankl (1963) has shown, faith is directed toward the future. Szondi concurs with that direction. The relationship of the ego to the future, in Szondi's terms, is of utmost importance from the standpoint of the individual's fate. The function of the ego is to serve as a bridge between the spirit and the inherited instinctual forces. The spiritual fate of the human being is capable of turning a person into a real human being. The strength of functional faith and its quality are dependent on the strength of the ego in terms of its libido, mental energy, interests, and the social environment. If the ego disperses its energy to satisfy the instincts, its chances to become sick are great. In order to prevent mental illness, the ego needs to give control to the spirit, rather than to materia, and only faith can help the ego to attain that function.

Szondi's Mental Picture of the Human Being

The question of "how does an individuum become a human being," or the process by which a person attains the designation of a "human being" (in the spiritual sense of the word) has been raised by the leading "depth psychologists" over and over. Freud's discovery of the unconscious and its many manifestations and expressions via dreams, symptoms, and via the "psychopathology of everyday life" has opened new perspectives for psychology. Psychoanalysis, in Szondi's approach, affected the mental picture of the human being in two ways: one, by discovering the irrational forces in the unconscious, which, if unchecked by the ego, may cause serious harm to both the individual and the collective; and two, by the "reality principle" (of Freud), by which the founder of psychoanalysis tried in vain to educate mankind to adapt to reality in order to escape the dangers inherent in irrational forces.

Szondi saw in fate the sum total of existential possibilities given to human beings by way of this genetic and social inheritance. Between those possible ways of existence, both in a positive and in a negative sense, that people bring with them from birth, in a healthy condition, man can freely choose his fate and his existence. This freedom is expressed in man's ability to overcome the forced nature of his fate with the help of his spirit and the strength of his ego. Those people who are incapable of doing so will fall victim to their "forced fates" and become neurotic or even psychotic (Szondi, 1996a).

When human beings are born, they bring with them the forced fate of their ancestors. Later, with development, as they pass through the first four phases of life, they may become "homo electors," that is, people who choose, or elect, their own fate. This election is possible only when individuals are able to use their Pontifex ego. In Szondi's theory the Pontifex ego is analogous to Freud's super-ego, as well as to Adler's "compensations," and to Jung's "myself." Each of these "higher egos" relate to the highest aspect in the structure of the human psyche (Szondi, 1996c). The structure of both forced and elected fate decides one's overall fate.

Szondi emphasized that a person has not only one fate, as the old anancology taught, but several "fate possibilities," which are sometimes of opposing directions (Szondi, 1996c,). The highest form of being, Szondi claims, once people are capable of being themselves, is to return to the collective, the love of mankind. This is the main task of the "homo elector." This is the difference between the "homo individuator" of Jung and the "homo elector" of Szondi. The former refers to those who are basically narcissistic, who love themselves, whereas the latter refers to those who expand their love to others, as in Frankl's concept of "self-transcendence." But attainment of the "homo elector" is not yet the highest achievement on the way to become a human being, says Szondi. "Homo liberator" and "homo humanisator" are two concepts that more than anything else, express Szondi's faith in humankind. Both stations can be achieved by human beings whose faith, in the spiritual sense, in a loving human collective means liberation from the confines of their instinctual natures and from the loneliness of self-love (Szondi, 1996c).

Szondi's Approach to Meaning

Szondi's basic assumption was that there is no clear border between the healthy and the sick personality, and that meaning in life is dependent on the choices we make – despite the biological heritage we all carry. His training in biology led him to think in terms of biology, or rather instincts. In Szondi's works we can discern four major instincts. Each of them is divided into two possibilities, and these eight possibilities influence an individual's fate: the "circular" instincts can take the direction of depression or mania; the "schizophren" instincts can become either catatonic or paranoidic; the "paroxic" instincts manifest themselves in either epilepsia or hysteria, and the "sexual" instincts can lead to sadism or homosexuality.

For each of these instincts Szondi has found positive and negative traits, and they can affect the meaning an individual assigns to them and to life. Thus for example, the sexual instinct is expressed in femininity and masculinity, in tenderness and aggression, in humanism and violence, in passivity and activity, and so on. In each of the four central instincts there is a struggle between the opposing forces. These forces represent the human versus the animal aspects of man (Szondi, 1996b).

FRANKL'S LOGOTHERAPY

Logotherapy's Philosophical and Guiding Principles

Logotherapy is built on "three pillars"; on the freedom of the will, on the will to meaning, and on the meaning of suffering. In developing logotherapy, Frankl intended to complement Freud's "depth psychology" with "height psychology," a psychology that, in Frankl's words, "would do justice to man's higher aspects and aspirations" (Frankl, 1967). Frankl cites the astronaut John H. Glenn, Jr. who said that "what is needed is a basis of convictions and beliefs so strong that they lifted individuals clear out of themselves and caused them to live, and die, for some aim nobler and better than themselves" (Frankl, 1967, p. 18).

The guiding principles and philosophy of logotherapy have been discussed by Guttmann (1996a), and can be summarized as follows. Life has meaning – as long as one is conscious – in all circumstances, and the will-to-meaning is the main motivating factor in life. People have the freedom to find meaning in life, and the defiant power of the human spirit is a potent force in the struggle for survival. Furthermore, choices are present in all situations. They are expressed in our attitudes to the alternatives we select for making decisions. Another important principle is that human beings have biological, psychological, and spiritual dimensions and all of them must be considered in any treatment. People should never be referred to as "nothing but"; that is, they should never be reduced to just one of the dimensions listed, or seen as machines in need of fixing. Still another element in logotherapy's philosophy is that the human spirit is the healthy nucleus in all sick people; that we can transcend ourselves for the sake of another human being in need, by the virtue of love, and that we can detach ourselves from constant self-preoccupation by laughter and humor. Our existence in the present is determined not only by our past but also by what we wish to become in the future, for each individual is unique and cannot be substituted. Meaning is present in each and every situation. The individual decides whether to use, or to lose, the opportunity to find meaning in any circumstance. The meaning of the moment is not always clear. We must be patient in order to discover it. Tension and stress are part and parcel of human existence. Spiritual tension strengthens the "spiritual muscles" of the person and helps in the quest to lead life in the way it could be rather than as it is. Responsibility is the ability to respond to the demands of life in a given moment. Growth and development are the results of change. Therapy is needed only when the change is not accompanied by growth. And finally, life does not owe us pleasure – only meaning that we must find. Happiness and pleasure are by-products of finding meaning in life. In the words of the great poet and philosopher Goethe: "Life is not something – but something for ...."

Frankl saw the issue of responsibility as one of the central tenets in psychotherapy. In his view, it is the patient or client who has to decide what he or she is responsible for, and how life's demands are perceived at any given moment. Frankl also discussed the methodology by which the patient's sense of responsibility can be heightened and coined the concept of "logotherapy" to emphasize a meaning-centered approach to psychotherapy. Frankl was aware of the separation between human dignity and psychotherapy, and used the concept of responsibility to reconnect these two elements. Frankl said:

> Convenient psychotherapy is content with making people "free from" psychological and physical inhibitions or difficulties and with extending the sphere of the ego as against that of the id. Both logotherapy and existential analysis seek to make people free in another and more basic sense: "free to" take their responsibility upon themselves. (1986, p. 273)

Logotherapy is neither a philosophy by itself nor a psychotherapy that stands apart from other established schools (Kovacs, 1985). Rather, it is a way of thinking and a methodology combined together in a process aimed at enabling clients to discover meaning in their lives. Logotherapy's clientele constitute a rather large group of people. In addition to helping those suffering from various forms of nöogenic neuroses, or neuroses that originate in the nöetic or spiritual dimension, logotherapy has developed methods for dealing with clients who suffer from phobias in their sexual behavior, for those with incurable diseases, and for those who lead empty and meaningless lives. Logotherapy can also serve to complement and/or supplement conventional methods of psychotherapy in cases of addictions, victims of accidents, the physically disabled who have lost limbs, and others, especially in cases in which the losses are accompanied by lack of meaning in life.

The Concept of Meaning in Logotherapy

The Meaning of Life. Meaning, Frankl states, exists under all circumstances. "That meaning must be specific and personal, a meaning which can be realized by this one person" (Frankl, 1986, p. xvi). Meaning can be achieved by realizing creative, experiential, and attitudinal values. Frankl claims that:

> Even a man who finds himself in the greatest distress, in which neither activity nor creativity can bring values to life, nor experience give meaning to it – even such a man can still give his life a meaning by the way he faces his fate, his distress. By taking his unavoidable suffering upon himself he may yet realize values. (1986, p. xix)

When people are unable to discover, recognize, and accept meaning they find themselves in an "existential vacuum." This vacuum cries out for fulfillment. Those who are unable to fill their lives by finding meaning are apt to pay a price in the form of psychiatric symptoms, such as anomie, addiction, and aggression, which in their severest forms lead to what Frankl has termed as "existential neurosis." These people suffer from anxiety and depression.

Meaning can be found in many ways: by doing a deed or by a creative enterprise; by experiencing a value; or by relating to people and to causes. We can find meaning by "symbolic growth": by discovering ourselves; by choice, or by making a decision; by acting on our uniqueness and by our response-ability; by self-transcendence and by our attitude to guilt, pain, and suffering; and by our attitude to death (for a detailed account of these avenues to meaning, see Fabry, 1988; Frankl, 1963; Lukas, 1986).

The Meaning of the Moment. Problems in living are part and parcel of everyday life. At every moment we may be called upon to make decisions in many areas. Some of these may be very simple, while others can be complex with far-reaching consequences for the individual, the family, and even society. Thus life may be perceived as a never-ending chain of decisions to assure our survival and to give content to our days upon this earth. Each situation in life is unique. It cannot be substituted for someone else's. Nor can someone else take on our lives or problems.

The meaning of the moment stands between past accomplishments that are safely stored away in our memory and future possibilities that are waiting to be grasped. It is transitory, cannot be repeated, cannot be postponed or delayed. Life forces it upon us whether we like it or not. Potential for meaning is always present in a given situation. We are required to discover it – and to act for its realization (Guttmann, 1996b).

The Supra or Ultimate Meaning. As an abstract concept, the term *ultimate meaning* is hard to grasp, and yet its existence is evident. We just have to look around in nature to see that there is some order in the world, both on our own planet and beyond. How did this order come about? How does it work? How does it affect the lives of the people on Earth? These are some of the questions that the greatest philosophers, humanists, and psychologists have asked, and continue to ask from one generation to the next (Einstein, 1934). No one has real answers, and yet there are opportunities when one can experience something extraordinary that reaffirms the existence of that special dimension.

Whether or not one believes in God is a personal matter, and a private value. However, for a professional there is a need to formulate a worldview, a basic perception of this world, that provides him or her with a sense of security. Moreover, professionals have to internalize values that are an integral part of their respective professions. At times these values may be similar, even identical to personal values, but it is possible that personal and professional values do not correspond. In such cases professionals can find themselves in a value conflict. Frankl's "mental picture of the human being" can help those professionals and laymen alike who are in doubt.

Frankl's "View of the Human Being – Homo Paciens"

Frankl is the originator of the concept of "the tragic triad," which consists of pain and suffering, guilt, and death. These are experiences that we all have to encounter at some time in life, but the way we encounter these trying events depends upon the attitude we take toward them. For in all of them there are opportunities for finding meaning in life. Frankl (1963) claims that we have the ability to turn tragedies to human achievements – by virtue of finding a meaning to our suffering. We can turn guilt to a lever of true repentance and service to others, and we can accept death as inevitable, as our fate, and as a motivating factor to make our life meaningful. There is value in "homo paciens," the suffering man, so long as it changes us into better human beings. Understanding the concept of the "tragic triad" is important for the terminally ill and their therapists, while for the families of the sick it is absolutely necessary. Therefore, no psychotherapist can disregard the logotherapeutic approach to that concept.

Frankl stated: "Suffering is an ineradicable part of life, even as fate and death. Without suffering and death human life cannot be complete" (1963, p. 154). Albert Schweitzer (1974), the great physician and humanist, said that there is a brotherhood among all those, whether White or Black, who have experienced great suffering. Diseases and illnesses cause as much pain to the former as the latter, for all human beings are ruled by the terrible power called suffering. Members of this brotherhood of pain are marked with a stamp. It is invisible to the naked eye, yet it chains together all those who have experienced great anxiety and undergone physical suffering.

Frankl (1967) emphasizes that people are ready and willing to shoulder any suffering as soon and as long as they can see a meaning in it. For without this discovery suffering can turn into despair and self-destruction. In his writings he also speaks of three types of suffering: that which is associated with an unchangeable fate; that which comes as a result of an emotionally painful experience; and that which arises out of the meaninglessness of one's life.

The avoidance of misery and human unhappiness is a goal shared by all the helping professions. Various schools of psychotherapy aim to reduce the causes and treat the symptoms of suffering and pain. They tend to see in psychic misery only the negative aspects, those that can be eradicated by science, while the creative powers inherent in human suffering, and the bravery required to confront it, are largely ignored. Logotherapy, on the other hand, perceives unavoidable suffering as an opportunity to demonstrate the person's capacity to rise above pain, above suffering, by making use of the "defiant power of the human spirit," a concept coined by Frankl to demonstrate human achievement. For Frankl, "the right kind of human suffering is facing your fate without flinching. This is the highest achievement that has been granted to man" (Frankl, 1986, p. xix).

Logotherapy's insistence on the unconditional meaningfulness of life – even against the reality of death – is based on Frankl's analysis of the meaning of death for all human beings. Frankl claims that we are the only creatures upon this earth who are aware of their own death. And this discovery should lead us toward the reawakening of the responsibility toward life – instead of denial of death's existence.

Frankl's attitudinal values toward life and toward death are always aimed at others – rather than to one's self. It is the caring for others, for their welfare, for their peace of mind, for their comfort, and for their consolation that raise attitudinal values high above all others. To make this caring meaningful is the aim of the logotherapist.

SUMMARY

The "view of the human being" of two major psychologists are compared and contrasted with respect to their approaches to psychotherapy. Szondi's "Homo Elector" is based on his "family unconscious" and genetic inheritance. These include both positive and negative traits that people bring with them into the world from their ancestors, as well as all the possibilities for choice. According to Szondi, the fates of people in five major areas of life, namely in love, friendship, occupation, sickness, and death, are not predestined. People are able to choose their fate despite the oppressing forces of inheritance.

In summing up Szondi's work, one is struck by the duality of man's nature: "forced fate" versus "selected fate." Szondi claims that people can continue to adhere to murderous inclinations, as contained in his "Cain's fate" (Szondi, 1987), or can use their conscience to recognize this tendency to sin and contradict it, his "transformation to Moses." The tendency to kill is as old as human history, says Szondi, and therefore it is ever present. But the recognition of sin is also present from ancient times in the human soul. A person can lead a life in which he or she aims to become like Moses, who struggled with his Cain's spirit and sin, and came out glorious, meaning that he turned his murderous past into the highest achievement that a human being can attain – to become the founder of law and morals.

Frankl's "Homo Paciens" is one who has to confront suffering that cannot be changed or cured by way of conventional medicine. In his logotherapy, the meaning-centered psychotherapy, the person can use his or her unique capacities of "self-transcendence" and "self-detachment" and elevate him- or herself to a spiritual height in the struggle with the forces and the vicissitudes of life. People have the freedom to decide which stance they wish to take; to succumb to fate, or to use freedom of choice. The meaning assigned by people to what happens to them, and their search for a meaningful life, are central concepts in Frankl's approach to psychotherapy.

In summing up Frankl's work in relation to meaning and to the picture of the human being, one can say without hesitation that Frankl has basically continued to elevate the person to a higher plateau than the one contained in "fate-analysis." While both Szondi and Frankl agree that people have both potentialities within themselves (to be a saint or a swine), Frankl's approach to human destiny is much more positive than Szondi's. Frankl has shown that the person always has the freedom to choose a meaningful life – even under the most trying of circumstances. Frankl's unconditional faith in human freedom, in human choice, in self-transcendence, and in the defiant power of the human spirit make logotherapy into a valuable tool for psychotherapy and a philosophy for survival in an increasingly impersonal, cruel, and cold world.

Both Frankl and Szondi have enriched our knowledge of the human being, each in his own unique approach. Yet common to both of them is a deep concern for the fate of humankind. These two outstanding human beings represent two important avenues to psychotherapy, and they have left behind them theories that light our ways in the present and give hope for the future.

REFERENCES

Einstein, A. (1934). *How do I see the world*. Budapest: Gladiator. (In Hungarian.)

Fabry, J. B. (1988). *Guideposts to meaning: Discovering what really matters*. Oakland, CA: New Harbinger.

Frankl, V. E. (1963). *Man's search for meaning: An introduction to logotherapy*. New York: Washington Square Press.

Frankl, V. E. (1967). *Psychotherapy and existentialism: Selected papers on logotherapy*. New York: Simon & Schuster.

Frankl, V. E. (1986). *The doctor and the soul: From psychotherapy to logotherapy*. New York: Vintage.

Guttmann, D. (1996a). *Logotherapy for the helping professional: Meaningful social work*. New York: Springer.

Guttmann, D. (1996b). The meaning of the moment and existential guilt. *Journal des*

Viktor-Frankl Instituts, 4(2), 54-64.

Kovacs, G. (1985). Viktor Frankl's "place" in philosophy. In Viktor E. Frankl – 80 years (Special issue). *International Forum for Logotherapy, 8*, 17-21.

Lukas, E. (1986). *Meaning in suffering, comfort in crisis through logotherapy.* Berkeley, CA: Institute of Logotherapy.

Schweitzer, A. (1974). *Ma vie et ma pensée.* Budapest: Kossuth. (In Hungarian.)

Szondi, L. (1937). Analysis of marriages. An attempt at a theory of choice in love. *Acta Psychologica, 3(1)*, 1-80.

Szondi, L. (1944). *Schiksalanalyse.* Basel: Schwabe.

Szondi, L. (1963). *Schiksalanalytische therapie.* Bern and Stuttgart: Huber.

Szondi, L. (1987). *Kain, a torvenyszego, Mozes, a torvenyalkoto.* Budapest: Gondolat. (In Hungarian.)

Szondi, L. (1996a). Fate-analysis and self-disclosure. *Thalassa, 96(2)*, 5-38. (In Hungarian.)

Szondi, L. (1996b). The languages of the unconscious: Symptom, symbol, and choice. *Thalassa, 96(2)*, 61-82. (In Hungarian.)

Szondi, L. (1996c). The way to manhood. *Thalassa, 96(2)*, 39-60. (In Hungarian.)

PART IV

OVERVIEW AND
NEW DIRECTIONS

CHAPTER 13

Existential Meaning: Reflections and Directions

Gary T. Reker and Kerry Chamberlain

The contributions presented in this volume cover a diverse arena and raise a variety of issues and debates around existential meaning. An examination of these contributions reveals a number of themes that underlie the discussions and provide a general framework for approaching existential meaning. These themes in their turn suggest implications and offer possibilities for future development in the area. In the first part of this chapter, we attempt to explicate the common threads that unite the chapters and highlight issues of particular relevance. Then we offer a consideration of current theoretical and conceptual developments in existential meaning and future directions for research. Finally, we explore applications of meaning, including ways of maintaining meaning and of facilitating the process of meaning-making for individuals undergoing a crises of meaning.

COMMON THREADS

Theme 1: Existential Meaning as an Essential Concern of Human Life

One issue that unites these contributions, perhaps above all others, is the consensus that existential meaning is a fundamental and essential human process. Although there are differences in understanding about how meaning is attained, contributors are united on the notion that finding or creating meaning is an essential issue in human living, applicable across racial, ethnic, and cultural divides. That is to say, they generally accept the notion of a will to meaning proposed by Frankl (1962). Although several contributors comment on the issue of meaninglessness, it is clear that this is regarded as a negative and incomplete way of living and that a person is limited and partial if lacking in meaning.

Theme 2: Existential Meaning as Personally Constructed

Existential meaning is personal; it is private and subjective. People find and lose, discover and create meaning as they progress through their lives. The processes by which people discover or create meaning are the subject of debate and investigation, but it is clear that meaning is derived from a diversity of sources and in response to a variety of life demands. Regardless of sources or circumstances, meaning is personally constructed by individuals living their lives. However, this subjectivity of meaning should not be taken to imply that it cannot be investigated or that it is essentially individualistic in nature.

Theme 3: Existential Meaning as a Relational Construct

People do not exist in isolation. Meaning is personally constructed, but also socio-culturally situated. As Kenyon notes in Chapter 1, meaning cannot be considered apart from the paradox of existence, that the person is simultaneously individual and social. The notion of meaning can only make sense within the nature of existence. Hence existential meaning is also a relational construct, achieved and facilitated in a sociocultural context of interrelations. Several contributors to this volume explicitly document how existential meaning is established within the context of significant others who, in part, help define one's personal existence.

Theme 4: Existential Meaning-Making as a Developmental Process

Meaning is personal, constructed, and ever-changing. Therefore the attainment of existential meaning is an ideal goal that is never completely realized, and constitutes a life-long task. The attainment of meaning differs as life progresses and is necessarily a developmental process. Many of our contributors exemplify this with a focus on specific times of life, such as midlife or old age, or on the occurrence of life crises. These times are seen as highly salient periods that provide leverage for increased understanding of meaning-making.

Theme 5: Existential Meaning as Amenable to Investigation

Existential meaning has often been regarded as the preserve of the philosopher rather than the social researcher. However, the contributors leave us in no doubt that existential meaning can be investigated and that it deserves investigation. Many lament the paucity of research and the lack of interest in the topic until quite recently, but the contributions all document a commitment to inquiry into existential meaning. They adopt a variety of ontological and epistemological positions on how meaning should be conceptualized and investigated, but there is consistent agreement that the undertaking is valuable and important. Furthermore, the contributions demonstrate how this can be achieved from a variety of perspectives and approaches.

FUTURE THEORETICAL AND CONCEPTUAL DEVELOPMENTS

Theory forms an important focus of the contributions in this book, and between them they present and exemplify a broad diversity of approaches that may be taken to existential meaning. Some of the contributors report on the difficulty of choosing between existing theories, and others offer new theoretical directions that are deserving of further attention. Others again opt for a measurement framework for their inquiry and essentially avoid the issue of theory choice. All this reflects the current situation: that there is no agreement on a dominant theoretical framework for existential meaning. This is not surprising given the relative recency of social research into the construct, but perhaps reflects more strongly on the fact that existential meaning, by its nature, is a difficult conceptual area. Given that there is no one "best" theory, further attempts at theoretical expansion should be embraced and encouraged. Different perspectives will support different orientations to and objectives for further research, and enhance the complexity and richness of our understandings of existential meaning.

As this book is focused substantially on life-span development, it is interesting to note that existing theory has not been strongly informed by any overarching life-span developmental theory. In spite of the broad agreement on existential meaning-making as a developmentally important process, existing theoretical approaches have not attempted to incorporate developmental issues and concerns into any general existential meaning theory, although there have been some efforts to relate existential meaning processes to specific stages of life such as old age (e.g., Reker, 1997). Kenyon's work (see Chapter 1) offers some interesting proposals concerning personal existence, the storied nature of life, and the interrelation of existential meaning and time that have potential general application in this regard, but that require further unfolding to inform and develop a fully developmental theory of existential meaning.

Conversely, we could ask whether existing developmental theories have potential for building theoretical accounts of existential meaning. In this regard, Tornstam (1997) has offered the concept of gerotranscendence as a general theoretical guide to understanding the process of living into old age. Gerotranscendence captures the contemplative nature of human aging as characterized by "a shift in meta-perspective, from a materialistic and pragmatic view of the world to a more cosmic and transcendent one, normally accompanied by an increase in life satisfaction" (Tornstam, 1997, p. 143). Gerotranscendence emphasizes change and development and is regarded as "the final stage in a natural progression towards maturation and wisdom" (p. 143). Change is described as occurring along two dimensions: cosmic transcendence and ego transcendence. Thus, according to the theory, a gerotranscendent person experiences feelings of cosmic communion with the spirit of the universe, a redefinition of time and space, life and death, and a redefinition of the self (Tornstam, 1994).

The theory of gerotranscendence shares much in common with the construct of existential meaning and existential meaning-making. Both attempt to describe and account for how an individual comes to a new understanding of existential questions and experiences. Both are personally constructed, relational concepts that undergo dynamic change over time, leading toward the attainment of a higher end-state that extends beyond the self. As a contemplative dimension of aging, the theory of gerotranscendence is broad enough in scope that it could easily incorporate the processes of existential meaning-making (such as transformation and transcendence).

Gerotranscendence shows promise as an overarching theory of life-span development, particularly as it applies to the later years of life. Although there is general support for the theory, the findings are not always consistent, either within or across cultures (Thomas, 1997). Nevertheless, the theory merits further consideration and investigation in that it may provide a broader theoretical context for future studies of existential meaning. It is only through further conceptual and theoretical work of this nature that we will develop improved theories of existential meaning from a developmental point of view.

FUTURE DIRECTIONS IN RESEARCH

The contributions to this book open up the diversity of approaches that can be adopted for inquiry into existential meaning. Recently, social science researchers have been moving to incorporate qualitative approaches more strongly into their research, and the contributions here certainly highlight that movement. An examination of the content reveals that those contributions that use quantitative approaches alone (Chapters 3 and 4) are outnumbered by those using or advocating qualitative approaches (Chapters 1, 2, 5, 9, and 10). Other contributions (Chapters 6, 7, and 8) use a combination of quantitative and qualitative approaches within the same study.

Qualitative Approaches

Qualitative approaches to research are diverse and premised on a variety of epistemologies. There is no agreed definition of qualitative research, which makes it very difficult to summarize and comment on qualitative approaches in a way that successfully captures their essence. However, Morse (1992) has suggested three characteristics that distinguish qualitative from quantitative approaches: they value the participant's rather than the researcher's perspective; they seek a holistic, integrative interpretation that includes the social context of the phenomenon rather than stripping the context away for purposes of control; and they utilize inductive rather than deductive processes in data analysis and theory building. In general, qualitative approaches shift away from quantitative approaches in emphasizing understanding over measurement, the significance and meaning of action over causation, and interpretation over statistical analysis.

The diversity of qualitative approaches is illustrated by the contributors to this volume who draw on different perspectives in their research and analysis. Much of the qualitative research presented here is premised on some form of content analysis, but several chapters offer alternatives. For example, Debats (Chapter 6) and Coward (Chapter 10) both focus on experience and draw on phenomenological approaches, O'Connor and Chamberlain (latter part of Chapter 5) privilege language in presenting a discursive analysis, and Kenyon (Chapter 1) and Hermans (Chapter 2) both argue for the storied nature of life and the use of narrative and dialogue, respectively. All of these approaches have value for investigating existential meaning and we foresee a considerable contribution arising from further research that explores existential meaning from a variety of qualitative perspectives and research approaches. In fact, because so much of existential meaning is experiential, constructed, and linguistically accessed, these approaches can be seen to have particular promise in opening up the field and extending our understandings substantially.

Quantitative Approaches

In contrast to qualitative research, which frequently operates from constructionist, critical, and postmodern paradigms, quantitative research is typically premised in a positivist paradigm, assuming the existence of a real world that can be revealed through accurate, controlled research using reliable and valid measurement. Much research into existential meaning has proceeded from this perspective and provides valuable information about the nature of the construct, its function and content, and its relation to other constructs. However, there are a number of issues that can be raised with the objective of improving this type of research into existential meaning.

First, there is a need for conceptual refinement of the meaning construct. Much of the research reported in this volume has used a variety of measurement instruments that all purport to tap the construct of existential meaning. While specific individual measures have been shown to be reliable and valid, it is not known whether the measures, collectively, converge to form a unitary, coherent construct. Studies are needed in which data from several measures of existential meaning are examined for their underlying structure, using factor analytic procedures, for example. Findings from such research would enable us to determine whether existential meaning is a unitary or multidimensional construct.

Conceptual refinement in this form would enhance our knowledge base by allowing meaningful comparisons to be made across studies that use different measures of existential meaning.

Second, and complementary to the first point, there is a need to develop context-specific measures of existential meaning for use in particular research contexts. In his review of measures, Reker (Chapter 3) highlighted the need for more domain- and context-specific measures of existential meaning, particularly in relation to life-threatening illnesses such as cancer or AIDS. The work of Prager, Savaya, and Bar-Tur (Chapter 8) underscores the need to develop scales that are culture-specific and culturally sensitive. Further, care must be taken to ensure that our measuring instruments reflect and accommodate ethnic differences in the way meaning is experienced. The research by Farran, Graham, and Loukissa (Chapter 9) clearly reveals the importance of differing ethnic perspectives in one specific setting, but this will be true of many others. Through the development of context-specific measures that are sensitive to these concerns we will be better able to investigate existential meaning in diverse contexts and enhance our knowledge of how it functions in them.

Third, there is a need to disentangle the causal relationship between existential meaning and other facets of life. Many studies have now reported a strong association between existential meaning and various other indicators, such as measures of physical and mental health, psychological well-being, life satisfaction, happiness, morale, or self-esteem. However, the cross-sectional and non-experimental design of most studies limits clear delineation of cause-and-effect relationships. For many researchers, it is tempting to conclude that existential meaning precedes these "outcomes" rather than the other way around, or perhaps that the influence may be bidirectional. Van Ranst and Marcoen (Chapter 4) and Debats (Chapter 6) explicitly raise these issues. Van Ranst and Marcoen find an association between existential meaning and death attitudes and between existential meaning and coping with aging, but correctly conclude that the direction of influence could go either way. Debats provides more direction by concluding that the cause-versus-effect problem in correlational research can be more adequately addressed through longitudinal, prospective studies. It is also possible that the issue could be explored experimentally. For example, it may be possible to manipulate existential meaning by having participants engage in either low, moderate, or high levels of meaningful activities (relative to their normal standard) over a period of time followed by an assessment of their physical, psychological, mental, and spiritual well-being. In this way, statements about causality could potentially be attributed to existential meaning.

Fourth, there is a need for more use of longitudinal designs in meaning research. The reasons for this include the concerns with untangling cause and effect discussed above, but go beyond that. Currently, much of what is known about existential meaning is based on cross-sectional research. Thus, findings of developmental trends may pertain more to age or cohort differences than to age changes per se. This is problematic, for existential meaning is likely to be influenced by a variety of internal and external factors, including developmental stage, transition points, different points in an illness trajectory, differing levels of physical and mental health, and related factors. To examine this fully, future research needs to assess existential meaning at a minimum of two, and preferably more, points in time within the same individuals. Longitudinal designs have the advantage of "profiling" changes in existential meaning as well as in related factors such as sources of meaning across developmental stages, over the course of an illness, and between developmental transitions (e.g., retirement). An additional advantage of longitudinal designs is the opportunity to collect normative data that more accurately portray the level of stability and/or change in existential meaning over the life span.

Combined Approaches

The use of a combination of qualitative and quantitative approaches within the same study has been promoted by some researchers, and *triangulation* has been used to characterize the process of combining methods. Triangulation is based on the assumption that any biases inherent in data sources, investigator, and method will be neutralized when used in combination with other sources, investigators, and methods (Jick, 1979). In short, through triangulation the researcher makes use of multiple methods of data collection and analysis and seeks convergence of the results. The notion of triangulation is contentious because it contains positivist assumptions of bias and 'truth.' However, there are additional reasons for combining methods in a single study. These include using one method to complement the other, using the first method in a sequential manner to inform the second, the ability to identify contradictions and emerging perspectives, and the prospect of expanding the scope and breadth of the study (Greene, Caracelli, & Graham, 1989).

Creswell (1994) has advanced three models of combined designs: the two-phase design, the dominant-less dominant design, and the mixed-methodology design. In the two-phase design, the researcher conducts a qualitative phase and a separate quantitative phase of the study. In the dominant-less dominant design, the researcher relies heavily on one method with a smaller component drawn from the alternate method. In the mixed-methods design, the researcher moves freely between both methods at all stages of the research from the introduction to the reporting of the results.

These designs are all represented in the present volume. For example, Debats (Chapter 6) uses a dominant-less dominant model to identify, qualitatively, the constituents of the experience of meaningfulness and meaninglessness and relates this to a quantitatively derived measure of existential meaning. Prager et al. (Chapter 8) demonstrate a two-phase mixed-methods design in the development of a measure of sources of life meaning that is culture-specific and culturally sensitive. In the first phase, a qualitative approach was used to gain a broad-based, deeper understanding of meaning from the participants' perspectives; in the second phase, a quantitative approach was used to develop a psychometrically sound instrument to assess sources of meaning in life. Dittmann-Kohli and Westerhof (Chapter 7) provide a good example of a mixed-methodology design. Here, individuals' personal meaning systems were assessed through self- and life descriptions (qualitative) that were subjected to an elaborate category scoring system to delineate the content and structure of personal meaning (quantitative). In this way, Dittmann-Kohli and Westerhof were able to chart both qualitative and quantitative age differences in domains of meaning across the life span, thereby expanding the scope and breadth of the study.

The advantages of using combined designs are evident in these studies. Combined designs offer a way to capture the dynamic, complex nature of existential meaning and the different ways in which meaning can be experienced. Future studies that take advantage of these ways for blending methods will enrich our understanding of existential meaning.

FUTURE APPLICATIONS

Enhancing Meaning Therapeutically

In this volume, a number of contributors implicitly or explicitly refer to the use of a variety of meaning-enhancing interventions. Hermans (Chapter 2), in his case study presentation, offers a form of therapy utilizing the self-confrontation method which contributes to the organization and reorganization of the individual's valuation (meaning) system. The insight gained in the therapeutic relationship allows the client to transform specific valuations referring to the past, present, and future into responsible action. Hermans' method of intervention, from assessment to therapeutic change, offers a refreshing approach to help clients better understand their own valuation systems and to lead more meaningful lives.

Logotherapy is closely aligned with existential meaning and is referred to and drawn on by several contributors. In particular, Guttmann (Chapter 12) identifies depth psychology and logotherapy as two important approaches to meaning and to psychotherapy. Of the two, Frankl's logotherapy, which describes both a theory and a method, has the most direct application to existential meaning as conceptualized in this volume. As Guttmann points out, logotherapy is neither a philosophy nor a psychotherapy that is independent of other therapies, but an approach that enables clients to discover meaning in their lives. Logotherapy is an open system, applicable to every individual whether receiving conventional therapy or not.

Recently, Wong (1998) proposed an extension of the basic tenets of logotherapy, with its emphasis on existential issues and the central role of personal meaning, to incorporate cognitive-behavioral processes that allow key concepts to be operationalized. The main focus of Wong's hybrid model of meaning-centered counseling is on discovering "the deep structures of personal meanings" (p. 404) and on "realizing meaningful life goals" (p. 404). Wong's approach is similar to Hermans' intervention in that both combine assessment strategies with counseling techniques such as self-valuation and social validation.

Many case studies and anecdotal reports on the effectiveness of logotherapy and related interventions in restoring a sense of meaning and purpose and in promoting positive mental health have been published, but more extensive studies establishing the value and effectiveness of these approaches in a broad range of contexts and for a wide range of people would be valuable. Future applications of meaning-enhancing therapies for restoring a sense of meaning in life are extremely desirable, along with rigorous research demonstrating the extent to which health and well-being can be achieved through meaning.

Facilitating the Process of Meaning-Making

The relational nature of existential meaning was identified earlier as an important theme, and it has implications for facilitating the process of meaning-making. For example, McFadden (Chapter 11) describes how persons of faith construct a sense of existential meaning through religious beliefs, feelings, and values and share these with other members of the worshipping community, including persons who are frail, weak, and suffering from disease. Within the religious context of commitment, a sense of meaning and purpose can be maintained and an individual's feeling of worth can be affirmed.

In a different example, Coward (Chapter 10) discusses how health professionals can facilitate the process of meaning-making within the structured environment of support groups. Her research focuses specifically on how self-transcendent views and behaviors are facilitated among cancer support group participants and how such facilitation is related to improvements in emotional well-being. According to Coward, the mechanism for the healing that occurs in the group environment appears to involve the expansion of self-boundaries through the sharing of common experiences, the giving of support to others, and having a sense of common purpose. Meaning-making might also be facilitated in less formalized environments, such as self-help groups in which members all share a common purpose. Self-help bereavement groups are just one example. Future investigations need to explore the many different ways in which self-transcendent views and behaviors can be facilitated in group environments.

However, interventions at an individual level also deserve consideration. Although many of these may involve formal therapy, as discussed above, other avenues have been suggested for promoting meaning-making. For example, Lichter, Mooney, and Boyd (1993) suggest that conducting a life-review process can function in this way. They facilitated a life-review for terminal cancer patients in a hospice setting by providing them with assistance to write a biography. They argued that this process provided a range of benefits, but predominant among these was finding meaning. The challenge ahead is to determine and evaluate interventions and to ascertain which processes in which circumstances offer the best prospects for maintaining, restoring, or facilitating a sense of meaning in the individual.

Cross-Cultural Applications

Several chapters in this volume allude to the supposition that existential meaning and meaning-making are universal processes that are recognized by individuals from varying ethnic, race, and cultural backgrounds. What may differ among these backgrounds are the contents of existential meaning and the ways through which meaning is ultimately expressed. This is evident in the work of Prager et al. (Chapter 8) as it relates to differences in sources of meaning between Jews and Arabs, and in the work of Farran et al. (Chapter 9) as it relates to race differences in sources of meaning in the caregiving experience. The work of Dittmann-Kohli and Westerhof (Chapter 7) on personal meaning system development across Dutch, Zairian, and Indian cultures clearly demonstrates this point at the cultural level. Future applications of existential meaning might explore how meaning is experienced by persons exposed to different cultural models, particularly pertaining to individualistic versus collectivistic orientations.

IN CONCLUSION

The chapters in this book have documented a wide range of material in relation to existential meaning. Although much has been covered here, much remains to be done. The inquiry into existential meaning has a relatively short history, and in many respects we are at an early stage of the venture. Throughout this chapter we have suggested a range of future directions and opportunities for enhancing our understanding of existential meaning. We hope these comments, along with the substantial contributions in this book, will serve to provoke and stimulate further activity toward advancing theory, research, and applications of existential meaning.

REFERENCES

Creswell, J. W. (1994). *Research design: Qualitative and quantitative approaches.* Thousand Oaks, CA: Sage.

Frankl, V. (1962). *Man's search for meaning.* New York: Simon & Schuster.

Greene, J. C., Caracelli, V. J., & Graham, W. F. (1989). Toward a conceptual framework for mixed-method evaluation designs. *Educational Evaluation and Policy Analysis, 11*, 255-274.

Jick, T. D. (1979). Mixing qualitative and quantitative methods: Triangulation in action. *Administrative Science Quarterly, 24*, 602-611.

Lichter, I., Mooney, J., & Boyd, M. (1993). Biography as therapy. *Palliative medicine, 7*, 133-137.

Morse, J. M. (Ed.). (1992). *Qualitative health research.* Newbury Park, CA: Sage.

Reker, G. T. (1997). Personal meaning, optimism, and choice: Existential predictors of depression in community and institutionalized elderly. *The Gerontologist, 37*, 709-716.

Thomas, L. E. (1997, November). *Gerotranscendence: A cross-cultural investigation.* Symposium. Annual Scientific Meeting of the Gerontological Society of America, Cincinnati, OH.

Tornstam, L. (1994). Gerotranscendence: A theoretical and empirical exploration. In L. E. Thomas & S. A. Eisenhandler (Eds.), *Aging and the religious dimension* (pp. 203-225). Westport, CT: Auburn House.

Tornstam, L. (1997). Gerotranscendence: The contemplative dimension of aging. *Journal of Aging Studies, 11*, 143-154.

Wong, P. T. P. (1998). Meaning-centered counseling. In P. T. P. Wong & P. S. Fry (Eds.), *The human quest for meaning: A handbook of psychological research and clinical applications* (pp. 395-435). Mahwah, NJ: Lawrence Erlbaum.

AUTHOR INDEX

Abelson, R. P., 175
Achenbaum, A., 12
Agren, M., 15
Almond, R., 46, 47, 49, 61, 81, 95, 96, 102, 103
Andeberg, M. R., 127
Anderson, N. B., 144-146, 150, 153
Anderson, R., 165
Antonovsky, A., 101, 111, 160
Atkinson, B. E., 176
Austin, J. T., 107

Bakhtin, M., 24-26
Baldwin, M. W., 29
Baltes, M. M., 109, 120
Baltes, P. B., 59, 109, 120
Bastin, E., 62, 64
Batson, C. D., 177
Battista, J., 46, 47, 49, 61, 81, 95, 96, 102, 103
Baumeister, R. F., 60, 62, 108,123
Baumgartner, I., 68
Beck, S. L., 140
Bellah, R. N., 173, 174
Bentler, P. M., 40, 46
Birren, J., 15, 59, 124
Bloom, J., 165
Bolt, M., 44
Bouffard, L., 62, 64
Bowman, P., 150
Boyd, M., 207
Braden, C., 165, 166
Brandstädter, J., 59, 109, 120
Breytspraak, L., 123

Brody, E., 139
Bross, L. S., 68
Bruner, J. S., 8, 27, 29
Buehler, C., 99
Burbank, P. M., 62
Burman, E., 81
Butler, R. N., 68

Calman, K., 164
Campbell, D. T., 105
Campbell, R. J., 146
Caracelli, V. J., 205
Carey, S., 109
Carr, D., 8, 14
Cassirer, E., 28
Caughey, J. L., 28
Cella, D., 165
Chamberlain, K., 2, 40, 42-44, 46, 47, 64, 93, 99, 124
Chatters, L. M., 142, 143, 146
Chiriboga, D. A., 124
Cohen, R. D., 179
Cole, T. R., 18, 172, 173
Courtney, C., 175
Cousins, J. B., 46
Cousins, N., 165
Coward, D., 159, 161, 162, 165, 166
Crandall, J. E., 44
Creswell, J. W., 205
Crumbaugh, J. C., 45, 46
Cunningham, A., 165

Damasio, A. R., 175
Davies, B., 81

211

SUBJECT INDEX

Printed in the United Kingdom
by Lightning Source UK Ltd.
128604UK00002B/208-213/A

9 780761 909941